The Institutional Repository

CHANDOS
INFORMATION PROFESSIONAL SERIES

Series Editor: Ruth Rikowski
(email: Rikowskigr@aol.com)

Chandos' new series of books are aimed at the busy information professional. They have been specially commissioned to provide the reader with an authoritative view of current thinking. They are designed to provide easy-to-read and (most importantly) practical coverage of topics that are of interest to librarians and other information professionals. If you would like a full listing of current and forthcoming titles, please visit our web site **www.chandospublishing.com** or contact Hannah Grace-Williams on email info@chandospublishing.com or telephone number +44 (0) 1865 884447.

New authors: we are always pleased to receive ideas for new titles; if you would like to write a book for Chandos, please contact Dr Glyn Jones on email gjones@chandospublishing.com or telephone number +44 (0) 1865 884447.

Bulk orders: some organisations buy a number of copies of our books. If you are interested in doing this, we would be pleased to discuss a discount. Please contact Hannah Grace-Williams on email info@chandospublishing.com or telephone number +44 (0) 1865 884447.

The Institutional Repository

RICHARD JONES
THEO ANDREW
AND
JOHN MACCOLL

Chandos Publishing

Oxford · England

Chandos Publishing (Oxford) Limited
Chandos House
5 & 6 Steadys Lane
Stanton Harcourt
Oxford OX29 5RL
UK
Tel: +44 (0) 1865 884447 Fax: +44 (0) 1865 884448
Email: info@chandospublishing.com
www.chandospublishing.com

First published in Great Britain in 2006

ISBN:
1 84334 138 7 (paperback)
1 84334 183 2 (hardback)

© R. Jones, T. Andrew & J. MacColl, 2006

British Library Cataloguing-in-Publication Data.
A catalogue record for this book is available from the British Library.

Typeset by Domex e-Data Pvt. Ltd.
Printed in the UK and USA.

Contents

Acknowledgements

Richard would like to thank

Jim Downing, Cambridge University Library
William Nixon, Glasgow University Library
Morag Greig, Glasgow University Library
Ruth Lewis, University of Edinburgh

Theo would like to thank

Leah Halliday, EDINA
Bill Hubbard, University of Nottingham
Liz G. Stevenson, University of Edinburgh

John would like to thank

Stephen Pinfield, University of Nottingham
Paul Ayris, University College London
Sheila Cannell, University of Edinburgh
Fred Friend, University College London

All the authors would like to thank

The Joint Information Systems Committee (JISC)
Ariadne Magazine
Program: electronic library and information systems journal

List of figures

List of tables

Preface

In 1878, Daniel Coit Gilman, the first President of Johns Hopkins University wrote 'It is one of the noblest duties of a university to advance knowledge, and to diffuse it not merely among those who can attend the daily lectures – but far and wide'. At the time, over 100 years before the development of the Internet, Gilman's words related to the concept of the university press. In the digital era, however, the idea can equally apply to institutional repositories.

Institutional repositories provide an opportunity for an institution to share its intellectual wealth with the worldwide community of scholars, allowing all interested readers access to the discoveries and insights produced by its members. They form a 'shop window' for the endeavours of the institution and ensure the long-term preservation of vital academic results.

Increasingly, the possibilities of institutional repositories are being realised by researchers, librarians, university administrators, and the funders of research. They fit with the researchers' desire for the increased dissemination and impact of their work, with the librarians' desire to meet the information need of their users, the administrators' desire to increase the visibility of their institutions (locally, nationally, and internationally), and the funding bodies' desire to both track and evaluate research outputs and to increase the return on their investment in research. Soon the institutional repository will be seen as a vital and integral part of every academic institution's infrastructure.

For many, the ideal home within an institution for the institutional repository is the library. The library already possesses many of the skills needed to set up and run an institutional repository – including handling of information, metadata creation (cataloguing), and archiving. While some have predicted the decline of the academic library in the digital age, the development of institutional repositories gives the library a central role within the institution. Naturally, this will require (at least in part) a shift in how we view libraries: from a body that takes external information and makes it available to members of the institution, to a body that makes information generated at the institution widely available to the world beyond. This is the 'diffusion' of knowledge described by Gilman.

In many ways, institutional repositories are simple in concept and execution. However, as ever, the devils are in the detail. The University of Edinburgh has been one of the innovators in the field of institutional repositories. By drawing on their own experiences, as well as those of other innovators and early adoptors, Jones, Andrew, and MacColl have given us a comprehensive outline of the main issues to consider when setting-up and developing an institutional repository – from making the case within the institution and choosing suitable software to formulating workflows, policy, and advocacy plans. In doing so they have ensured that others will be well equipped to ask the right questions, formulate suitable answers, and implement institutional repositories tailored to the needs of their own institutions, so making them better able to fulfil Gilman's 'noblest duty'.

David C Prosser, Director, SPARC Europe

About the authors

Richard Jones is currently a senior engineer at the University of Bergen Library, in Norway, where he works with the Bergen Open Research Archive (BORA) and related repository projects. He was formerly an information systems developer at Edinburgh University Library where he worked developing the Edinburgh Research Archive through the Theses Alive and SHERPA projects and beyond. There he developed the technological, and procedural aspects of the institutional repository, before taking up the post in Bergen. As a member of the DSpace core development group he has contributed code to the development of this open source repository platform, and is an active member of the user and developer community. His professional background is in web application development and information systems and he holds a degree in astrophysics from the University of Edinburgh.

Theo Andrew completed his doctorate in geology/tectonics at the University of Edinburgh. It was during this period of research that Theo became interested in investigating the role of digital media and the Internet in enhancing scholarly communication and publication. He subsequently became involved in a number of JISC-funded projects at Edinburgh University Library. His work in the JISC-funded Theses Alive project helped initiate the successful electronic theses programme at the University of Edinburgh. This has led him into a number of related activities, including, as part of the SHERPA project, investigating policy, workflow and intellectual property issues in setting up institutional e-print repositories. Currently Theo is responsible for managing the Edinburgh Research Archive and coordinating the related academic liaison and advocacy activities.

John A. MacColl is Head of the Digital Library Division at the University of Edinburgh, where he has worked for the past seven years. His work involves the strategic management of library systems, e-resources and help services. He is also closely involved with the development of an Edinburgh-based consortium of libraries sharing digital services. His career has been spent in the universities of Glasgow, Aberdeen, Abertay Dundee and Edinburgh, working in libraries, converged information services, a computing service and a UK Data Centre. He was the founding editor of *Ariadne* magazine in 1996, and his experience in digital and research library issues has led to consultancies in different parts of the world. He has served on various national committees dealing with research library issues, and has extensive experience of JISC-funded projects in digital libraries, scholarly communications and e-learning.

The authors may be contacted in care of:

Richard Jones
University of Bergen Library
Norway
E-mail: *richard@oneoverzero.com*

The institutional repository in the digital library

We begin by looking at the concept of institutional repositories within the broader context of digital libraries. 'Digital libraries' can mean many things, but we consider them to be libraries first and foremost, and built upon the enduring principles of information management which have lain at the heart of the practice of librarianship for hundreds of years. We look also at the significance of the qualification which defines the scope of this book – the institutional repository. Libraries are themselves repositories, and have always dealt in the management of repositories for their users. With libraries now routinely managing repositories of various types in digital format, what does it mean to qualify 'repository' with 'institutional'?

We examine the particular value of institutional repositories to research material, and look also at the other types of material for which institutional repositories are increasingly being used. There are considerable implications for librarians in managing digital material as full-text, where the digital item is the item being curated and managed over time, rather than a printed item with some digital metadata. The institutional repository movement has played a large part in making librarians face up to these implications in their entirety, and one of the first to be encountered is the question of metadata. What needs to be described for a digital object to be made findable in the present and into the future, when the environment which sustains and creates it may change and change again many times?

We complete this first chapter with a consideration of the real motivation behind the dissemination of research on the Web – research impact. Studies are beginning to show just how much more impact research can have when it is 'unlocked' from commercial journals and made available for everyone to find on the Web.

Digital libraries in a digital world

In the past ten years, the concept of the 'digital library' (or the 'electronic library') has been increasingly used, and now crops up relentlessly in the professional literature. This is not surprising, as the combination of low-cost computing and high-speed networking now affects all areas of life in the developed world. 'Digital banking', 'online shopping' and 'digital television' are transforming the ways in which we transact our daily business and consume entertainment. We also book holidays online, gamble on the Internet and conduct hundreds of other activities online. Increasing numbers of people work from home, using telecommunications to recreate their office environments in virtual space. As content goes online, and the means of access to it becomes as available and familiar as clicking on the television set, so it is a natural expectation that libraries too will join the interconnected web world.

Librarians are, however, well aware that there are also dangers surrounding the concept. It is often stated that the World Wide Web, or the Internet itself, is one huge electronic library. This is only true in the most general sense that it requires navigation aids in order to discover particular content. In fact, the Internet is no more a library than is a city or a country. Of course the Web contains masses of documents of all types, and in that sense it is like a library – but all libraries – even 'universal libraries' such as the Library of Congress – are based on selections. The Library of Congress's website admits that it does not collect everything, and nor would it want to: 'The Library's collections are based on the Jeffersonian ideal that all subjects will be of interest and value to Congress and, by extension, to the scholar and researcher'.

On the basis that it reflects the culture of a nation, universal libraries sometimes collect material which it is hard to imagine being of interest to scholars and researchers. The National Library of Australia, for example, reported in 2002 that it was now harvesting pornography published on the Australian web domain, for the use of researchers (BBC, 2002). It had not at that stage developed a policy on how to allow access to the material, however. It was also careful to confirm that it would be collecting only legal pornography. The Internet, as is well-known, contains both legal and illegal material.

Ross Atkinson emphasises the key library activity of selection:

> The network is not a digital library. We cannot sit back and imagine that what is on the network is in the digital library ... A

library, digital or otherwise, is always a highly selective subset of available information objects, segregated and favored, to which access is enhanced and to which the attention of client-users is drawn in opposition to objects excluded. (Atkinson 1996)

Definition of a 'digital library'

So it is false to think of the Internet as itself a digital library. As we, therefore, have to refine the concept if we wish to talk about digital libraries, how do we do so? Writing in *Library Journal*, Cloonan and Dove (2005) reminded readers of the 'Five laws of library science' expounded by the great Indian librarian Shiyali Ramamrita Ranganathan, in 1931. To this day, many librarians accept Ranganathan's five laws as a perfect conceptual summary of the aims of librarianship. Written in a period before gender-neutral language was expected, the five laws are:

1. Books are for use.
2. Every book its reader.
3. Every reader his book.
4. Save the time of the reader.
5. A library is a growing organism.

Cloonan and Dove then look at Google, the world's most popular search engine and, therefore, the most obvious candidate to be a universal catalogue of the Internet, and ask whether it meets the test of Ranganathan's Third Law. Does Google find, from the mass of digitised documents which exist on the Internet, not only the specific item for which a user may be searching, but also related items which they may want to consult without previously knowing about them as they begin to search? In the days of print librarianship, the Third Law was met by the use of robust cataloguing and indexing standards, including cross-referencing from within catalogue records. Librarians have yet to replicate these standards and their reach in the digital world. The authors conclude:

> Most information seekers using Google never go past the first page of results. Google's criteria for what goes on that first page are popularity and payment for placement. It is unlikely Google will

> change that. Library resources should match Google's ease of use but not its criteria for first page listing. Library tools must exhibit all the qualities of what Ranganathan calls a 'well-arranged collection'. (Cloonan and Dove, 2005)

It is tempting to use the term 'digital library' about any collection of digital objects which have some means of navigation and retrieval, but approaching the question using Ranganathan's Laws would suggest that a collection of items is not a digital library merely by virtue of the items being digital. Rather, a digital library is such by virtue of its being a library first and foremost. An academic or research library is organised for use in the pursuit of human advancement. The fact that its contents – or a large proportion of them – are digital is merely an accident of history. Digital libraries are, therefore, much more than aggregations of documents on the World Wide Web, whose navigability and discovery services can be left to commercial companies interested in maximising income from advertisers with product information which can be made particularly eye-catching. A true digital library has to be organised for its purpose, and must not be randomly heterogeneous and indexed as a commercial by-product. Nor should it be simply a desperate response to digital deluge and budgetary inadequacy, as Robin Alston suggests:

> If a librarian found juggling resources difficult in 1980, when the first storm clouds began to appear, by 1990 not even those who approached budgeting with imagination could balance the books. The concept of the digital library was born in desperation. (Alston, 2002)

Michael Lesk, however, in his authoritative book on the subject, disagrees:

> The answer should not be despair but organization. A digital library, a collection of information that is both digitized and organized, gives us powers we never had with traditional libraries. (Lesk, 1997)

Yet even today there is still no common consensus to define a 'digital library'. One reason for this is that the term was adopted by the computing science community while librarians were still talking about 'electronic libraries' and 'hybrid libraries'. The National Science Foundation's 'Digital Libraries Initiative', launched in 1996, funded six projects, one each in environmental planning and geographic information systems, spatially-referenced map information, digital video creation, federated repositories of scientific literature, intelligent agents and 'interoperation mechanisms among heterogeneous services'. Its website gives a description of digital libraries which puts their creation firmly in the hands of software engineers:

> Digital libraries basically store materials in electronic format and manipulate large collections of those materials effectively. Research into digital libraries is research into network information systems, concentrating on how to develop the necessary infrastructure to effectively mass-manipulate the information on the Net. The key technological issues are how to search and display desired selections from and across large collections.

Bearing out this definition, the annual Joint Conference on Digital Libraries (JCDL), which has been running since 2001, is a collaboration between the Association for Computing Machinery (ACM) and the Institute of Electrical and Electronic Engineers (IEEE). However, in the years since it began, the conference has gradually become more accommodating to librarians and information scientists. For example, the JCDL 2004 conference catered for an audience which was a mix of librarians and computer scientists, with the latter group still probably outnumbering the former on the basis of the papers presented. Its themes plainly sought to encourage attendance from both communities, however, with titles such as 'Educational aspects of digital libraries', on the one hand, and 'Mining and disambiguating names' on the other.

What happened, then, during the few years which saw the first burst of energy associated with this new idea of 'digital libraries', was that research was done by computer scientists in order to provide solutions to the problem of putting research-quality digital content on the Web, with sufficient functionality to replace its normal format as print, or images, or laboratory instrumentation, together with some innovative new functionality never previously available. The collections of content which formed the testbeds for this research effort were, in effect, subject-based digital libraries. Once a collection of high quality content had been mounted on the Web – the maps of the Alexandria Digital Library, for example – they were there for all to use. In time, logically, it seemed that all knowledge domains could be represented by digital libraries, making institutional libraries redundant in the process.

Repository locus: institution vs discipline

When we talk about the 'institutional repository', we use 'institution' to refer the educational or research establishment which is the library's parent body. Institutional repositories have emerged from universities, but are spreading into other types of educational organisation too, such as colleges and research institutes. However, research repositories were until quite recently based only around disciplines. The first and still best-known disciplinary repository to emerge was arXiv (*www.arxiv.org*), a repository of research papers in particle and high-energy physics, based originally at the Los Alamos National Laboratory. arXiv has been running for some 15 years, and is widely used by physicists across the world. Over time, it has expanded its coverage to embrace associated disciplines such as mathematics and computer science, and it has also changed its physical location, moving to Cornell University Library a few years ago.

While arXiv has been successful in capturing the market for deposited e-prints in these particular domains, it has been somewhat surprising to observe that it has not served as a model for many others. Economics has been partly successful, with EconPapers (working papers in economics – see *www.econpapers.repec.org*), and the literature of cognitive psychology is captured in e-print form in CogPrints (*www.cogprints.org*). In medicine, the PubMed Central service is somewhat different in that it provides digital copies of papers only after their publication in printed journals. As the e-print movement gathered pace in the late 1990s, promoted tirelessly by evangelists such as Professor Stevan Harnad of Southampton, who was inspired by the example of arXiv to call for it to be replicated across all subject disciplines, it became clear that methods of working by researchers in different disciplines were themselves sufficiently different that we could not cover the entire world of research by means of the physicists' model.

There are significant differences in the ways in which academic and researchers work in different domains. For the purposes of managers of institutional repositories, the most significant relate to the place of peer review – the process of 'refereeing' by which research is validated by peer experts, or referees, and thereby permitted to enter the discourse and body of knowledge of a particular knowledge domain. What all domains hold in common is their need for peer review, if only to allow the researchers to point to citations in reputable journals in order to prove their credibility in the field, and to enhance their career prospects. Physicsts, however, tend to be happy to have their research papers circulated widely while the research described in them is still unvalidated, and, therefore, tentative. This form of paper, known in pre-digital times as the pre-print, is normally eventually replaced with a refereed version. Prior to the Web, scientists would send copies of pre-prints to fellow researchers working in institutions across the world, or distribute them at conferences, and thereby seek early feedback. Physicists, particularly in high-energy and particle physics, work at rapid speed, and are not content to wait for official peer review by journals to validate their ideas. In arXiv, many papers are submitted initially as pre-prints, and later replaced with 'post-prints' (refereed versions) which come complete with citation details to the published journal in which they appear. The substitution is not always applied, however. Some physicists are happy to let unrefereed papers remain in the repository, or to add refereed versions rather than replace one with the other.

In other disciplines, pre-prints are scarcely used (perhaps only to a small and very select group of peers), and research is carefully guarded until after refereeing, when the researcher, satisfied to have their work validated, will release it to the world in the form of journal publication. Not surprisingly, the fields of medicine and life sciences research behave in this way. The consequences of unverified medical hypotheses leaking into the public domain and creating hysterical stories in the press can obviously be very serious for a researcher. In these post-print oriented domains, repositories are still very useful, if only because the paper, once refereed, can then be placed immediately into a repository and made findable on the Web. Journal publication, even in electronic form, has an associated time-lag between acceptance and publication which can be many months, and researchers want their work to appear as early as possible.

It was in response to the growing awareness of the importance of arXiv that the institutional repository movement was created, and along with it the Open Archives Initiative (OAI), beginning with a conference in Santa Fe, New Mexico, in 1999. The rationale for this was that if academics working within disciplinary boundaries did not feel motivated to deposit copies of their pre- or post-refereed articles in such disciplinary archives as existed for them (if any), then their institutions could provide facilities to make the process easy, and might indeed eventually require the population of institutional repositories as a contractual obligation.

The consequence of the OAI has been the appearance across the globe of many hundreds of institutional archives, alongside the disciplinary archives which continue to exist. This has presented a dilemma for some researchers who – where the choice exists of both types of repository – have not been sure which one they should choose in which to deposit their paper. Repository managers have urged them not to worry, and to deposit in both, as the search services being developed can cope with redundancy and apply de-duplication of identical results in some cases. In this way they have brushed aside the legitimate confusion of researchers due to the urgency of the need they perceive to prove the open access publication paradigm change by means of capturing content on a large scale. Yet the confusion persists, and academics will rightly ask why, in a system designed to maximise efficiency, they should be asked to negotiate two separate submission interfaces in order to deposit a single paper. Submission interface design needs, therefore, to advance in order to cope with this dilemma, and this is one of the research and development challenges still facing the open access movement at the present time.

Repositories and digital libraries

Academic libraries today are increasingly involved with the digital library agenda represented at conferences such as JCDL because they see that there is a need to develop institutional digital libraries alongside subject-based digital libraries. The institutional library needs a presence on the Web – a place to describe its print and web-based services, and to bring together the content it makes available to its users. It needs to present its catalogue but also its other finding aids – to its collections of e-journals, its collections of digitised materials from its treasures, and other lists which are most usefully presented separately, such as electronic reserve texts or past exam papers. Institutional libraries also are growing the range of services they can offer via their website. Examples of these include interlibrary loan request – sometimes by electronic full-text delivery; requests to retrieve store items; book loan renewals and electronic reference support. In addition, library services need to be distributed out to other useful environments, such as student virtual learning environments and university portal sites. They need to be 'skinned' in various ways, and to be capable of being searched in an aggregated and in a user-defined sub-aggregated fashion. Some of the technology involved in providing these apparently obvious functional enhancements is astonishingly complex and difficult (such as federated searching across a heterogeneous commercially published database environment).

Digital libraries, then, belong both to knowledge domains and to institutions, in the same way as do repositories, which are constituent elements of each. Table 1.1 breaks down both digital libraries and repositories by institution and discipline. The libraries, on the left, depend more and more on the repositories, on the right, to provide them with the selections of collections they present as libraries, whether institutional or disciplinary.

There has been a great deal of experimentation and research into digital library developments across the globe in the past 15 years, and these days, as some of the experimentation and research begins to blossom into genuinely new and important services, academic libraries are employing a higher proportion of staff with IT experience and qualifications. This is particularly true in larger libraries. The consequence of this is that library managers need to understand the technologies of digital libraries, at least conceptually, and so plan for

Table 1.1 Examples of digital libraries and repositories

Digital libraries	Repositories
Disciplinary	
Alexandria Digital Library *www.alexandria.ucsb.edu*	arXiv *www.arxiv.org*
Perseus Project *www.perseus.tufts.edu/*	PubMed Central *www.pubmedcentral.nih.gov*
Digital Scriptorium *sunsite.berkeley.edu/Scriptorium/*	EconPapers *econpapers.repec.org/*
Center for Electronic Texts in the Humanities *www.ceth.rutgers.edu/*	CogPrints *cogprints.org*
Institutional	
California Digital Library *www.cdlib.org/*	Edinburgh Research Archive *www.era.lib.ed.ac.uk*
Illinois Digital Academic Library *www.idal.illinois.edu/*	DSpace at MIT *dspace.mit.edu/index.jsp*
	Nottingham Eprints *eprints.nottingham.ac.uk/*
	LSE Research Articles Online *eprints.lse.ac.uk/*

their future development along a trajectory which, for some, might see their goal as being transformed in their entirety into digital libraries, but for all must mean that over time their services are converted gradually to a basis in digital library technologies.

While for many this may seem like a threatening picture (James Thompson terrified librarians as far back as 1982 when he published a book called *The End of Libraries*), in fact libraries have always developed by importing technologies from elsewhere. Cataloguers and classifiers have relied for decades upon technologies developed by bibliographers, documentalists (an American term, referring to professionals who had 'the delegated task of creating access for scholars to the topical contents of documents, especially of parts within printed documents and without limitation to particular collections' (Buckland, 1997)), information scientists and, of course, more recently by computer scientists. These technologies have produced standard tools such as the Dewey Decimal Classification (DDC) system, Library of Congress Subject Headings (LCSH), Anglo-American Cataloguing Rules, 2nd edition (AACR2) and the Machine Readable Cataloguing (MARC) manual.

Perhaps the difference with the digital library technologies now being developed is that there is no automatic assumption that they will be handed to librarians to use, or at least, perhaps only to certain types of librarian – many of whom might not be expected to work inside campus library buildings. The digital library, in such a context, becomes something which takes some shape from the traditional library, and some shape from other sectors and disciplines. Several writers have likened the concept of the 'digital library' to that of the 'horseless carriage', a term which was a clumsy attempt to describe a new invention – automobility – by reference to what was familiar. Automobiles, of course, are much more than horseless carriages, as an enriched world of accessible content is much more than a digital library. Whether a new term emerges or not, it seems likely that digital libraries will be part of the bloodstream of knowledge at an earlier stage and in a more integrated way than libraries of printed objects ever were.

Repositories of research papers

Repositories are simply databases, and what distinguishes institutional repositories is the idea that an internal database can serve more than an administrative purpose, and can constitute a building block in a distributed international service which is a virtual database composed of a user-defined set of cooperating databases on the network. This is, therefore, an essentially subversive technology, capable of allowing grassroots publishing by non-publishers, and delivering a service with the same functionality and feel as large commercially published databases. The idea is not unique. The UK's Joint Information Systems Committee (JISC) funded a number of 'CLUMPS' projects as part of the Electronic Libraries Programme (eLib) in the late 1990s. These created federated databases of academic library catalogues. However, that was a more straightforward undertaking, as the library catalogues involved were already central university services, available to the outside world for searching over the Internet. The breakthrough was to make them searchable using the federated search technology of the z39.50 standard. With institutional repositories, however, the challenge is greater, as the databases must first be established locally, then opened to the Web, and then configured for harvesting in order to provide the shared database facility.

Institutional repositories are perhaps particularly applicable in the context of research publications, as they emanate from institutions, and with the right technology in place can be caught at source and built into services. An institutional repository can, therefore, serve as a publisher of research materials – peer-reviewed papers, e-prints, theses, reports, conference papers, working papers and other types of document.

Repositories of other objects

In its seminal analysis of trends in the library and information world published in 2003, the Online Computer Library Center (OCLC) reported on feedback obtained from surveying librarians and users about the relevance of libraries to digital content. One response highlights the need for librarians to address new custodial challenges:

> Librarians are way too focused on published material: they should leave that to the Amazons and concentrate on the hard stuff. (Online Computer Library Center, 2004)

By 'hard stuff' might be meant the types of content which are generated in academic institutions but which are not destined for publication. There are three reasonably well-known examples of such types of content, though the potential clearly exists for many further types which may have more limited appeal as part of distributed services.

Learning objects

Whereas the development of repositories for research content represents a relatively intuitive migration from pre-digital to post-digital research publishing practices, with many of the same landmarks still visible (pre-prints, peer-review, journal titles and impact factors), when we move into the realm of teaching we find a much less coherent transition taking place. The development of teaching material in digital form embraces both institutionally-authored material – lecture notes, image collections, animated programs, assessments as revision aids – and externally-published material (typically textbooks). So, while it is conceivable that an institution could eventually capture all of its research outputs in an institutional repository, it is much less easy to see how its learning material could be captured so extensively. Copyright presents a major hurdle to this in itself, and institutions are not in as strong a position to seek copyright exemptions – even for textbooks to which they may have contributed – as they are with research papers written by their own academics.

Nonetheless, there is an obvious argument to be made for storing such teaching material as can be stored, in order that it can be reused by colleagues and future teachers, or modified and reused in new teaching contexts. 'Learning objects', however, are a heterogeneous group of materials (which is why such a clumsy, abstract name has been adopted for them). They vary enormously in format, in metadata requirements, and in size. Pulling them all together into a single repository presents considerable challenges. The advantages in doing so, however, are the same as those which apply to research outputs. It makes more efficient use of the institution's resources; allows the digital content to be preserved over time; provides a comprehensive view of institutional product; supports high-quality searching; and permits interoperability with similar repositories across the Web, so contributing to a global service.

In the same way as applies with research outputs, learning object repositories can also be classified into disciplinary and institutional. In contrast to the situation with research materials, however, we find that institutional repositories of learning objects are relatively uncommon. It is rare as yet to find institutions which view the aggregated collection of their learning objects as having a useful 'showcase' value. In addition, whereas research materials are likely to be quite widely read by other members of a disciplinary community across the world, the value in learning objects lies in their capacity to be re-used. For that reason, we find that disciplinary repositories of learning objects predominate, with a few cross-disciplinary services emerging, sometimes national in scope, such as the UK's JORUM repository, funded by JISC. The software platforms used for these repositories are not as standardised as are those for repositories of research materials, and are not all capable of being harvested via the Open Archives Initiative Protocol for Metadata Harvesting (OAI-PMH). This imposes limits upon their value as part of a comprehensive virtual database of freely available learning materials.

Table 1.2 **Examples of learning object repositories**

Learning object repositories
Disciplinary
Several UK Higher Education Academy subject centres provide repositories of learning objects, including:
Bioscience: Imagebank *www.bioscience.heacademy.ac.uk/imagebank/*
Management and Accountancy: Learning and Teaching Resources *www.business.heacademy.ac.uk/resources/landt/*
Geography, Earth and Environmental Sciences: Resource Database *www.tellus.ac.uk/*
Health Sciences and Practice: Learning-Teaching Web-Resource *www.health.heacademy.ac.uk/site/ltresource/index.php*
Information and Computer Sciences: Learning Objects for Introductory Programming *www.ics.heacademy.ac.uk/Resources/Learning_Objects/index.shtml*
Languages, Linguistics and Area Studies: Materials Bank *www.llas.ac.uk/resources/bankcontents.aspx*
Materials Education: Database of Resources *www.materials.ac.uk/resources/index.asp*
Physical Sciences: Courseware *www.physsci.heacademy.ac.uk/Resources/Courseware.aspx*
Psychology: Resources *www.psychology.heacademy.ac.uk/html/resources.asp*

Table 1.2	Examples of learning object repositories (*cont'd*)

Learning object repositories
Disciplinary (*cont'd*)
Perseus Project *perseus.csad.ox.ac.uk*
Dr J's Illustrated Guide to the Classical World *lilt.ilstu.edu/drjclassics/*
Images from History *www.hp.uab.edu/image_archive/index.html*
NORINA: The Norwegian Reference Centre for Laboratory Animal Science & Alternatives *oslovet.veths.no/NORINA/*
DERWeb: Dental Educational Resources on the Web *www.derweb.co.uk/*
Institutional
The University of Birmingham School of Dentistry Ecourse and CAL downloads *www.dentistry.bham.ac.uk/fordentists/caldownloads.asp*
University of Leicester School of Archaeological Studies, Departmental Image Collection *www.le.ac.uk/archaeology/image_collection/*
LORE: Learning Object Repository for Edinburgh University *www.lore.ed.ac.uk/*
Cross-disciplinary
JORUM *www.jorum.ac.uk*
SCRAN *www.scran.ac.uk*
Cooperative Learning Object Exchange (CLOE) *cloe.on.ca/*
HELIX Image Service for Higher Education *helix.dmu.ac.uk*
Multimedia Educational Resource for Learning and Online Teaching (MERLOT) *www.merlot.org*

Corporate assets

Another role for institutional repositories is in the management of corporate assets. This is the territory of the archivist first and foremost, and embraces institutional records, including curricular descriptions (calendar, prospectuses), examination results, annual reports from the institution and its subdepartments, and many other records. Clearly, much of this material is confidential or sensitive, and, therefore, not to be made available in the public domain. There is nevertheless a desire to make available, within a single campus, as much information of this sort as is consistent with devolving responsibility for its creation and maintenance to the most appropriate point of data entry. This is desirable for reasons of efficiency, as it reduces indirection. So, wherever possible, academics in their role as Directors of Studies, for example, should input information regarding the course choices of individual students directly into the database which acts as the source repository for the institution, rather than send details to a secretary or administrative officer to input. The development of web-based intranet environments is allowing more and more efficiency in operations involving corporate assets.

The archival function, which is often managed by the library, requires that these corporate assets – now in digital form – be subject to archival process. This means that they need to be appraised as to their future value for the institution, and then preserved for a defined period, which may in fact be an indefinite period of time. Because they are now digital, inevitably they contain the ability to be linked to associated documents which may be held in other institutional repositories potentially available on the Internet. Repositories of past exam papers, of course materials, or of prospectuses, are all examples. Some assets will only be available to authorised staff within an institution, and the most sensitive information will be available only to particular members of institutional staff with accorded privileges. Each category of material must take account of relevant legislation to protect the rights both of the data subject (e.g. the

Table 1.3   Examples of corporate assets in a linked repository environment

Preservation period	Public domain	Institutional domain	Protected domain
One-year or less	Prospectus	Student course records	Student financial records
Several years	Calendar	Student exam results	Staff salary records
Indefinite	Past exam papers	Student personal details	Staff appraisal records

Data Protection Act in the UK), and of the enquirer seeking access to corporate information for a valid reason (e.g. the Freedom of Information Act in the UK). Being digital, the assets themselves can be preserved, and can be interlinked in ways which make efficient use both of them and of the time of staff maintaining or accessing them. This requires that a lifecycle approach to assets be adopted by the institution, and at the present time few institutions are doing this optimally.

Granular content

Another challenge for the architects of systems based around repositories is presented by the granularity within objects. Documents are often compound objects, and so composed of more than a single file. A research paper may have colour photographs embedded within it, or an associated table of data. Learning objects, in particular, have a troublingly elastic definition. A learning object can be as large as a year-long course of study in a subject, or as small as a single image file. It is important that institutional repositories have the means to describe their objects both at the highest level of granularity – the document level – and at the lowest level for each constituent part which, for a variety of reasons, requires independent description.

Repository objects are, therefore, often hierarchies in themselves, sharing the character of archival records more than individual object catalogue records. Each constituent record of a document or object requires its own metadata and this has to show both the relationship of the part to the whole record, and also the rights which inhere in its referent. For example, a PhD thesis may include photographic images where the copyright is not owned by the author. The cataloguer of this thesis then has to try to identify the rights ownership. This is not an easy task, and it is often solved for repository managers by devolving it to the authors themselves. Authors are clearly better placed to establish the copyright in embedded objects than are cataloguers, and a workflow step to require this is regularly included.

What role do institutional repositories play?

While institutional digital libraries are making inroads into the consciousness of their users, it is nevertheless true that the march of digital content via the Web makes many of their services less vital than they were, and even redundant to a growing proportion of users on campus. The concept of institutionality is an increasingly fragile one when we consider digital content and digital libraries, and we, therefore, must ask whether we should be developing institutional repositories at all. Are they an attempt to shut the stable door after the horse has bolted? All institutional digital library services face a tough battle in being accepted on campuses because alternative systems usually exist, and their shortcomings are not always obvious. Institutional repositories are not an intuitively necessary development in the minds of most academics. Few people yet feel they do not need a physical library on their campus doorstep, but many – particularly those experienced in using subject-based repositories such as arXiv – are surprised to hear librarians arguing for the creation of institutional repositories as new services.

Might it not be better for publishing agencies – content aggregators – to work on behalf of subject disciplines directly in the development both of repositories and broader digital libraries, with institutional digital libraries requiring only a minimal presence? After all, repository and digital library development to date has been more successful in the disciplinary than the institutional sphere, and has been driven directly by academics themselves. Libraries, by trying to create generalised institutional services, are confronted by the twin difficulties of acting as third-party agents between academics and their content and so being perceived as unnecessary, and of seeking to impose conditions upon academics in order to attract content, which may be resented.

It is not yet clear whether institutional repositories will take root and flourish in the digital knowledge landscape. As an innovation, they are still at an early stage of diffusion. What is clear is that they are regarded as a strong and important new idea by many organisations which are concerned with the dissemination of research outputs. Their appeal lies in the idea of 'groundedness'. Institutions are themselves the ground from which emerge the outputs of research – ideas, proposals, hypotheses, experiments, data and reported results. These outputs now share a common DNA in digital representation. It is this common base format which allows institutions to look more closely at their traditional way of managing research outputs – using print and microform – in order to discover whether there are new and more efficient modes of operation. 'Research outputs' traditionally are just that – research publications which are 'put out', given away to third parties for further processing. In such a process there is a loss of control, by the institution and the research funder, and with that loss of control come the problems which libraries are well aware of, as are increasing numbers of academic staff and researchers: the loss of the alignment of the output with the aims of the research funder; and the partial loss of the output to research generally across the world, because publishers require payment for their efforts in dissemination. The outputs, now in the hands of publishers, have to be 'bought back'. Inevitably, this means that only some researchers will benefit. But if the outputs are of near-publication quality while still 'on the ground', because of their digital DNA, then what new opportunities are opened up?

In pre-digital times, when researchers wrote up their results for publication, they would have been posted, hand-written or in typescript, to a publisher – the only agent with the technology to present the finished paper in a pleasing form, and to reproduce it in multiples sufficient to meet the likely demand across the world, in their journals. Publishers also managed a third very important process – that of verification that the research was of a quality which made it valuable to other researchers. This is achieved by the system of peer review, and is critical to the advancement of knowledge, and, therefore, to the careers of researchers as they develop. If a piece of research is flawed or unoriginal, then the advancement of knowledge is stultified or even damaged, and at some future point this fact is likely to become obvious to other researchers, so that the researcher responsible is tarnished in the eyes of their peers – with obvious consequences for personal self-esteem and career development.

In the digital age, the presentation and reproduction functions do not require the intermediation of a publisher. This is what an institutional repository can do. In doing so, the institution is granted a capture function similar to the archival functions which have long existed – in pre-digital time also – for corporate records. Sending research papers to publishers immediately they have been written was a necessary process, but not an ideal one. If the overall work required is not made noticeably more arduous, how much better to record the outflow of the institution's research as it leaves the premises, stamping it at source with the institution's imprimatur, and asserting ownership rights over it – either for the institution or for the author themselves. In the words of Herbert Van de Sompel, 'Scholars deserve an innately digital scholarly communication system that is able to capture the digital scholarly record, make it accessible, and preserve it over time' (Van de Sompel et al., 2004). Van de Sompel's analysis is founded on a concern about data loss and the need to provide effective data curation, but it implies an emphasis on the role of the institution in the lifecycle nonetheless:

We feel this loss needs to be remedied in a future scholarly communication system by natively embedding the capability to record and expose such dynamics, relationships, and interactions in the scholarly communication infrastructure. Recording this body of information is synonymous to recording the evolution of scholarship at a fine granularity. This will allow tracing the origins of specific ideas to their roots, analyzing trends at a specific moment in time, and forecasting future research directions. (Ibid)

This new functionality is obviously desirable but was given little attention in the past because it was virtually impossible to administer, and there was no obvious benefit in any case. Institutional repositories now make the administration relatively simple, and the future benefits have come dramatically into focus in recent times. These benefits derive mainly from the extraordinary potential of repository networking which has been made possible through the development of the OAI-PMH protocol.

Herbert Van de Sompel, developer of OAI-PMH, has regularly described how the invention has the ability to serve the purposes of the academy – and the interested public – without sacrificing any of the tried and trusted elements of the research dissemination and publication process. He quotes the scholarly communication lifecycle model of Roosendal and Guertz, with its five key components (Roosendaal and Guertz, 1997):

- *Registration*: allows claims of precedence for a scholarly finding.
- *Certification*: establishes the validity of a registered scholarly claim.
- *Awareness*: allows actors in the scholarly system to remain aware of new claims and findings.
- *Archiving*: preserves the scholarly record over time.
- *Rewarding*: rewards actors for their performance in the communication system based on metrics derived from that system.

In the traditional print world, registration and certification require publishers, and awareness and archiving are carried out by libraries. Rewarding is done by a variety of actors, both institutional (e.g. promotion by the university) and at national and international levels, through rewards such as increased funding for research, visiting professorships, and invitations to contribute to scholarly works and conferences. In what Van de Sompel elsewhere describes as a 'decomposed scholarly communication system' (Van de Sompel, 2000) involving repositories on the Web, there is no longer a need for separate agents responsible for each stage in the process. Instead, the repository, working in concert with other compliant repositories across the Web, becomes an 'interoperable grid' supplying in itself all of the elements of the system – registration, certification, awareness, archiving and rewarding.

Van de Sompel also presents librarians with some serious food for thought. The migration of the scholarly process onto the Web, with a central role for the institutional repository, raises questions about the continued role of the library as an agent for the purchase of published material:

> It has become increasingly difficult for libraries to fulfil their fundamental role of safeguarding equity of access ... At the core of the problems that libraries are facing is the total dependency on information held upstream in the information chain. (Van de Sompel, 2000)

In other words, they are in danger of becoming redundant – in at least those of their functions which depend on content held elsewhere. But there is some good news for libraries if they can seize the initiative presented by institutional repositories and ensure that they run them on behalf of their organisations. Libraries are close to authors, and so in 'a great position to fulfil the registration function i.e., obtain institutional material.' They are also clearly well qualified to archive this material. They are 'fast at embracing new technologies', and full of very knowledgeable people. However, there are some dread warnings as well:

> As organizations libraries are slow movers, hosted by slowly moving institutions. Libraries are slow to recognize the fact that a new technology may allow [or beg] for a new mode of operation. The information world runs on Internet time (Van de Sompel, 2000)

This slow speed of response might be fatal for libraries. They may have the technology at an early stage, but they generally do not use it to engender change in their host institution's organisational practices, and so they run the risk of losing out to other players in the digital content marketplace. The greatest challenges of all for university libraries wishing to populate institutional repositories within their digital libraries may, therefore, be outreach and liaison. These are not activities which are normally given high priority, and this must change if libraries are to claim a key role in the scholarly communication lifecycle.

Metadata

There are two main components in the construction of digital libraries. One is technologies, several of which have been spawned by the digital library community itself. The other is metadata. Metadata has long been the 'bread and butter' of libraries. 'Data about data', as it is commonly described, metadata creation involves the production of records which act as proxies to the holdings of libraries, allowing those holdings to be discovered, whether the searcher is looking for a known item, or an item on a particular subject, or by a particular creator. For hundreds of years, cataloguing (still the favoured term by many librarians, rather than 'metadata creation' which can sound like an attempt to give a core library activity a pseudo-scientific digital age identity) was a local activity, designed to make usable the particular collections held by particular libraries in particular places. With the scale increase in volume of holdings typically held by libraries in the twentieth century, however, it soon became obvious that much of this labour could be shared so that the same items were not being separately catalogued in many different places. Subject indexing had already been standardised through the widespread adoption of the Dewey Decimal and Library of Congress schemes, among others, and cataloguing likewise became a standardised activity for an increasing proportion of the total, as libraries saw the benefits in sharing their efforts. Catalogue records, including standardised subject codes and headings, were initially posted out to subscribing libraries on cards, but were to become distributed over wide area networks from the early 1980s onwards, as the first generation of computer-based catalogues appeared in libraries.

The MAchine Readable Cataloguing standard (MARC) evolved as an international standard, and is still massively used across the world for the cataloguing of books and journals according to a very detailed *schema* (defined set of record elements). MARC can be used for the description of items other than books and journals, but it falters in its capacity to describe the requirements of digital objects, and has been supplanted in digital repositories by other, more appropriate standards – none of which yet has the universality of use of MARC.

Designers of databases or repositories of digital content have had to give very high prominence to the importance of metadata in their undertakings, however reluctantly. Although traditionally a professional library activity (which means that cataloguers require a degree in library science, or a degree in another subject together with a postgraduate library science qualification), cataloguing is generally not considered to be at the glamorous end of information work, and yet metadata is the key to unlocking the digital content which institutions – via their libraries – are so keen to make available. It is ironic that, just as the combination of shared cataloguing and Internet connectivity was in the process of diminishing the relative importance of cataloguing as a locally-based activity, and deprofessionalising it in some libraries, the digital order has revealed content which is much more complex to describe than print. This is due to the fact that digital documents are illusory objects, presentations or performances composed of many layers of technology.

The document that one reads on a computer screen is assembled from a stack of machine protocols, a particular operating system, and applications software. The work may be stored in a single file, or be composed of several interrelated files. Each file will have a particular file format. Each of these components has a generation number. Besides that, an authoritative copy of the document may be stored in a digital store somewhere (or should be), and it will have a number of rights which exceed by some distance the relatively simple copyright with which the print world was familiar. There may be the separate rights of one or several creators, as well as the rights enjoyed by the reader of the document, and rights belonging to the institution which hosts the copy a reader may happen to be using. In short, for digital content, the description of the object – who created it, what it is called, what it is about, where it was published – is only one of many dimensions of metadata which need to be recorded in order for identification to take place.

The first generation of institutional repositories used the Qualified Dublin Core metadata schema to describe the content of their objects. Qualified Dublin Core is still widely used, mainly because it is specified by the OAI-PMH as a 'lowest common denominator' format well suited to supporting harvesting into a commonly structured repository, and, therefore, supporting discovery interoperability. Qualified Dublin Core utilises a 15-element record. A typical QDC record for an institutional repository item is shown in Table 1.4. This is the record for a biological sciences paper held in the Edinburgh Research Archive.

Table 1.4 **QDC record from the Edinburgh Research Archive**

DC Field	Value	Language
contributor.author	Byrne, Mary E	–
contributor.author	Barley, Ross	–
contributor.author	Curtis, Mark	–
contributor.author	Arroyo, Juana Maria	–
contributor.author	Dunham, Maitreya	–
contributor.author	Hudson, Andrew	–
contributor.author	Martienssen, Robert A	–
coverage.spatial	5	en
date.accessioned	2005-02-08T17:10:54Z	–
date.available	2005-02-08T17:10:54Z	–
date.issued	2000-12-21	–
identifier.citation	Byrne ME, Barley R, Curtis M, Arroyo JM, Dunham M, Hudson A,	en
	Martienssen RA, NATURE, 408 (6815): 967-971 DEC 21 2000	
identifier.uri	*www.nature.com*	–
identifier.uri	*http://hdl.handle.net/1842/687*	–
description.abstract	Meristem function in plants requires both the maintenance of stem cells and the specification of founder cells from which lateral organs arise. Lateral organs are patterned along proximodistal, dorsoventral and mediolateral axes (1,2). Here we show that the Arabidopsis mutant asymmetric leaves1 (as1) disrupts this process. AS1 encodes a myb domain protein, closely related to PHANTASTICA in Antirrhinum and ROUGH SHEATH2 in maize, both of which negatively regulate knotted-class homeobox genes. AS1 negatively regulates the homeobox genes KNAT1 and KNAT2 and is, in turn, negatively regulated by the meristematic homeobox gene SHOOT MERISTEMLESS. This genetic pathway defines a mechanism for differentiating between stem cells and organ founder cells within the shoot apical meristem and demonstrates that genes expressed in organ primordia interact with meristematic genes to regulate shoot morphogenesis	en

Table 1.4	QDC record from the Edinburgh Research Archive (*cont'd*)

DC Field	Value	Language
format.extent	369139 bytes	–
format.mimetype	application/pdf	–
language.iso	en	–
publisher	Nature Publishing Group	en
subject	Asymmetric	en
subject	leaves	en
subject	mediates	en
subject	leaf	en
subject	patterning	en
subject	stem cell	en
subject	function	en
subject	Arabidopsis	en
title	Asymmetric leaves1 mediates leaf patterning and stem cell function in Arabidopsis	en
type	Research Paper	en

Gradually, however, the multidimensionality of digital objects is bringing new metadata schemas into play, which provide for the 'packaging' of metadata from a variety of schemas suited to the different dimensions of objects – descriptive metadata, technical metadata, rights metadata and other dimensions in some cases. There are a few such schemas now in implementation, including METS, MPEG-21 DIDL and SCORM.[1] They are commonly referred to as *complex object formats*. The frontrunner among them at the present time for institutional repositories of research materials is METS, the Metadata Encoding and Transmission Standard, jointly developed by OCLC and the Library of Congress.

The METS standard is structured into seven sections, as follows:

1. *The header*: metadata describing the document.

2. *Descriptive*: this section may point to external descriptive metadata (such as a MARC record), or contain internally embedded descriptive metadata, or both.

3. *Administrative metadata*: this section provides information describing how the files were created and stored, intellectual property rights, etc.

4. *The file*: lists all files containing content which comprise the digital object.

5. *The structural map*: this outlines a hierarchical structure for the object, and links elements to content files and related metadata.

6. *The structural links*: this records the existence of hyperlinks between nodes in the hierarchy outlined in the structural map.

7. *The behaviour*: this can be used to associate executable behaviours with content in the METS object.

For learning objects, the IEEE Learning Object Metadata (LOM) standard tends to be used as the source schema. LOM implements the IMS Content Packaging standard, and so performs a similar task to METS in supporting the cataloguing of compound objects but within a pedagogical context. The LOM standard, for example, has nine categories (General, Lifecycle, Meta-Metadata, Technical, Educational, Rights, Relation, Annotation and Classification). Educational and Annotation are clearly categories which are quite specific to learning objects.

Cataloguing for the digital library requires skilled practitioners, and this may create a tension in libraries as traditional library cataloguing in the past few decades has increasingly been taken up by computer-based shared cataloguing systems which have reduced the burden of original cataloguing, and turned the bulk of print cataloguing activity into a relatively routine operation. By contrast, a metadata editor needs to know several different metadata schemas, and to apply them – or, often, to interpret them in a standardised way – to a heterogeneous range of digital object formats. The dominance of the age of MARC is over, when a single schema served for the description of any book or journal, and also for a few other things besides – realia (concrete objects housed in libraries, such as toys, or exhibition objects), and early websites among them. Now the metadata editor or creator has to be an artisan, with a variety of tools in their workshop, appropriate to the digital object in hand.

This adjustment is difficult for libraries because it requires a changing of organisational shape, and a reclustering of professional posts around the activities of the digital library. Few libraries have yet made the switch to this mode of hospitality to digital data. One reason for this is that it costs extra money to do so, as printed items are still flowing into our libraries in numbers at least as great as they ever did. The second reason is that there is no established workflow for the capture of records for digital materials. Libraries physically need to unpack printed items, and they ensure that the items are catalogued and classified before they leave the back-of-house to take their place on the shelves. This is essential in order to make a library out of a chaos of materials. In the digital realm, however, the materials which are added to a library repository are in many cases already findable on the Web. They need to be made more findable, and consistent with each other – not simply because librarians like order and consistency, but because knowledge machinery (such as the OAI-PMH) relies upon standard ways of description in order to generate meaningful indexes.

Repositories and research impact

Researchers are rewarded for their work not financially but through its impact. They want their research to be read, consumed and understood. They want their peers to comment on it, credit it and add to or extend it. Naturally, they want to receive credit for adding to human knowledge of the world; equally naturally, they want to help make the world a better place.

The conventional method of research dissemination via publication in journals is much more limited in its possible impact (through market forces) than is the new method of publication of the same research in open access repositories. Studies have already shown that open access research papers are read more widely, and, therefore, cited more frequently, than papers which are not housed in repositories. The consequence of this is that they have greater impact.

The Institute of Scientific Information (ISI) has produced impact rankings for scholarly journals for many years, based upon its series of citation indexes, now web-based and known as *Web of Knowledge* (*wok.mimas.ac.uk/*). Impact factors are based upon the average number of times that papers in a given journal title are cited by other papers – a fair measure of their research impact, though not without some distortions, as ISI itself points out in its regular publication which presents impact rankings, the *Journal of Citation Reports*, where its online help text states:

> You should not depend solely on citation data in your journal evaluations. Citation data are not meant to replace informed peer review. Careful attention should be paid to the many conditions that can influence citation rates such as language, journal history and format, publication schedule, and subject specialty.

This methodology is not an appropriate way to measure the impact of open access research papers, however, as it is based on journal titles rather than individual papers. While a growing number of open access journal titles now exist, by which is meant that they are published free on the Web with the costs of publication met by authors paying to publish, these are generally a poor measure of comparison because they are newly-founded journals competing against existing, established titles, and, therefore, almost inevitably producing less impact. Harnad and Brody point out this limitation, and suggest a way in which impact can be measured for papers deposited in open access repositories:

> To get a realistic estimate of the effect of OA on impact, it is not enough to compare only the 2% of ISI journals that are OA journals with the 98% that are not, to find that they are equal in impact (for this may well be comparing apples with oranges, even if you equate for subject matter). (Harnad and Brody, 2004)

What further needs to be compared is:

> (1) the citation impact of the much higher percentage (perhaps as high as 20–40% according to Swan & Brown's (2004) sample) of articles from the 98% non-OA journals that have been made OA by their authors (by self-archiving them)
> with
> (2) the citation impact of articles from those very same journals and issues that have not been made OA by their authors. (Ibid.)

Building on Steve Lawrence's seminal paper, 'Online or invisible' (Lawrence, 2001), Harnad and Brody's analysis of the physics literature for 2001 revealed that the ratio of open access article to non-open access article citations varied from 2.5:1 to 5.8:1. They are now extending the analysis to other disciplines. Kristin Antelman uses the same evidence in order to draw a significant conclusion for libraries. If they learn more about the working methods of the researchers in their institutions, they can provide a strong impetus to the adoption of open access repositories by researchers:

> Librarians must be able to draw on a sophisticated understanding of the scholarly communication practices of individual disciplines even as they are rapidly evolving, including scholars' use of prepublication research material not traditionally part of the domain of libraries in a print environment. If we choose to

implement institutional repositories, we also must be able to persuade faculty, many of whom are for a variety of reasons quite reluctant, to contribute their prime research output. Data showing that freely available articles in their discipline are more likely to be cited is powerful evidence of the value of repositories as well as other open-access channels. (Antelman, 2004)

Antelman studied the relevant impact of open and restricted access papers in four disciplines – philosophy, political science, electronic and electrical engineering, and mathematics. She found that, while mathematics had the highest overall proportion of papers available on open access (69 per cent), the discipline in which the comparison between open and restricted access shows the greatest difference in impact measured by citations was in fact political science, which only had 29 per cent of its papers available on open access.

Scientists and social scientists are becoming more and more comfortable with reading articles in online form as a preference. The evidence from the arts and humanities does not yet bear this out, but Antelman believes that the behaviour of researchers in those fields will also change once a critical mass of papers is available in open access repositories. Lawrence points out the part that is played by convenience in the higher impact of open access papers. If papers are easy to get hold of, by being fully available from a usable online source, then they are more likely to be cited, particularly by researchers in a hurry. Libraries need to provide speedy access as part of their service (Ranganathan's Fourth Law), but they also observe a duty to ensure that the material they provide represents a balanced provision. It is ironic that one of the complaints made about some of the largest commercial publishers is that they have manipulated the convenience factor in order to serve their own commercial advantage, by putting their own journal articles within such easy reach of academics that they can benefit from the growing profile of their own titles whose impact factors are thereby boosted. Jean-Claude Guédon points this out in his seminal 2002 work *In Oldenburg's Long Shadow: Librarians, Research Scientists, Publishers, and the Control of Scientific Publishing*:

> If, through the manipulation of the number of articles in a given database, a publisher manages to affect the rate of use of its own articles, it also stands to reason that this publisher is able to affect the citation rate of its articles. If this situation leads just one Ohio scientist to cite one more Elsevier article in one of his/her articles, this affects the impact factor of the journal where the article

appears. Of course, with one citation, the effect is too small to be detected, but imagine now that event repeated an untold number of times in Ohio and across other similarly structured consortia. It will lead to increasing the number of citations to Elsevier articles. As a result, the impact factor of Elsevier journals should begin to go up. As a consequence, these journals begin to attract more authors; but then, with a greater choice of authors, the quality should go up. In effect, a kind of quality pump has been successfully primed and it begins to propel the journal up the pecking order ladder among the core journals. (Guédon, 2002)

What holds true for a commercial publisher with a vast number of full-text articles available to subscribing institutions could equally hold true for a large, interoperating, worldwide network of open access full-text institutional repositories. As Antelman remarks, the comprehensiveness of this network is likely to have a beneficial consequence for the quality of research:

> One may speculate that when articles are only a mouse click away, 'bad' author behaviors that have been described in the citation analysis literature will be less common. One example is citation bias, where authors reference only journals they can access. (Antelman, 2004)

The provision which librarians wish is one whose underlying motive is aligned to the motives of authors in publishing their research in the first place, and the 'quality pump' maintained by libraries managing institutional repositories can then serve the advancement of knowledge rather than publisher profit.

Conclusion

A growing proportion of the research community has discovered the utility of the Web for the dissemination of their research outputs, and has now been using it – for many years in the case of some disciplines. The approach has been somewhat haphazard, however, as scholars are neither publishers nor librarians. The library community, increasingly focused on a digital library agenda, has understood the need to intervene in order to ensure that the material being disseminated is managed successfully through proper description, indexing and storage for long-term preservation. The approach which has now proved its value and begun to gain ground for research outputs is also now being used for other types of material which are generated within institutions.

The marriage of research generation by academics, with output management by librarians, has created a new form of publication, with open values, which presents a growing challenge to the commercial publishers which have controlled research publication for many decades. Commercial publishers operate on the assumption of a profit motive both for themselves and for their authors. As this motive is absent in the case of academics seeking the publication of their research, it may be that with this new form of publication in repositories owned and run from within the academy, research publication has finally found its most appropriate form.

Note

1. For definitions, see MPEG-21 (2003) 'Information Technology, Multimedia Framework, Part 2: Digital Item Declaration', ISO/IEC 21000-2:2003; Advanced Distributed Learning (2003) 'The Sharable Content Object Reference Model (SCORM) – Version 1.3 – WD'.

2

Establishing a repository

Most universities and research institutions should now be actively considering the establishment of an institutional repository, if one does not already exist. If research is being conducted in the institution, then its outputs are undoubtedly being stored somewhere – probably in a variety of digital locations which will not support either ease of access to the potential user base, nor maximum impact for their authors.

Recognising the benefit of an institutional repository, and actually setting up one, are of course two entirely different things. In this chapter we look at the practicalities involved in setting up a repository. We begin with some general reflections on the importance of research and its wide dissemination, which should serve as motivation to act with some urgency if a repository does not yet exist. We then move on to examine the vital question of costs. For library managers, this is likely to be the overriding consideration. In looking at it, however, we realise that we cannot consider only the cost of setting up a new service, without at the same time addressing the longer-term question of the cost of research to our libraries and our institutions if we do not take some action of our own. The cost of research is unjustifiably high and rising, skewing our budgets to absorb it and unbalancing the library services we provide too far in support of research. As we read in Chapter 1, a library is a growing organism, in the words of Ranganathan, but unbalanced growth – too much of the budget devoted to research – makes a library fail in its endeavour to make fair and equitable provision for the needs of its users.

Much of the analysis of this chapter is based upon our own experience in setting up a repository for the University of Edinburgh, which is described in greater detail in Chapter 7. In assessing the cost elements involved for this chapter, we have sought to extrapolate these for general application. Finally, we consider the other implications for our existing library services – promotion, the design of the repository, the scoping of its contents and the question of absorbing the workload within the institution once the initial set-up and service establishment phase has ended.

The case for a repository

Why set up a repository? It cannot be done without incurring cost, and, to date, institutional repositories have not established themselves so indelibly within the landscape of academic library services that their creation is a simple expectation. It is certainly the case that institutions now produce a considerable quantity of digital data, but that has been true for many years. The normal pattern until very recently has been for that data to be housed in databases maintained in the creating departments. Academic computing services may have been considered as appropriate central services to manage some types of locally-produced data which merited the provision of a shared access facility – particularly if they ran data libraries, such as the University of Edinburgh's Data Library service. But libraries were not considered the appropriate location for data repositories.

This was because the data produced was not of the sort with which libraries were considered competent. It was statistical, or symbolic data, managed within departments by administrators or computing officers, or else fed into large national data services at hub facilities. Where research outputs were concerned, once they began to appear in digital form, as a successor to the circulated pre-print, they were often not brought to light in that form at all, because authors were content to persist with their trust in the scholarly communication process in which journal authors took care of bringing their work to public attention, and any prior attempt would present work which had no credibility as a finished output. Physicists, however, did believe strongly in circulating pre-prints speedily among themselves, and so invented arXiv to permit them to do so. Authors in other disciplines may at best have had the ability to post their papers onto departmental servers, from where they could be accessed, once the Web arrived, by a custom-written front-end.

Yet it was the arrival of the Web into this scenario which changed it and which has led to an increasingly urgent pressure now for institutional repositories of these outputs. Our concept of immediacy has been irretrievably altered by the combination of digital information, computer networking and hypertext navigation. Quite simply, we are not prepared to wait any more. The days when a paper was despatched to a publisher and, therefore, out of sight, often for many months, have gone, and as an academic I am likely to feel that if a paper I am anxious to read is sitting on a colleague's hard disk in Prague, there is no reason why I shouldn't have a copy of it a matter of seconds after requesting it from them. With a repository system in place, academics now expect that immediacy of access to papers even by fellow researchers whom they do not know. arXiv has set new expectations of immediacy of indexing, navigation and access for research publication systems, pushing publication functions further up the research process chain, to the point where a paper should be able to be published almost immediately after the author completes it, and pushes the 'Save' button.

These new systems are designed to serve the impatient, and the cynical view might be that this impatience derives from academic self-serving career ambition – the faster I can get hold of the results of other people's research, the faster I can shape and then publish my own, and so derive the credit and reward which follows. But there is another, genuine reason for injecting speed into the research publication business too, and it is one which reflects the essential value of research for humankind. Put simply, we need research. The faster the research is known and understood, the faster we all benefit. Research lubricates progress – in medical advances, in engineering new aids to human endeavour or leisure, in understanding the natural world, the motivations for the shape taken by recorded events, human belief systems, and the illuminations of artists. The speed at which a cure is found for the disease from which my child is suffering can never be great enough. Similarly, we can never arrive too quickly at a comprehensive understanding of a catastrophic failure of human politics resulting in human injury and death on a massive scale, so that we can be warned of how not to repeat it. Speedy, universal publication of research is a crucially serious business, and the humble institutional repository, in playing its part in its acceleration and general broadcast, should not be underestimated or trivialised.

The cost of scholarly journals

There are, of course, more mundane reasons also. The traditional research publication system is straining to breaking point at the present time, as library purchasing power falls further and further behind the rate of price increase of journals, and the rise in the number of these journals due to research specialisation. The Scholarly Publishing and Academic Resources

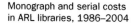

Figure 2.1 ARL analysis of serials costs 1986–2004

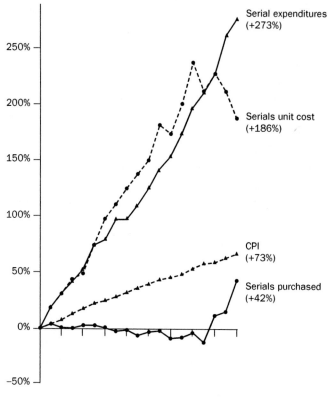

Monograph and serial costs
in ARL libraries, 1986–2004

Coalition (SPARC) has been particularly effective at drawing attention to this crisis in recent years. SPARC was established by the US Association of Research Libraries (ARL), which also runs a longitudinal survey of US library budgets and costs. Figures from 2005 on monograph and serial costs in its member libraries over an 18-year period show very vividly why the system is in crisis. Serials have risen by 273 per cent in those 18 years – almost four times as much as the Consumer Price Index, which roughly reflects the rise in university library budgets (Figure 2.1).

This is obviously unsustainable, and university libraries are, therefore, driven to investigate new forms of scholarly publishing as much by the need to survive as by any higher motive.

University libraries, particularly in research-intensive universities, have become familiar with these issues through the activities of bodies like SPARC and the ARL, and funding initiatives in many countries to explore open access publishing. In the UK, for example, JISC set up the Focus on Access to Institutional Resources (FAIR) programme in 2002. Libraries have, therefore, felt under pressure to respond to the suggestion that they should set up an institutional repository themselves, and to investigate the implications of doing so.

Costing a repository

Before we look at the costs of setting up an institutional repository, it is worth looking at the cost structures libraries are already familiar with when they purchase electronic research outputs from journal publishers. These reveal that the arrival of research publications in digital form has pushed libraries into a very weak position as purchasers, and show why the motivation to reach an alternative system of research publication is such a strong one in the academic library community.

The cost of buying a bundled e-journal service from a publisher is not straightforwardly measurable in the way the purchase of printed journals is, with payment for each individual title being made normally to a subscription agent, who would often offer a discount for bulk orders. What both forms of journal have in common is that the cost of the purchase is expressed in terms of the content, and the period of time over which that content will be accessible. In that sense, both forms appear to have only two axes. Printed journals have only ever been sold on an annual basis, with libraries free to cancel any individual title in any given year because of low use, or high cost. E-journal services, however, are frequently sold on a multi-title, multi-annual basis, with libraries tied in to purchasing a larger set of journals than they need for a longer period than they want. The product sold in this way is popularly known as the 'Big Deal', and is only possible because the market for research publications is supplier-led.

With all library resources, there are hidden costs to factor in as well. With printed journals, these are the cost of cataloguing and binding the journals, of replacing stolen or missing parts, and of displaying and providing access to them per square metre of shelving. In addition, there is the cost in staff time of issuing them, if we allow that, and of reshelving them from the photocopying room.

E-journal services have their hidden costs also. The cost per megabyte of caching them; the cost per fraction of public PC time in providing access at PCs over campus networks; the cost of training users, and of producing documentation which helps to train them. These are all *local* hidden costs, and we consider them a valid additional cost which we should bear in our libraries, as service providers, as they are an inevitable consequence of purchasing content which then has to be promoted and delivered in our own local environments.

But e-journal services also come with another dimension, which is the hidden cost of the Big Deal, where the publisher presents an incentive to the customer to purchase the entire database of content rather than just a subset of it – the incentive usually being that there is no saving to be gained in buying a subset. Often, for example, a proportion of the cost of our printed journals is really a hidden cost of the Big Deal, because the price we pay is based upon a formula which assesses our print spend as a proportion of the total possible print spend, from which is derived the additional premium we pay for access to the online corpus. Put more simply, the less we spend on print, the more we will be charged, relatively, for the electronic Big Deal. We might call this the 'proportion of total' cost. Hidden costs of this type are not local, but rather could be seen as premiums levied by publishers for the way in which content is now being delivered in new packaged aggregations. However, they are additional to the publicised 'e-journal premium' fee which publishers also levy.

Then there is the hidden cost which we might think of as a reverse loyalty charge, and which exploits the multi-annual nature of the Big Deal. In order to benefit from the Big Deal, we must show loyalty to the supplier by undertaking not to cancel more than a tiny fraction of the journals we purchase in print in our annual review of journal titles for cancellation. This charge, which arguably exploits monopoly power, means the opposite of what 'loyalty' means in our local supermarket, where the purchaser is rewarded for loyalty by being given discount on purchases. In the case of such Big Deals, our loyalty as customers rewards the supplier with extra revenue, on the grounds that however bad a deal the Big Deal may appear to be, it is not as bad as choosing to buy only the subset of the corpus that we actually want, as that would be more expensive still.

E-journal costs are, therefore, more complex than traditional print journal costs, because they contain two dimensions of hidden costs rather than just the one cost of the local dimension. The second dimension has no parallel in the print journal world. It represents the exploitation of customers through the practices of suppliers who have realised the power they now wield over revenue generation through the combination of the absence of competition and the attractiveness of a web-accessible database of multiple journal full-text content. Of course e-journal aggregations, as they are databases, can appear to be a wonderful solution, so time-saving and so easily searchable. We might, therefore, think of this second dimension as being *databased costs*.

By far the greatest element of the cost to libraries in acquiring closed-access journals, of course, is the cost of the content. We say 'That journal costs £400 a year' or 'That journal costs £4000 a year', and we ignore the hidden element. In the case of open-access content, however, the cost appears to be only the hidden element, as the content is free. And in that case, we might wonder whether it is even worth talking about. Here, of course, we are leaving aside consideration of any 'author pays' costs which might apply in the case of open-access journals, as there are too many unknowns there. For example, will these costs continue to be met by libraries at all? And if they are, what would be the overall reduction in the journals cost burden for an average research library if all journals went open access? There is a variety of opinions on that question.

Generally, libraries set up repositories themselves. There has been little opportunity to date to have a service set up on their behalf, with the repository hosted and facilities-managed by a third party (though this model has been applied in one or two JISC-funded projects, such as SHERPA and IRI Scotland). One commercial publisher, the open access journal publisher BioMed Central, does offer a hosted repository service, Open Repository (*www.openrepository.com*), and a service based on the GNU EPrints platform from the University of Southampton has just been announced.

There are a number of reasons why institutions are more likely to develop their own repositories over using a hosted service. It may be that, by their very nature, institutional repositories are 'home-made' alternatives to third-party agents of dissemination. But if institutions are to run them for themselves, they need to consider the total cost of ownership (TCO) of a repository service. As the content is free, what non-content costs are there?

First, there is the cost of two servers (one to run the service, and one to provide a test environment). Most of the remainder is staff time. But this is significant, and considerably less absorbable into existing library costs than the staff time costs in the case of commercial e-journals.

To begin with, there is the cost of technical support. The cost of installation of any of the available open source platforms is not trivial at the present time, and the local customisation of the software might easily require six months of a system developer's dedicated time on interface development. It might require even more if the library concerned is interested in enhancing functionality – by writing new code which is then released to the relevant open source community at large – which thereby benefits all users of the software. Such an act of philanthropy goes unrewarded in any direct way in the world of open source, as there is no cooperative market operating in open source of the type which operates in cataloguing cooperatives because of the different nature of the products involved. The open source economy works differently, with all benefiting from the work of the enthusiastic and well-resourced few – a sort of 'trickle-down' rather than the more straightforward 'buy or sell' model of cataloguing cooperatives. It does have a payback, however, in the goodwill generated towards those institutions which shoulder the brunt of the work. In addition, while it allows the overall improvement in research publication to be expedited for the benefit of institutions whose academics have most to gain in access to research, it does so through the efforts of those institutions whose academics have most to gain in impact.

Then there is a metadata cost. Depending on how many deposits a given repository receives in a year, we might require, say, in a university of around 1,500 researchers, 0.25 FTE of a cataloguer to create original metadata and quality control work on author-provided metadata. A quarter of a post is high for this, but in these times of moving from the uniformity of MARC to the plurality of schemas for a large range of digital object types, the business of cataloguing has become considerably more complex, and slower. We should also recognise that the complexity of the cataloguing effort required would suggest a professional-grade post.

Finally, in assessing staff costs, there is the effort required to garner the content at all. Our experience tells us that in this endeavour it is not enough simply to host a couple of half-day seminars in the library. By and large, the research community is not nearly as interested in self-archiving or open access journal publishing, as is the library. Academic authors do not flock to half-day seminars organised by the library on these topics, nor in any great numbers leave the events wiser and resolved to make wholesale changes in their research lifestyles.

Acquiring the content is slow and laborious work, and at the present time we pay for it with the sweat of our brow, rather than by dipping into our materials budget. It involves – in addition to seminars in the library – working though lists of academics with research management responsibilities, research journal editors and senior managers, as well as 'common or garden' academics. It requires the organisation and tenacity (and thick skin) to lobby powerful committees, to meet academics in their own territory – in departmental meetings, and at lunchtime seminars held by research groups. It requires the hunting down of unorganised self-archived work, and the corralling of it within the institution's managed repository. It requires the capture of author permissions and an awareness of publisher policies on copyright transfer. It involves knowledge of licensing as it applies to self-archived and open access content. And most of all, perhaps, it involves the practice of constant repetition of the same message over and over many thousands of times, often to the same people, because the issues are difficult and non-intuitive to academic authors. This is liaison work, and in a large research university it can easily cost a full-time professional member of staff.

There will hopefully come a 'tipping point', of course, when the acquisition of content suddenly becomes much simpler because of paradigm shift, and authors begin naturally to send their newly completed research straight to the repository without a second thought. Breaking the long-established pattern of submission direct to publishers will indeed be perhaps the most important achievement of libraries in this culture shift in which we are engaged, and we might here make the more general observation that, in the world of digital content, libraries need to intervene in the direct supplier-to-user link at various points. An institutional repository is the result of just such an intervention. This provides them with the challenge of doing something which is counter to the ethos of many organisations in adopting the Internet, which is to 'cut out the middleman'. In this new environment, libraries have somehow to be invisible, or at least unobtrusive middlemen, who still manage the relationship of users and content in accountable and efficient ways.

This library intervention may have to be human, as in the case of making decisions on whether an article destined for a given journal can be self-archived as a pre-print, and what copyright transfer assertion may need to be made; or it may be applied at the machine-level, as in the deployment of OpenURL link resolution to channel a link request to a repository object rather than direct to a publisher's server. In the near to medium term, some of what would currently require human intervention will switch to machine intervention, as machine intelligence is more commonly applied in these contexts.

But the tipping point is not yet here, so for the time being, the establishment of an institutional repository is likely to require the services of a full-time professional liaison librarian across a medium-to-large research university.

Other costs remain. There is the large and still largely unknown cost of digital preservation, which is likely, once business models emerge, to require some local professional staff time in selection and metadata generation, and a storage cost which might be borne locally, or might be a fee levied by a digital vault service. The activity of digital preservation is at the present time too experimental, with too many models operating for costs to be definable. For longer-term planning purposes, we suggest that at least 10 per cent is added to the overall cost of its institutional repository to allow for preservation of the archived items.

On top of all of these 'lifecycle' costs for our digital object management, there is of course the cost of management time to ensure that progress is made, that staff are in post at the appropriate points and are productive and motivated, and that targets are set and achieved. So we have identified technical, metadata, liaison, preservation and management activity which by our estimate would add up to around 2.25 FTE professional staff. That is a significant additional cost on the budget of a research library.

Making the case for a repository

Arguing for additional resource for a repository from the university or the cost centre in which the library belongs, is not an easy matter, particularly when the urgency of the requirement may be difficult to convey. What might help, however, is the recognition that the cost involved is not necessarily all additional. In academic libraries at the present time, managers are generally engaged in strategic development which involves a radical look at historically-based budgets to derive savings from the de-emphasis or even the abandonment of some activities, and the reallocation of those savings to new activities – such as the creation and maintenance of institutional repositories. Thus, many academic libraries began a few years ago to purchase self-issue and discharge machines to handle much of their circulation. As they move beyond the capital investment phase in these machines, there ought to be some recurrent saving. Similarly, they are tending to scale back on their use of front-desk reference staff, and instead equipping newly-built library web portals with functionality which allows their users to send queries to subject librarians to be answered either synchronously or asynchronously. The asynchronous service will normally have a cost-saving attached.

Such savings are few as yet, and they are not always easily reallocated to digital library development costs, but it is too simplistic a view of library economies to say that the costs of implementing institutional repositories are all additional. What the decision to implement an institutional repository is likely to do, however, is to catalyse the radical review of budget allocations in a library. A library with a culture which permits a budgetary reorganisation to happen that way is likely to have an institutional repository ahead of a library that requires the reorganisation to be complete before spending on the repository. Much will depend on the library director's freedom to act within an overall budget from the planning group to which the library belongs, and smaller libraries are likely to find it more difficult to introduce initiatives which impact on their budgets.

We need a range of new skills in our library staff today. We need programmers, web designers, and experts in multiple metadata schemas. We need state-of the-art digital object archival skills. We also, arguably, need more staff with disciplinary knowledge to do effective liaison. As we need more staff with those skill-sets, so we need fewer MARC cataloguers, and fewer library assistants on issue desks; however, we don't need to do the sums to see that overall the savings, which are generally made from lower-paid staff, will not offset the additional costs, which are generally for staff with more expensive skills.

Where do we find this additional money? Only an optimist would argue that it is likely to come from savings in the materials budget as open access and self-archiving transform the economics of research publication. Even accepting that that whole enterprise should ultimately become cheaper as the proportion of materials spend which goes to the shareholders of private publishing companies falls, hopefully dramatically, we are still some way off that 'windfall saving'. We are not in the business of promoting open access and self-archiving primarily in order to save money, though it is reasonable to expect that at the very least we will reduce the rate of the excruciating erosion of purchasing power which has been caused by monopoly pricing far in excess of inflation over the past couple of decades.

Some of the funding for repository development is already coming from sector-wide agencies interested in promoting innovations for the sake of improved service and cost-efficiencies in the longer term. In the UK, the FAIR Programme has provided funding for a number of institutions to develop repositories as part of projects that have been resourced to generate experience which can be shared with the UK higher education community as a whole. Some elements of a national infrastructure have also been funded, such as a service provider search service (e-prints UK, see *www.rdn.ac.uk/projects/eprints-uk/*), and the GNU EPrints software development. Project SHERPA (*www.sherpa.ac.uk*) was funded in order to kick-start repositories in a number of research universities across the UK, with coordination coming from a single project manager, and a similar project which embraces research institutes and further education colleges as well as universities is just beginning in Scotland (*www.jisc.ac.uk/index.cfm?name=project_iriscotland*).

There are two obvious ways in which a university library can fund a new venture into digital repositories for university output. One method is to bid to the parent institution for funding, and the other is to find the funding from within the existing library budget.

The first route is not always successful. At least until recently it has been difficult for libraries to explain to the academic community why they believe repositories are important. This changed in 2005, however, within the UK at least, due mainly to announcements in support of open access publishing from research funding bodies such as the Wellcome Trust and Research Councils UK. What has also brought repositories to the attention of academics and university managers is the possibility of using a repository in the submission process for the UK's Research Assessment Exercise in 2007–8. Nevertheless, librarians know how much academics resist having to change their behaviour and for them to be persuaded to give even a few minutes of their precious time over to a new regime for capturing their output will not be easy. It is important for the library to find academic champions in senior positions in order to persuade waverers. If the arguments for a repository are opposed by sceptical academics in senior management decision meetings, the prospect of receiving additional funding for a repository may be a remote one.

Librarians must be prepared to be patient. They will find themselves having to rebut common misconceptions about open access publishing and open access archiving time and time again. Some academics will declare that all Internet publishing is non-refereed and, therefore, valueless. They need to have the difference between pre-prints and post-prints explained to them. Some will state that mixing non-refereed with refereed papers on the Web will devalue the latter. They need to be told that the two can be kept entirely separate by search services. Some others will say that the whole initiative will put publishers out of business. The counter to that line is that publishers who price responsibly will still be able to sell their products, and that a new market is in any case developing in open access publishing, in order primarily to allow publishers to continue to perform peer review via their journal titles.

It is not surprising that academics misunderstand the issues; their jobs require them only to use the services of publishers, not to understand the whole scholarly publishing business. Yet it is a fact peculiar to universities as organisations that the correction of these misconceptions has to be made repeatedly, and that broadcast and printed information from the library on the subject will not be sufficient to allow the library to take the position that all of the organisation's staff are now in possession of the facts.

The second route has a greater chance of success – but even there, the library usually has to obtain permission from a library committee or equivalent to permit it to divert its own funding into this purpose. One of the most effective ways of doing this is to demonstrate demand for the new service which is being argued for. Demand can be shown via project work, and it is certainly true that most of the repositories now active in UK university libraries emerged from previous projects – funded either by JISC, or funded internally in some cases. The project can then demonstrate the demand as well as the full scope of the service, and can initiate a fledgling service. Once the demand has been proved, a library committee can find it very difficult to say 'no' to the diversion of funds from elsewhere into maintaining a service which is appreciated.

But what are the costs, and how can they be found within a large university library budget? Given that it is accepted that a library should run an institutional repository, which services can it give up, or run in a different way, to realise the saving required? This is a fairly contentious topic, and can lead to heated discussions in library management meetings. Before we turn to the savings opportunities, however, we need to calculate the costs of setting up and running a repository.

Table 2.1 shows the cost elements which applied in Edinburgh University Library. Costs were projected over an initial five-year period. The software platform chosen by the library was DSpace, an open source system, hence there is no costing for the application software.

In making the case for an institutional repository in terms of value for money, we looked at how its costs impacted on the total budget, in order to see whether it could be funded from strategic change savings arising in other areas. We found that the staffing cost, in Year 1, was just below 1 per cent of our overall library staff budget; by Year 5, that had risen to 1.13 per cent. The creation of a repository, of course, can also be considered as a cost on the materials budget, in which context it could in theory be offset against savings to be made over time as open access publishing either drives down journal publisher costs, or else permits

Table 2.1	Cost elements involved in establishing an institutional repository over five years

Item	Notes
Servers (2) + open source operating system support contract	Capital cost of servers; annual maintenance costs; contract paid annually
System developer	Estimated at 0.8 FTE in Year 1 (installation and development), 0.5 FTE in Year 2, and then 0.3 FTE in succeeding years (mainly support)
Liaison officer	Estimated at 0.8 FTE every year
Metadata editor	This requirement scales up considerably over time; estimated at 0.1 FTE until Year 3, then rising over two years to 0.5 FTE
Management	Arguably this cost is higher in initial 1–2 years, but is generally at a low level – estimated at 0.07 FTE of a senior manager's time

journal cancellations. The total cost of the repository, at 2004 prices, was approximately £47,000 per annum in Year 1, and £54,000 per annum by Year 5. This represented 1.43 per cent of our materials budget in Year 1, and 1.64 per cent by Year 5.

Such figures persuaded the University of Edinburgh Library Committee that spending on an institutional repository was justifiable. Repository growth needs to be brought into the calculation for costing, and we based our figures on the next few years, when we assumed that the content would begin to flow properly into the repository. Our model made a knowingly optimistic assumption that by Year 5 the maximum possible number of items each year would be deposited in our institutional repository. The University of Edinburgh has roughly 1,400 active researchers, each producing an average of two publishable papers per year (allowing for disciplinary culture differences which mean that the very prolific scientific domains are balanced out by the arts and humanities where journal article publication is often not a standard research output). As our repository also ingests PhD theses, and approximately 600 of these are produced each year, this amounts to a maximum of 3,400 items per year.

Since the metadata work for each item is quality control work, rather than original cataloguing (because the depositor adds the metadata at the time of submission), the metadata labour involved should not rise substantially. Estimating 15 minutes per item, for 3,400 items per year, means that a half-time post would be required. On the hardware front,

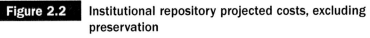

Figure 2.2 Institutional repository projected costs, excluding preservation

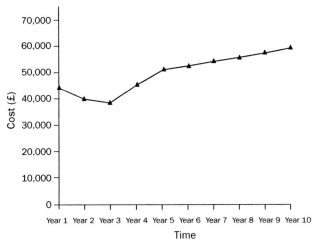

we purchased both a development PC and a production server. The latter was equipped with 183 Gb of storage. Taking a cautious average size per deposited output of 1.5 Mb, this would mean that even after five years, the server's storage capacity would have reached no further than 20 per cent full. However, the savings to be made by buying less storage were not significant, and it was decided that we should allow for the fact that deposited outputs might begin to diversify over time, to encompass data sets, for example, a higher preponderance of high resolution images, or more substantial items, such as monographs.

Basing the model on a maximum input projection allows decision-makers also to see the annual total cost once the fledgling service has moved into a stable mode of existence. We then projected the model forward by a further five years, to show the 'steady state' costs (Figure 2.2).

Costs begin higher, during the project phase. There is also likely to be an initial glut of already-produced content, sitting in departmental publication systems or in academics' own web pages. Costs then reduce for a couple of years due to a drop in the number of deposits and in the reduction in the number of programmer hours required. They rise again, however, as the content increases towards its maximum, and thereafter (Years 6–10) the increase is only that required to keep pace with inflation.

A truer picture includes also the cost of digital preservation. This is a cost which we do not know as yet, but if we assume that it will be known after five years, we see costs rise steeply at that point, and then achieve

Figure 2.3 Institutional repository projected costs, including preservation

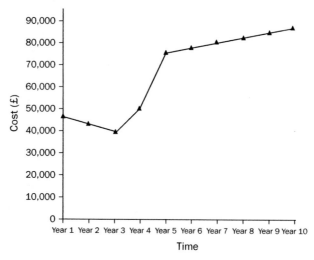

steady state. Figure 2.3 shows the effect of a 10 per cent rise in overall costs to cover preservation. Some analysts believe the percentage rise could be much higher than that. Our figure of 10 per cent is based on the assumption that preservation will be delivered in a collaborative environment of some sort.

Returning to the question of whether any elements of these costs can be considered substitutional, as stated above, the most obviously related saving – in the cost of journals – is not a reality yet, although it might conceivably be so in a few years' time. There are likely to be savings, however, in the concentration of repository services into one point, as it is frequently the case that academic departments have embryonic repositories already in place, and it is certainly very common for individual researchers to have copies of their own papers on servers in their offices or departments. Quantifying the cost of that disparate provision, and of the resource to sustain it (such as departmental computer officers) would be difficult to do exactly, but it may be worthwhile for a library to estimate the cost saving to the institution as a whole by creating a single institutional repository in the library.

Securing the innovation

An institutional repository is an innovation in library service, and it needs to be nurtured and husbanded carefully in its early days. Library managers will require the repository to make a reasonable impact early on, in order to persuade the institution to support the repository, both with funding and with content. Their first priority will be to secure a good quantity of content quite rapidly from early adopters, in order to be able to demonstrate to more cautious academics and academic managers that the repository has validity elsewhere in the university, and has proved its feasibility in a short space of time. There will also need to be a sustained effort of promotion of the service, best achieved by targeting specific departments and research groups 'on the ground'.

On the other hand, several decisions need to be made at the outset, which require careful thought, and which – if made wrongly – could endanger the whole project in the longer term. Of these, three in particular stand out. These relate to structure, to validity of deposits, and to metadata.

The structure

How is the repository to be organised? Most repository applications will allow a considerable degree of freedom in how to set up a repository for a particular institution. Institutions then need to decide whether to recreate the whole organisational form (e.g. faculties, departments, research groups) in their repository structure, or to adopt a different approach, such as by subject. In reaching this decision institutional politics will need to be considered. Departments that deposit a high quantity of material, for example, are likely to want their relative weight to be labelled with their departmental name. Libraries must take care to consult on structure at an early stage, as decisions taken at the outset will be difficult to change later.

Object validity

What formal requirements will be made for objects entering the repository? It is likely that repository managers will wish to limit the number of file formats which can be accepted, mainly because of the need to provide a facility which provides a guarantee that the objects will be preserved into the long term. This is a guarantee which many academics may require before they begin to use the repository, and is likely to be a clear reason for them to prefer a centralised service to one that they might operate themselves in their own department. Some file formats are better future-proofed than others, being based upon open standards.

Another aspect of validity relates to data level. Will a repository accept deposits which are of metadata only? Here there are two questions to consider. First, will the software technically permit the deposit only of meta-information, without an accompanying bitstream that represents the described object? If not, are there ways around this limitation to deal with cases which might appear reasonable, such as the case of those electronic theses which are restricted for a number of months due to the need to protect commercial confidentiality? Managers will need to decide whether a metadata record only in such instances is preferable, say, to showing the record in the library catalogue instead. This decision will necessitate an overview of a library's full repository architecture, including its central bibliographic database, so that the presentation of records, both metadata-only and full-text, can be efficient (avoiding duplication) and coherent for users.

Some repository managers might decide that they can accept metadata-only records. This would be useful as a means of recording an institution's total research output at a meta-level, but is nonetheless likely to be frustrating for users, particularly if they cannot predict whether a given record is likely to have a full-text object attached.

Metadata

Finally, there is the question of metadata. Libraries must be aware that, if they do indeed find content beginning to arrive in their repository quite quickly, they must have a way of recording it to a given level of metadata quality. Basic metadata will be provided by authors, but library staff will need to perform a quality control check, make corrections, and add missing fields. It is both practically very difficult, and unhelpful to the objective of maintaining repository users, to accept poor quality metadata initially and then to go back at a later date in order to improve it.

One person managing the entire repository may quickly be swamped, particularly if departments make a wholesale switch of policy from maintaining their own separate repository to using the library's new service instead. In such circumstances too, there may be a large retrospective load of material to ingest. Libraries, therefore, need to have cataloguer resource standing by, able to be drafted in as required. Planning for this can be difficult, particularly when the cataloguers required are likely to have already existing hefty workloads, and may require training in a new schema. But it is unrealistic to think of a repository manager as being a 'one-man-band', incorporating the skills of academic liaison and outreach with those of cataloguer. It is likely instead that there will need to be a transitional period, which may be lengthy, during which the requirement to draft in cataloguing support will fluctuate often quite dramatically, before ingest stabilises to steady-state, and planning can be done more easily.

Conclusion

The creation of an institutional repository can be a costly business, even though it may seem trifling when set against the serials spend of a medium to large research university. A thorough understanding of the economic and the ethical arguments for open access and open archiving are essential if libraries are to receive institutional support to set up a repository. With such understanding, the advocacy work of promotion and liaison which are vital at the outset will stand a good chance of success.

Once a repository is established, it will remain an additional cost on the library for some time to come. Ultimately though, there should begin to be savings in the cost of published research as publishers respond to the competition afforded by repositories. Libraries have to be prepared to be patient as they wait for the 'tipping point' in their repositories, and for savings to be made in their journals spend to offset the TCO costs of their repository. Setting up the workflow measures to deal with a growing number of repository items year by year will ensure that they are able to realise the full benefits of an open access culture of research at the earliest possible opportunity.

3

Technologies and technicalities

In this chapter we examine the processes that an institution may need to go through in order to understand and specify the technical aspects of their institutional repository.[1] This includes an examination of general requirements of the software based upon its very nature; to help us define this set of requirements we recourse to current thinking regarding the scope of the institutional repository. Once we can provide a general outline of the functionality we desire or expect from the software, we can employ use case modelling to see how it sits within the institution's local requirements, and see how these use cases translate into literal software requirements. Then we can show how evaluation of available packages, and specifically a comparative evaluation, can be performed in order to ensure the adoption of the most appropriate technology, or even the decision to develop in-house.

Underlying this chapter there is a discussion of the technical issues facing repositories as pieces of software and the design processes that need to be gone through by both developers and implementers. We will take a closer look at the Open Archives Initiative Protocol for Metadata Harvesting (OAI-PMH) which is proving to be very popular among repositories of all types, and how this can allow us to create both external and internal information networks consisting of data sources above and beyond simply the institutional repository. This allows us to see the bigger picture by placing the repository among the many other forms of information systems on a global scale. We also examine the basic concepts of digital preservation; we look at the Open Archival Information System (OAIS) reference model, and some practical activities in which repository managers can engage at the outset to minimise the risks to holdings.

Throughout the course of the chapter, and indeed this book, we will primarily focus on open-source software (OSS) as the provider for technical solutions. There are many reasons for adopting open source, especially in an academic environment; it is often produced by a collaboration of interested parties working towards similar goals; it does not suffer from the risks of being tied to a single vendor for the life of the system. In addition, the goals and ethos of OSS are similar to those of open access (Jones and Andrew, 2005), making them natural partners in this kind of endeavour. For the purposes of this book we will consider *open source software* to mean that the software has been released under either a permissive or copyleft licence.

The nature of institutional repository software

The functional scope of an institutional repository package is fairly loosely defined; many features will be specified not by the nature of the software but by the specific requirements defined by implementing institutions. We can define a set of features that may be generally useful for software of this nature, but at no point do we suggest that this set is either complete or definitive. Here we will introduce these features, justify them, examine how institutions may decide on which elements are important for them, see how use cases can be utilised to extend the required scope as defined by local requirements, and subsequently how evaluation of software can be performed to ensure that the resulting software adoption (or choice to develop in-house) is successful.

Throughout this chapter we will avoid referring to any specific institutional repository software, but descriptions of some of the packages currently available under open-source licences are contained in the appendices.

General institutional repository feature set

To define any kind of feature set for a piece of software it is necessary to think about the scope of the resulting package, and how it will be used in its target environment. Although local scoping will play a primary role in the final evaluation of any package, there are general features which we can require by the very nature of the objective: being an institutional repository. We have seen that the institutional repository is only one form of a super-class of other digital object/asset management systems, and we are not, therefore, forced to address all repository-like issues as they may not belong within the remit of our system.

Current thinking suggests that the institutional repository should be able to meet the following criteria (Genoni, 2004; Johnson, 2002; Lynch, 2003):

1. institutionally defined;

2. scholarly;

3. cumulative and perpetual;

4. open and interoperable;

5. digitally capture and preserve many events of campus life;

6. search with constraints.

Examination of each of these criteria gives us more of an idea of what we would like to achieve and some clues as to how it might be done. For example, *institutionally defined* indicates that there are no extra-institutional issues that need to be dealt with, as there may be in subject repositories. This means that we are probably looking for something easily integrated into our existing systems framework, both in terms of style, semantics and technology.

For the system to be *scholarly* we do not demand that all content be of a publishable level, but that all of the material therein be of some value to academics. We are not requiring that the information be of specific interest to the public. That is, although *open* (point 4) it is primarily aimed at academics, and this will have repercussions with regard to the way that information is presented and organised; academics will be used to working with certain data forms and scholarly communication standards which the public will not, and the institutional repository may leverage these semantics.

Point 3, *cumulative and perpetual*, addresses the related issues of accumulation of material and the subsequent preservation of that material in perpetuity. We are neither aiming to gather a set of artefacts initially and hold them for all time nor to continually accept new material, allowing the old to slip away; we must always be looking to expand the collection and ensure that all holdings are viewable or recoverable effectively forever.

When we consider whether a system is *open* as per point 4, we mean that the access to the system is unfettered, and thus that the content, insomuch as is legally permissible, is freely available to anyone with access to the Internet. At first glance it would not necessarily be obvious that an *open and interoperable* system is in any way a requirement of an institutional repository. A laudable objective, no doubt, but perhaps not a requirement? In reality we can justify this in a number of ways, not least that the purpose of scholarly communication is to allow scholars to communicate, and as the institutional repository is one of the many forms of scholarly communication, no viable argument can suggest its holdings be restricted. Indeed, much of the effort behind institutional repositories is in order to provide this very service. It is also a feature of many other types of repository and as there will no doubt be content crossover and content aggregation it is necessary that any one repository system be capable of sharing its contents with others.

More abstract arguments aside, it is also necessary that the institutional repository capture the relevant materials. Some debate with regard to the content types exists, with some repositories preferring to capture only certified research output such as e-prints, others preferring to also embrace so called 'grey literature' such as e-theses or conference papers and posters. Some might choose to distinguish between peer-reviewed journal articles and pre-prints, while others still believe that the role of the institutional repository should be able to absorb many of the digital assets produced in normal campus life (Lynch, 2003). These latter assets can go so far as to include teaching and learning objects, technical and working papers and even institutional administrative documents, as per point (5). Our definition, for the purposes of this discussion, will assume that you may wish to do any of these things with your institutional repository, and attempts to address the issues which arise with such diverse content types.

Once we have our repository populated with material we obviously need to expose the contents to the world in order to meet our stated objectives. Being *open and interoperable* is one thing, but allowing users to examine the data in an intelligent way and discover relevant and interesting items is another. This is where we request that our software have, and be aware of, its own internal structure so that it is capable of answering queries from both human and automated users (point 6). This does not necessarily mean that the software requires a pleasant user interface; instead it means that it needs one or more software interfaces which are capable of receiving and responding to queries in standardised forms. The addition of a user interface or a web service interface is relatively straightforward and of less overall importance once the underlying infrastructure is complete and stable.

A set of requirements derived from the general scope

Examining the scope presented in the previous section and combining it with standard requirements that might be expected from a piece of software, we can build up a fairly comprehensive requirements list that would, in general, form an excellent institutional repository. However, it is worth noting before we proceed that although we will present a long list of items, it is by no means definitive. Furthermore, much variation based on your exact use cases will no doubt be evident, and we should remember that not all of these will necessarily be required at all institutions.

Community support

Having the software developed and supported by a strong and active community can be a great bonus for any package. For the users it provides a place of technical support, source of development (which is often responsive to feature requests) and bug fixing. Users who are technically minded are also encouraged to feed their experiences back for the benefit of others. This is a particular advantage of using OSS.

Easily integrable

Local services will exist prior to any institutional repository software being installed, and it is increasingly necessary that systems fit well into existing infrastructures and designs. Both branding and interoperability are important to institutions and both of these require that new software be sufficiently customisable as to be seamlessly integrated. Concepts that aid this are customisable user interface templates, abstracted display styling (e.g. CSS), good standards compliance for interoperability and strong divisions between the application's layers.

In addition to this, the general software architecture should be modular such that local customisations, as will often need to be made, are pain-free. There should also be options to allow the system to plug directly into your local authentication system whatever it might be (e.g. single sign-on, certificate based system). With an adequately well layered system it should be possible to embed components in other systems and provide web service interfaces so that the repository can participate in genuine distributed application networks.

Authentication and authorisation

Authentication is the process by which a user is verified to be who they say they are. The most recognisable form of this is the provision by the user of a username and password. Other, more generalised solutions to this also exist, such as authentication against a Lightweight Directory Access Protocol (LDAP) server, or the use of some other certificate based system such as Kerberos. Most institutions will have global systems like these in use already, and the ability to connect directly to one of these would be a great asset.

The traditional partner to authentication, authorisation, determines what the authenticated users are allowed to do within the system. For this reason it can be very difficult to manage authorisations at a level higher than the application itself; applications often introduce new concepts or new ways of working which cannot easily be mapped from a standard authorisation system. Although such standard authorisation systems exist, and although it is technically possible to integrate them, it is still important that the application itself have a well designed internal system for managing authorisation settings no matter where they come from, and a separate interface upon which a local system could be implemented.

We may choose to link our authorisations through to many other institutional information systems, such as staff and student database or perhaps course lists. These might ultimately provide us with sufficient information for the system to automatically define authorisations using its own procedures. The problem with this, of course, is that a standardised way of doing this is virtually impossible at present, given the diversity of the data sets involved.

Content security and verification

Holding material in perpetuity has many complications, some of which will be discussed later in this chapter. One is ensuring that you are actually storing data which is correct and intended; there are a number of ways of achieving this, each with different strengths.

We can, for example, use checksums to verify the contents of a file. A checksum is the result of an algorithm which, when applied to a given digital stream (such as a file), provides an effectively unique identifier for each one. If this checksum is generated at ingest, then any re-application of the algorithm (which will be standard and trusted) should always yield the same results; if it does not then we know the file has been tampered with and cannot be assumed to be identical to the originally ingested one.

Another option involves placing provenance metadata alongside digital assets, to provide an electronic paper trail. If automatically applied by a trusted system then this information can help users understand the processes through which the information has passed and thus allow a degree of certainty to be placed on the authenticity of the item.

In addition to this, the actual structuring of the data needs to meet some digital preservation standards. These standards will be discussed more later on, but basic guidelines might be to consider whether the data, along with related metadata, is easy to recover without the application. This means that the files might have sensible names and be held in sensible directory structures, and that metadata for files and files themselves are stored together.

Administration systems

To successfully administer an institutional repository, which could contain a diverse set of information belonging to many different people, provided in several ways and forms, it is necessary to have a solid administrative tool to maintain the application quickly and easily. This is going to include the ability to manage authorisations, and may include convenience tools such as user grouping or cascading property changes. It should also be possible to support devolved administration; being institution wide, it is likely that departmental administrators will be interested in managing their own content, and the option to provide this, without compromising the overall integrity of the system, is important. It is easy to imagine many different kinds of administrative roles that intersect the system; super users to administer any of the following might be important: collections, users and groups, repository structure, general content or the entire system.

Content licences and restrictions

As material is being made available online in an open and interoperable repository it is useful and important to license the holdings correctly. As Chapter 6 notes, we can identify three parties involved in the act of depositing material in an institutional repository: the submitter, the institution and the end-user. It would be convenient for different licences to be in place for each of these parties' interests, and it may also be necessary to constrain the scopes of the licences. For example, we may choose one licence for on-campus access and another for off-campus, or we may choose to limit the time for which a licence applies, especially in the case where content is potentially sensitive for a period in time (e.g. commercial research), but whose content we do ultimately wish to curate.

It would, therefore, be desirable to have a system which allows us to build complex licences for our items, and to tie those licences to a restriction system which knows how to manage the content to ensure that the terms and conditions of the licence are met.

Web service enabled

Web services are becoming increasingly important in modern systems, and the institutional repository is no exception. Indeed, it is the best way to achieve open and interoperable behaviour, as it allows remote hosts to request information in a structured and manageable way. There are a number of web service protocols that might be particularly important for this sort of application, such as z39.50 at the heavyweight end of the scale through to simple HTTP used in a RESTful (Representational State Transfer, which, in a loose sense, describes any web service which uses XML over HTTP without the additional complexities of web service protocols such as SOAP) way at the lighter end. Of increasing importance are lightweight protocols such as Search/Retrieve Web Service and URL Service (SRW/U) and the OAI-PMH. It is useful for any repository to be able to support one or more of these sorts of protocols, with OAI-PMH being of particular interest; this protocol is discussed in more detail in due course.

Flexible metadata capture

The choice of a particular schema or form of metadata storage can be highly dependent on both the type of content being stored and the history and experience of the institution providing the storage. For this reason it is helpful if common standards are supported at the outset and are ideally sufficiently flexible to allow the addition of others at a later date. While adding new schemas is never going to be trivial, certain design decisions could enable the addition of new schemas, such as a high degree of modularity and a strong internal element mapping system, allowing a central metadata set to be exposed in the form of many others. This sort of cross-walk could be exemplified by the way in which repositories may take their internal metadata standards and transform them to be compliant with the simple Dublin Core format initially supported in OAI-PMH, as we will see later.

To enable the use of any one of a set of metadata schemas that we may be required to handle it would also be ideal to have a capturing mechanism which is equally customisable. This could involve being able to create submission forms dynamically, for example, or modify submission procedures 'on-the-fly'. Such a manner could potentially allow for different sorts of metadata to be used not only globally but dependent on where the item is submitted to or from or what sort of item it is. For example, an e-thesis will have different metadata requirements from a conference poster, while computer science contributions may have different requirements from administrative records. Ultimately, a good system will be able to combine the different requirements for each of the possible content domains to produce a metadata set to be collected which is exactly appropriate.

Given the propensity of users to write bad metadata it is also worth considering the requirement that authority control may be needed over some fields, and that some fields may also be pre-populated (although still modifiable by the user). In addition, metadata review by a qualified librarian is a great asset to any kind of catalogue, for which we may also require a post-submission workflow.

Federation, devolution and scalability

While centralised systems have their advantages, such as the ease by which centrally managed information can be dealt with, there are also many benefits to be obtained by using a federated model, especially with regard to scalability. Here we aim to distribute the repository's components into other systems and the domains of other academic units. This allows us, as the next point notes, to obtain and deliver content into a user's native environment, increasing the likelihood of uptake and acceptance; in addition, we can federate at the storage level as well, employing powerful distributed or grid storage mechanisms, which have the advantage of scalability and reliability which centralised storage cannot necessarily offer.

The number of options you may consider for federation are many, and we will not discuss this in great depth. Nonetheless it remains an active area of development in repository, and many other forms of software, and represents one of the major challenges being taken up in the area of digital curation. A good package will either support this sort of implementation or will have an architecture capable of being extended to this where necessary.

Ingest and egress

As with being *easily integrable*, the institutional repository needs to collect items for the archive. Given the content types, and the usage to which they are subject, it is reasonable that some sort of submission interface be available to users. Ideally this is via a web front-end (most packages support this as the primary method), but other forms of ingest are possible and desirable. Consider, for example, the need to batch import items from legacy systems, or to harvest or aggregate data from other similar systems; you could even employ technologies such as website 'scraping' or custom-written ingest procedures using the native API (such as would be used when developing devolved or federated components).

Similar comments to ingest apply for egress. One of the primary methods is no doubt via some kind of web interface as this is highly popular and easy for all users. Nonetheless we may also choose to bulk export our data for various reasons, or cross-walk our metadata for insertion into other systems; we may, again, wish to deal with harvesting or aggregation but this time being a data provider for another service, or to make our data available via any sort of customised system using an egress API (which could deliver content to devolved interfaces).

We should also not forget that the items contained in our repository should, in general, not only be metadata, but will actually come with one or more files attached. Procedures for ingest and egress must satisfactorily meet requirements for receiving and making files available. Several ways to do this exist, with possibly the most popular being to provide upload and delivery over HTTP or even to provide FTP access, although this may be less intuitive to users.

The archival information package

In archival terms, items are not singular entities. Instead they exhibit potentially rich internal structure and the institutional repository, like other complex digital asset management systems, needs to be able to understand the shape of the objects it contains. For example, a book chapter may consist of an access metadata record (enabling discovery of the item), metadata regarding the relationship this item has with other items (the other chapters of the book), a primary document which contains a representation of the chapter, and a number of image files which contain the figures used in the work (perhaps in a higher resolution). When storing this it is necessary to be clear about the structure of the item; we must be able to see which is the primary file, and in which order the figures should be presented; we must be clear about the place this item holds in the sea of other assets.

To do this we need to provide a 'wrapper' for the item, which encapsulates all of the information required to reconstruct the content in a meaningful way. This is important not only for immediate use but also for the purposes of digital preservation. One such encapsulation is the archival information package (AIP), and generally would consist of a complex metadata file and content files wrapped together. Technologies such as METS or MPEG-21 DIDL are becoming increasingly prevalent in this area as schemas which allow digital object structures to be accurately described in XML, and to allow the presence of multiple metadata records for an item. For this chapter, a METS file may contain access, relational and structural metadata describing how to find it, how it relates to other chapters and its own internal organisation (known as 'structure mapping'). The additional metadata which could aid the future digital archaeologist rebuild items stands a much greater chance of survival alongside the digital assets using this mechanism. Some of these issues will be discussed in the next point and later when we talk in more detail about digital preservation.

Digital preservation

With an increasing amount of material becoming purely electronic, and the rate of change of modern technology increasing, digital preservation is becoming a serious issue. While we will not go into detail here, it is worth noting that any kind of support for preservation-like activities is a definite bonus. Defining precisely what is meant by 'preservation-like' is difficult, but some pointers here are warranted (Wheatley, 2003).

Persistent identifiers are a good way to start a digital preservation strategy and are useful for providing a mechanism to locate online documents in perpetuity; it reminds us that having the item is only part of the problem, and that being able to locate it and continue to define its relationships with other items is another. We may also choose to migrate file formats to currently supported ones; this can be done on ingest, on request, or periodically. Tackling the problem from a different angle we could have the option to preserve file viewers or file viewer emulators which move the preservation requirements from an individual item level to an application level, thus reducing the number of preservation actions that need to take place. Nonetheless, similar problems still exist and are more complex to solve, although fewer in number. It is also worthwhile considering simply providing linkage to file format registries (e.g. the Global Digital Format Registry (GDFR)) which may, in the long term, provide a good starting point for unravelling at-risk materials.

Defining local requirements

When examining the way in which your institutionally-specific repository will be embedded into normal service, it should be relatively evident that not all of the requirements set out in the previous section are necessary for a particular instance; rather, they are general guides which would be fulfilled in an ideal world. We cannot wait for these to be met before we embark, though, and they will not be met if somebody does not forge ahead and develop the technology and the practices that drive the specifications.

Of primary importance is that the repository is appropriate for the institution and the purpose for which it is being adopted. It is no use having advanced digital preservation techniques for ephemeral content, or multiple metadata schema support for a single content type. Therefore in this section we will look at how you may gain some insight into your own scope, use cases and subsequently requirements.

Example use cases

Use cases are a particular method of examining how a system might be interacted with. They are particularly prevalent in software engineering and are used to inform system architecture in the early stages and provide a basis for subsequent evaluation. Expressed via the Unified Modelling Language (UML), use cases can be pictorially represented to help us understand the scope and the requirements that we have of any particular process; in this case that of our system.

We will look at two examples of how use cases might be used to examine the requirements of our institutional repository. This imaginary repository is going to be used to allow for electronic submission of e-theses and subsequent long-term storage and preservation; simultaneously it will want to expose that information to a number of services, such as a centralised e-thesis metadata registry or an OAI service provider. It will, of course, have many other requirements that we will not consider here – these are for individual institutions to specify for themselves.

Figure 3.1 considers a use case which shows a user submitting their e-thesis to the repository. Here the user is interacting with the system and being required to authenticate in order to do so. Everything within the rectangular box is part of the system, while the relationships between the actions (denoted by ovals containing descriptive text) are depicted by the arrows. *Authenticate User* and *Authorise User* are processes which are implicitly included in the action of *Submit Thesis* in that all theses submissions require authentication, although there is no direct relationship between the actions. *Commit to Archive*, meanwhile, is an extension of the *Submit Thesis* action, and is not necessarily something in which the *Postgraduate* is involved (e.g. there may be post-submission workflow).

In Figure 3.2, consider that we are exposing our data to an aggregating service which may or may not be an OAI-PMH enabled system; that is, we may be required to use another standard web service protocol or even to provide our own. The primary activities being examined *Get OAI Packet* and *Get Web Service Metadata*, both of which require a

Figure 3.1   Use case showing postgraduate submitting their e-thesis

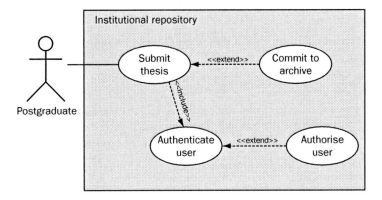

Figure 3.2 Use case showing exposure of data via web service layer to external aggregator

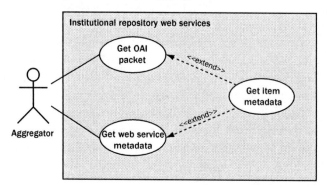

hidden activity by which the metadata are retrieved from within the system.

It is valuable to consult the people in your institution who will be involved in working with the repository and discussing what their requirements of the system actually are; attempting to second-guess their requirements is always risky. Using a standard such as UML allows this sort of research to be documented in a generally understandable way, and allows an evaluation process to be entered into with a good deal of confidence.

Example use case analysis

In the previous section we looked at two use cases for an example institutional repository with fairly sparse requirements. Now let us examine how these use cases might inform us of the functional requirements that are actually useful in our situation.

Let us start by re-examining Figure 3.1: this depicts a postgraduate student depositing their thesis in electronic form into an institutional repository. The primary objective of the student is to submit their thesis, so our repository clearly needs to have adequate e-thesis support. It also needs to be able to authenticate the user, and then to allow the user's thesis to pass into the archive. We will take a moment to consider each of these actions, and how they translate into the functional requirements we will demand of our software.

First, and possibly most complex, is the actual submission of a thesis itself. The process will consist of the definition of a set of metadata, the attachment of a number of files and almost certainly the application of relatively complex licensing. Our repository, therefore, must support a metadata set appropriate for e-theses (such as the electronic thesis or dissertation metadata set (ETD-MS) or the UK E-Thesis Core Set); if our repository is only to support e-theses then support of one format would be acceptable, but if we are to support other items, which may be apparent from other use cases, then we must consider multiple metadata schemas or a single flexible schema to be a requirement. It must also be able to capture this metadata either over the Web, if students are to submit their thesis themselves, or have a submission process which can easily be operated by non-technical administrative staff; in general we would expect the former. Also, we might expect large files to be uploaded so we may not be satisfied with a straightforward online (HTTP POST) upload form, which could be a usability or accessibility barrier, and prefer a much more definite FTP approach; it may even be that we prefer a thin client at the user end which manages the upload for them. Finally, the licensing for e-theses can be very complex (Andrew, 2004; Jones and Andrew, 2005), and if we find a package which exactly matches our institutional requirements we will be very lucky; instead better that our package is both flexible in its approach and easy to customise.

Second, authentication will not be an exclusive login event but also the attachment of a set of authorisations to the user. Given that we want to allow postgraduates to submit their theses, it would be ideal if the authentication and authorisations were tied into some kind of institutional database of users. Again, these are so varied and complex that a particular connector for your institution is unlikely; instead we will be mostly looking out for a degree of configurability and customisability in the software.

Finally, the thesis must leave the submission process and pass to the archive. This is potentially simple, if you are not interested in post-submission workflow. This, however, seems unlikely. If you are mandating e-thesis submission, and wish to verify metadata, add subject classifications, perhaps even perform marking procedures, then what happens between when the thesis is submitted and when the thesis arrives in the archive is very important. In this case we discover that our use case is accurate but insufficiently detailed and it will be necessary for us to delve deeper to discover our requirements.

If we now re-consider Figure 3.2, which shows a harvester or aggregator obtaining one of two things: an OAI packet or some other web service metadata packet. This indicates that our system must be able to support the OAI-PMH protocol initially, but also should be able to support some as yet undefined protocols. The result of this is that we expect some kind of API which each of the Web service delivery modules will utilise to access the definitive item metadata held in the repository; this is indicated by the lines annotated '«extend»'. Another product of this use case is that we would like a pluggable architecture in which, at a later date, we might deploy some other web service (e.g. an SRW interface) without the core of the system being affected, and with minimal configuration changes to the system environment.

Deriving example requirements from use cases

From the analysis in the previous section we can go on to list some things which are important to us, and which should ideally be addressed by any software that we adopt:

- flexible metadata schema or e-thesis schema support;
- customisable, accessible, web-based user interface;
- file delivery manager;
- customisable licensing system;
- authentication and authorisation systems and APIs;
- post-submission workflow;
- OAI-PMH web service protocol;
- pluggable/modular architecture.

To be able to set out your requirements fully it is necessary to carry out some form of use case analysis of all foreseeable uses of the system, and to produce a list similar, but no doubt much longer, to the above. You may, for example, consider how the repository's internal data representation should be; does it allow you to categorise your research, or provide research 'homepages' for departments? What other ways will users obtain content? Will the content need to be surfaced inside an institutional portal? Is full-text indexing important in your discovery processes?

Once you can answer these questions and others similar to them then you have an idea what it is that you are looking for and can start a structured evaluation procedure to ensure that your needs are met where possible.

OAI-PMH for inter-connectivity: the institutional repository in situ

A major objective for the OAI-PMH is to consolidate scholarly archives all around the world, providing free access to (at least) metadata; by providing a consistent interface to data and service providers it is a low-barrier access solution with minimal implementation effort. The basic format of data is in an XML representation of a Dublin Core metadata set and is traditionally transported directly via HTTP.

At either end of an OAI request you have a harvester (aka service provider) and a data provider. The harvester uses the query syntax over HTTP GET or POST to request data from the data provider. The data provider must then interpret the request, conduct a query on its native database, and return a correctly formatted XML document to the harvester; this process is depicted in Figure 3.3.

Furthermore, systems are not tied to being exclusively service or data provider and may, in fact, be both. Figure 3.4 shows the potential of such an architecture, where data and service providers live together on a network of OAI compliant repositories. We can easily imagine that each of the nodes in this network is one of many different types of repository, each exposing its own content and absorbing content from other repositories; meanwhile others might be pure interfaces to the network of open archives, effectively providing a search engine for scholarly content. Figure 3.5 shows how a real world OAI network might look.

Exposing one's archive to the world at large is certainly an objective we would like to achieve during creation of an institutional repository, but the appeal of OAI can go much further than that. Because it is lightweight and relatively easy to implement, it is not unreasonable to expect many

Figure 3.3   The relationship between the OAI service provider and data provider

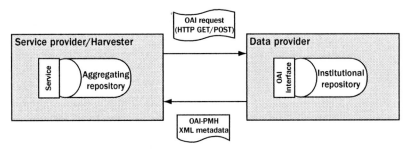

Figure 3.4 A latticework of OAI service and data providers interacting

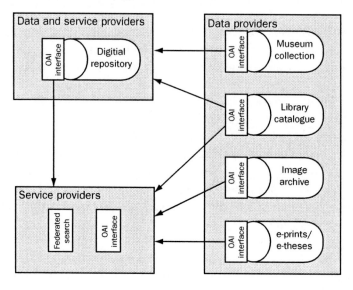

Figure 3.5 A realisation of an OAI compliant network

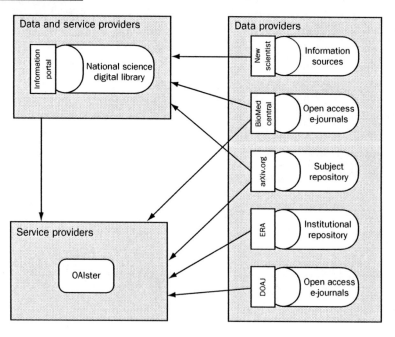

institutional systems to be able to exchange information using it as a communications protocol. Therefore, creating networks of institutional systems (of which the repository will be just one among peers such as library catalogues, departmental portals, collection gateways and online museum collections) using OAI-PMH as the communications protocol allows for a rich research environment. Departmental portals may choose to use the repository as a storage system for content, or collection gateways may aggregate metadata from several locations such as image repositories or museum collections to produce interrelated digital assets. Figure 3.6 provides an example of this.

Therefore, despite the argument that simple Dublin Core is insufficient for many purposes, using it in conjunction with the OAI-PMH is nonetheless an important data transfer toolkit and can dramatically improve inter-system communications to give the institutions internal and external data discovery and dissemination capabilities much greater impact. Its real strength lies in using a 'lowest common denominator' metadata set to provide a pathway back to the original resource and its locally held, rich metadata where appropriate.

This is the institutional repository in situ, integrated with many other types of local resources such as the library catalogue, each communicating via OAI-PMH to aid discovery of information from any one of the standard access methods employed on institutional networks. As a united front this internal OAI-PMH network can then expose its metadata to service providers allowing for a global audience for material which could have, initially, been difficult to locate.

Figure 3.6   **Internal OAI linked set of institutional resources**

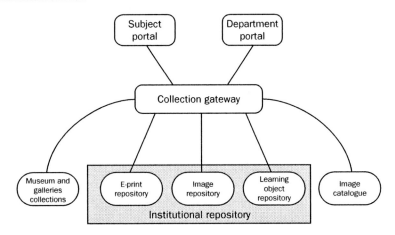

Technical notes on OAI-PMH

The OAI protocol supports six different ways of interacting with a repository (known as 'verbs' in the native parlance). Each of these is passed over HTTP GET or POST to the repository's OAI interface along with associated parameters which will not be discussed here:

- *Identify*: request a description of the archive being interrogated.

- *ListMetadataFormats*: get a list of the metadata formats being used by the archive being interrogated.

- *ListSets*: get information regarding the internal structuring of the archive.

- *ListRecords*: request a list of all the metadata records which match the query parameters passed.

- *ListIdentifiers*: shortened version of *ListRecords*.

- *GetRecord*: obtain a single metadata record from a repository, based on the identifier passed.

The simplest way to utilise these 'verbs' is to construct a URL which passes the query details along with the request for the web page. For example, to request a list of all the records in an informatics collection at the repository myrepository.ac.uk we would construct the URL: *http://www.myrepository.ac.uk/oai?verb=ListRecords&metadataPrefix=oai_dc&set=15*.

This accesses the OAI interface to the repository. We then specify the verb to be ListRecords, so the repository is prepared for the relevant parameters for this particular action. In this case we specify a metadata prefix, so that we know in what format we will receive the metadata, and only ask that the repository give us compatible metadata. We also tell the repository from which set it should give us the records; in this case '15' is the set identifier which can be obtained by requesting the ListSets action prior to ListRecords, and refers to an informatics collection in this case. There are also other parameters which we could pass which we will not consider here. It is then up to the repository to understand how to interpret these parameters in terms of its own functionality and construct a response which could look like Figure 3.7, showing a response with two records (with some details omitted to aid clarity).

We can see that full simple Dublin Core metadata records are returned for both items which match the request (the dc: prefix on many of the metadata tags indicates this). The listing has a header which identifies it as an OAI-PMH response along with the details of the query followed by

Figure 3.7 An OAI-PMH XML encoded response

```
<OAI-PMH>
 <responseDate>2005-02-08T16:11:10Z</responseDate>
 <request metadataPrefix="oai_dc" verb="ListRecords" set="15">
  http://www.myrepository.ac.uk/oai
 </request>
 <ListRecords>
  <record>
   <header>
    <identifier>123456789/100</identifier>
    <datestamp>2003-11-03T10:04:57Z</datestamp>
    <setSpec>15:12</setSpec>
   </header>
   <metadata>
    <oai_dc:dc>
     <dc:contributor>Researcher, A</dc:contributor>
     <dc:date>2003-11-03T10:04:57Z</dc:date>
     <dc:identifier>123456789/100</dc:identifier>
     <dc:description>
      The abstract, for example
     </dc:description>
     <dc:format>application/pdf</dc:format>
     <dc:language>en</dc:language>
     <dc:title>Theory of Relations</dc:title>
     <dc:type>Preprint</dc:type>
    </oai_dc:dc>
   </metadata>
  </record>
  <record>
   <header>
    <identifier>123456789/110</identifier>
    <datestamp>2004-04-07T11:20:28Z</datestamp>
    <setSpec>15:19</setSpec>
   </header>
   <metadata>
    <oai_dc:dc>
     ... Dublin Core Metadata ...
    </oai_dc:dc>
   </metadata>
  </record>
 </ListRecords>
</OAI-PMH>
```

the metadata for each record. It is clear from the layout that metadata schemas other than Dublin Core could be used to describe the items.

We can rapidly see how the OAI-PMH is useful for an institutional repository, and indeed any repository-like system, to support and how the information it deals with maps comfortably onto the information structures that we are likely to have in place already.

Evaluation

There are general evaluation procedures for choosing software both for a particular purpose and from a selection of options. In this section we will take a brief look at the processes you may have to go through to determine which package, if any, is good for your institution. It is worth bearing in mind that in-house development should always be considered if the resources are available and none of the packages considered meet your needs.

Figure 3.8 shows how the process of evaluation might be carried out for an institutional repository. You will notice that there is no particular reference to software vendors as we have made the implicit decision to

Figure 3.8 The institutional repository evaluation process

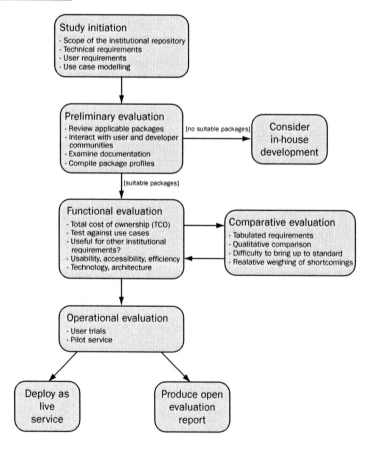

endorse open source, non-commercial solutions; you should be aware that adopting a commercial solution has different cost implications and other considerations which are not covered here.

Initialising the evaluation

In the early parts of this chapter we carried out what can be seen as the *study initiation*. We have looked at the sorts of requirements we will have for the software, and seen how to generate basic use case diagrams with a focus on providing an institutional repository service. The second stage, *preliminary evaluation*, is covered in the appendices, in which we summarise some common open source packages donated by their communities; this should allow you to make a start on software review and provide some insight into creating package profiles for consideration. Once you have examined the appendices you should continue your search on the World Wide Web as this area is rapidly developing and new packages will emerge while old packages may either become obsolete or change from the profiles we have collected. The objective of this stage is to rapidly eliminate software which is clearly inappropriate for your needs. Problems in this regard might be a dramatic difference in philosophy or methodology, architectural (i.e. that you feel the package is not sufficiently well written, or will not scale to your institution), purely functional (its focus lies elsewhere, or is too specific for your needs), or local practical considerations (e.g. the user interface is in a language other than your own, and translation would be difficult). Your requirements list will drive the final decision to a large degree, although consideration of the medium-term future of the package is also warranted; there is little point in adopting a package which will shortly be obsolete, even if it does meet all requirements (unless you intend to take over supporting it).

It may be that no packages meet your requirements, and in this case you may need to consider performing some in-house development. Before taking this decision many things need to be taken into account which are beyond the scope of this book, and a full understanding of the costs involved both in terms of resources and impact on other parts of the organisation are required. For the purposes of this chapter we will assume that two or more packages will pass the *preliminary evaluation* and move on to the *functional evaluation stage*.

Functional and comparative evaluation

Performing the functional evaluation is a time-consuming task and requires that you make test installations of the software packages which pass preliminary evaluation. It is also useful in the open source arena to be able to examine the code itself to ensure security, efficiency and stability; this will not always be possible, though, depending on your institutional resources. Certainly, having expertise in the operating systems and programming languages involved in the packages undergoing evaluation is a bonus.

A good way to make rapid headway with a functional evaluation is to work through your collection of use cases, seeing how well the software behaves under all the circumstances. For each of your stated requirements you can produce an entry on a comparison table which allows you to quickly and easily see how the relative performance of the software is going. Table 3.1 provides an example of how this comparative evaluation may be formalised.

Misleadingly, perhaps, within the functional evaluation we should also be calculating adoption costs, or the total cost of ownership (TCO). With open source, as we have already noted, these costs can be quite high, although in general are lower than purchasing from a vendor. Discussion of the costs involved in building a repository can be found in Chapter 2, while discussions of the relative cost of OSS to proprietary software can be found in many other texts.

Other factors to consider are whether the package can be used for other applications beyond that which you have already scoped. This is good forward planning and you will no doubt find many other applications of the same software once you are comfortable with the package you adopt. Having the additional, initially unused, features is a good secondary asset which will enable any service to be forward looking.

Table 3.1   Comparative evaluation table example

Requirement	Package 1	Package 2	Package 3
E-thesis metadata support	ETD-MS	Custom	None
Customisable licensing	None	None	Basic
Security	Good	Excellent	Excellent
OAI-PMH	v2.0	v2.0	v2.0

Once you have evaluated in as much detail as possible you will have a wealth of information in a similar form to that given in Table 3.1. A qualitative comparison of the packages will then be possible by examining the points raised, considering how important each requirement is to you (i.e. applying a weighting to the requirement) and attempting to rate the packages subjectively. As there are no quantitative ways of comparing such abstract objects as computer software, the next technique we employ is particularly important in the decision, especially when it is close. As per Jones (2004), we ask the following, 'How difficult would it be to modify Package X in order to bring it up to the standard of the other packages in the areas in which it is lacking?' (note that this requires you to undertake local development).

So for each package (X), we consider the difficulty or local development time to achieve the standard obtained by the leader in the field. If we examine Table 3.1 again we can rapidly draw up the supplementary questions that need to be answered:

1. How hard would it be to add e-theses metadata support to Package 3?

2. How hard would it be to provide basic custom licences in Packages 1 and 2?

3. What are the ongoing maintenance costs of any changes?

If we can produce answers to these questions with some degree of quantity, then the choices that we need to make are laid in front of us. Suppose that the answers to questions 1 and 2 are 'Not too difficult' and 'Quite complicated' respectively. These somewhat vague but partially quantified answers would lead us to suggest that bringing Package 3 up to the standard we require is much easier than bringing either of the other two up to its standard in other areas.

Question 3 is technically a subquestion for each of the first two, where we must consider the difficulty of, in this case, adding e-theses metadata support or custom licences to the relevant packages. The answer to this question will depend on the likelihood of your developments being incorporated into the code-base for your chosen package, or the ease with which additional modules can be written. For a well written package this may not be too difficult, but when you are modifying core behaviour there will always be maintenance issues.

If Package 3 is highly modular, then the maintenance of an e-theses metadata module should be straightforward, the outcome of this comparative evaluation would, therefore, be to choose it over Packages 1 and 2.

Operational evaluation

Of course, evaluation will not stop there. While Package 3 may well seem to be the most appropriate choice at this stage we should remember that information professionals and system users will have different perspectives and use methodologies which may result in a difference of opinion. If we follow the guidelines laid out above we should minimise the likelihood of future problems, but we should always be prepared for issues to arise and not be taken by surprise by them if they do.

For this reason we use an *operational evaluation* stage in which we run a test instance of the system, populating it with real data and giving it to a few typical users to use as though it were a real service. Here we should also test the system for appropriate scalability: bulk loading of data, load testing and so forth. If the system falls down at this stage it is relatively easy to return to the previous evaluation stage and reconsider our options; if the system is well received then we can move on to providing a pilot service which will leverage real users in real settings, but in controlled quantities, as the user test-bed; discussion of planning and execution of a pilot is covered in some detail in Chapter 7. Recovering from a failure at the pilot stage is not quite so trivial, but is also relatively rare, and with a solid functional evaluation there will be plenty of opportunity to re-trace and re-deploy with lessons learnt.

Digital preservation

One of the major benefits to an institution in having a repository of items that it has produced is that it provides a centrally managed service so departments need not worry about providing a repository for themselves. As central services with a traditional responsibility for bibliographic data management, libraries are in a position to offer expertise in centralised workflow management and metadata. Another service that libraries traditionally provide to their parent organisation is content preservation, and in seeking to attract content into a repository, the offer of a guarantee that the content will be available long-term is an attractive inducement.

In this section we take a moment to examine the overall idea of digital preservation and introduce the techniques that have been developed or proposed for managing this complex and ongoing problem. This chapter has already specified digital preservation as a desirable feature of an institutional repository, and Chapter 4 will go on to mention some of the concepts in relation to workflow development, and in particular the recommendations of the Open Archival Information Systems reference model which is described in the following section. A full examination of preservation is beyond the scope of this book, but this will provide a valuable starting point for anyone interested in taking the topic further.

The core requirements of any system or institution attempting to provide digital preservation for its assets can be broken into four objectives (Wheatley, 2004):

1. Data can be maintained without being lost, damaged or altered.

2. Data can be found and extracted for or by a user.

3. Data can be interpreted and understood by the end user.

4. That objectives 1–3 can be achieved in perpetuity.

Basic techniques for objective 1 are already commonplace, with technologies such as checksumming for verifying that file contents have not changed over time, as well as rigorous backup strategies for conviction that data will not be lost due to mere hardware failures. Whether this data still makes sense in years to come partly falls under objective 3, but some strategies, as discussed subsequently, will require the storage and maintenance of additional versions of the materials or further information concerning them.

The OAIS reference model, as discussed subsequently, forms a solid basis upon which to perform digital preservation activities. It aims to support objectives 2 and 3 by defined workflow, and has recommendations on how to support the preservation planning necessary for all the objectives. In addition, persistent identification of items will support objective 2 and is also discussed subsequently.

To ensure that data can be interpreted and understood by the end user (objective 3), significant challenges form the primary focus of digital preservation research. Digital materials as little as ten years old are already becoming obsolete so this is a pressing issue. The overview of preservation techniques introduces some of the most common forms of preservation activity, although we will not go into detail. It is the application of these techniques which will hopefully make objective 4 a reality. We should note that digital preservation is not, and most likely never will be, a one-stop solution, but an ongoing commitment by custodians of electronic materials.

The OAIS reference model

No discussion of repository preservation and workflow would be complete without at least a brief introduction to the OAIS reference model. Here we provide an overview of this model in order to show how it underpins much of the workflow processes presented in Chapter 4, and how it relates to digital preservation. This is recommended as current best practice, although no firm consensus has yet been reached.

The Consultative Committee for Space Data Systems (CCSDS), a forum for national space agencies interested in cooperative development of data management standards in space research, undertook the initial development of this standard to support long-term storage of digital data generated from space missions. In cooperation with the International Organisation for Standardisation (ISO) the reference model was approved as an ISO standard in 2002 (ISO-14721). Further information regarding this can be found in the CCSDS archives (CCSDS 650.0-B-1, 2002) or the Digital Preservation Coalition Technology Watch Report introductory guide.

The two primary functions of the model are to preserve and to provide access to information. Figure 3.9 outlines the entire OAIS functional model which sets out to achieve these broad aims, and thus, to a degree, defines

Figure 3.9 OAIS functional model

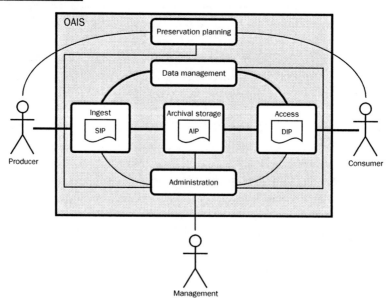

the approximate architecture of any software system hoping to meet this standard and any supporting workflows surrounding the repository.

The *producer* is the author or submitter, and provides items for the archive through the *ingest* process. The resulting Submission Information Package (SIP) is converted into the Archival Information Package (AIP) through the *post-submission* workflow and thus into *archival storage*. Simultaneously data concerning the items and the repository itself are kept organised by the *data management* section, which also aids in discovery and access. There is then a dedicated *administration* section attached to the *management* which would be our repository administrators and manager, and this section is related to the *data management* and the *preservation planning* sections. This is to allow for structural management, and also to aid in holding the AIPs over time.

To meet the various detailed requirements of this reference model, a repository system must capture all the relevant metadata to convert the SIP into an AIP with quality assurance and audit trails placed on the submission, as well as information such as file format standards and other technical metadata. The AIP needs then to be placed in archival storage, and references in the data management system need to be kept up to date. Archival storage then must support traditional verified storage techniques, as previously mentioned, such as backup and disaster recovery, content verification over time and migration between storage media.

Administration of the system requires the creation of policies and authorisations for access, and the management of the system configuration. It is also quite closely tied to the *ingest* process as it is within this scope that submission audit is defined, which ultimately becomes part of the AIP, and also the negotiation of the submission agreement, which is tied closely to licensing. In addition, OAIS recommends that administrators handle dissemination requests and deal with any customer service issues should they arise or be relevant to the repository.

Access to materials is provided to the consumer, who is defined by the reference model as a member of the *designated community*; this is a concept which exists to detail exactly who would be expected to understand the material. That is, if the archived research is in the field of astrophysics, then the designated community would be specified as 'astrophysicists' and, therefore, metadata and related documents concerning the meaning of the content are omitted on the grounds that the designated community will already understand. This community is provided with the DIP, which may be mediated by the administrators, or handled exclusively by the system. This DIP is obtained by performing a query on the data management module, which will in turn provide references to the AIPs that should be converted and delivered. The reference model also recommends keeping track of all requests for content which will be added to the AIP audit trail.

Spanning all of this is the *preservation planning* module whose job it is to develop preservation strategies and standards, monitor the state of the art for advances in the field, and monitor the designated community for change, so that any new required information can be attached to the relevant AIPs. The outputs of this module will guide the administrators in their policies, and ultimately lead to preservation activities undertaken on holdings; migration, and other format changing policies, it should be noted, require the generation of new AIPs, and absolutely not the modification of existing ones.

File formats

In practical terms, one activity in which repositories can quickly engage is file format mandates or conversions. That is, supported file formats are selected for the repository, and where possible files are provided in these formats. While it would be unwise and unsafe to define here a set of 'acceptable' file formats for preservation, we can ask a number of questions of a format to see if it is appropriate for storage as is, meaning that we do not have to have a list of formats that we accept, but a set of guidelines to follow when faced with a new one. These are (Jones, 2004b):

1. Is the file format an open standard/format?

2. Is the file format widely used?

3. Is the file format and associated technology likely to be preserved?

4. Are the contents of the file human readable?

5. Is the file format itself human readable?

Consideration of each of these will lead to a degree of certainty in the suitability for file format usability. Formats which fall into just one of these categories should not be considered 'safe', but inclusion in several of them will be a good pointer for their future. For example, the standard text document format Rich Text Format (RTF) would be covered by question 1, as the specification for this is open and anyone could implement an RTF reader should they choose to do so; there is no tie in to a commercial manufacturer who has control over the format specification, where the future of the format is determined by commercial interests and not preservation requirements.

The wide use of a file format (question 2) does not necessarily indicate preservability, but it does indicate the sorts of formats the repositories will be asked to deal with again and again. Preservation of formats that fall into only this category are absolutely not to be trusted, as these will often be commercial formats which again tie rendering to a specific package and platform, limiting the scope for long-term curation. Combined with a confidence that the format and the technology will be preserved (question 3), we may be more inclined to look more closely. For example, Adobe PDF is a commercial format which is an open *specification*. It is also so widely used that its preservation is extremely likely as there are many interested parties, and a variety of open source tools which will handle it.

The best sorts of formats are those where the contents and format themselves (questions 4 and 5) are human readable. To say 'human readable' in this context is a slight misnomer, as in reality no digital document is. Instead here we mean that the format markup and the contents are stored in the lowest possible denominator in computational terms: plain text (in a common encoding). Formats that meet these requirements to various degrees include LaTeX (or TeX), or anything written in a semantic XML format, such as DocBook or TEI.

For text-like documents the application of these conditions is relatively straightforward, but it rapidly becomes more complicated for multimedia objects, especially as few of them will comfortably satisfy questions 4 and 5; SVG (an XML vector graphics format) would be a notable exception, although whether the source would really count as human readable could be open to debate. Fortunately there are many good open standard image formats, and the same is increasingly true of video formats.

Whatever the final decision a repository manager makes with regard to supported formats, it is wise to store alongside any converted formats the original files also, to ensure that the risks involved in migration on ingest are minimised (see section on the overview of preservation techniques).

Persistent identification

One of the primary goals of digital preservation is not just to preserve the materials in perpetuity, but also to provide access to them on the same timescale. Much material on the Web is extremely ephemeral, as URLs change, and services come and go. Repositories can attempt to address this problem by providing persistent identifiers to their items, collections and even repositories as a whole. The basic principle is to provide a service-independent identifier which resolves to a particular instance of a service containing the requested resource. This has the advantage that services can come and go provided the local binding to the persistent identifier is maintained. Put practically, if we provide an identifier *xyz* which points to *http://www.myservice.ac.uk/xyz* and then we move the item to another service at *http://www.otherservice. ac.uk/abc* provided that *xyz* has its target updated to the new service, the end user should experience no interruption in the availability of the item, and never need to update their references.

Often systems that handle this sort of function automatically can suffer from what may be considered a Gödelian flaw in that ultimately the resolving service must be persistently identifiable without itself having a persistent identifier. We must, therefore, have confidence that our resolvers will always be available in the expected place, or else have a resolver which is beyond merely an automated redirection procedure (and even these could suffer problems of this nature in extreme circumstances). Effectively, though, by using this sort of system we are reducing the number of identifiers that need to be preserved to very few, which is also an approach that can be adopted in the preservation of digital objects as discussed in the next section.

Overview of preservation techniques

The philosophy behind digital preservation is that every preserved object can be reconstructed and performed by means of the packaged contents of object and tools – even if the software and hardware environment in which it was first produced has changed absolutely, or, indeed, no longer exists. Here we look briefly at some of the techniques that can be employed to achieve these aims.

- *Migration*: migrate the file formats to a supported format at ingest, or migrate the format to a required or requested one at delivery. Performing migration at ingest is practically straightforward, although the longevity of supported formats is still in question. If migration is done on request, then a tool to migrate the digital object to the current usable format must also be preserved alongside; the development and maintenance of this tool is related to both *viewers* and *emulation*. Either way, the original file and all subsequent migrated files should all be stored and maintained to aid in the preservation effort.

- *Viewers*: instead of migrating file formats, we can also reduce the preservation activity footprint by providing tools that know how to render the stored formats. The viewers themselves then need to be preserved, and maintenance is directed towards them rather than the source files.

- *Emulation*: similar to maintaining viewer tools for file formats, we may also choose instead to provide tools that emulate the original software platforms on which the items were created.

- *Universal virtual computer (UVC)*: this is an entire system designed as a preservable platform upon which emulation, viewing or migrating tools may be developed. This takes the point of preservation as far back as is possible, where there is only one system which needs to be preserved; naturally there is a corresponding increase in complexity.

- *Technical metadata*: as a supporting set of tools for digital preservation, technical metadata could encompass information such as the representation information for a file format and provide linkage to supporting databases of file formats and rendering tools.

Development of these tools is ongoing, and there is no clear path for digital preservation to follow as yet. Keeping the options for repository content as open as possible for as long as possible is likely to be the most prudent way to proceed, although not always practical.

Conclusion

We have examined the general requirements of the institutional repository and seen how we can employ use case modelling to scope our own requirements which will, in turn, provide the testing ground for an evaluation of the many packages available which may suit your needs. These are some of the main technical issues which surround the institutional repository and the way that it fits into the larger scheme of the digital library. Continuing work on the archiving process, especially in the field of digital preservation, and in the interoperability of systems, in this case led by the OAI-PMH, will see this field change radically over the coming years.

Although the stage for the institutional repository has been set, it has not yet reached maturity. While the core conceptual features of it contain no obvious challenges (collection, storage and dissemination of digital assets), the underlying technologies for all these systems are undergoing large changes. Developments in federated storage, leading into increased scalability can, and will, be implemented by institutional repositories, while digital preservation technology (relating to system backup, disaster recovery and long-term archival integrity) will also need to be noted if not integrated. In addition, data harvesting is a field with relatively minor technical challenges, but major information management challenges which need to be met and solved; all of this will be leveraged by the institutional repository.

If you have successfully evaluated and adopted a package then you will have overcome the main technical challenges of implementing your own institutional repository. At this stage it is important to produce an evaluation report showing how you came to the decisions you did, both for the benefit of others in similar situations and for yourself in the future when requirements or technology change and a re-evaluation may be required. It is also important in the world of OSS to feed your findings back into the communities, even if you did not adopt their package they will be interested by your comments and it will help in the long term to give us a wealth of diverse systems from which to share our information.

Note

1. Much of the underlying theory for evaluation presented in this chapter is derived from Brownstein and Lerner (1982) along with some of our own recommendations and adaptations. Meanwhile, further discussion of OAI-PMH can be found on the Open Archives Forum website *http://www.oaforum.org/tutorial/* and of especial interest is the 'OAI For Beginners' tutorial which can be found there. The digital preservation section of this chapter is owed, in no small way, to the OAIS reference model (CCSDS, 2002), and the associated Coalition for Digital Preservation Technology Watch reports on this (Lavoie, 2004) and on 'Institutional Repositories in the context of Digital Preservation' (Wheatley, 2004). Other works drawn on for this chapter include Crow (2004) and Nixon (2003).

4

Workflow and administration

In this chapter we look at the two concepts of workflow and administration to examine the integral relationship between them.[1] We will see how workflow provides an abstract, atomised set of general procedure flows, each stage of which can contain its own administrative tasks. Understanding how they are constructed then allows us to present some examples for different purposes that may be of use in an institutional repository. Once we understand how to generate workflow for our own repository we can then look at the administrative procedures which support these processes, and be relatively specific about the needs of the system in order for it to be sustainable. The topics covered in this chapter are the subject of extensive research which cannot be fully addressed here, but there is a large corpus of highly technical information available which this chapter reflects to a degree. Underlying most of what we are talking about relates to the Open Archival Information System (OAIS) reference model presented in the previous chapter, and reference to this will aid in a deeper understanding of workflow in general.

These related practices can be employed to allow both the providers and receivers of a service a smooth and rational interaction with a system. This, in turn, translates into greater productivity and adoption across the board. It is important, therefore, to understand where within the institutional repository these can be applied to streamline and rationalise complex procedures, including situations such as verifying the validity of submissions or managing and naming user groups.

An understanding of each of these issues is becoming increasingly important in modern times given the quantity of information and the number of distributed individuals who have some involvement in the running of such services. These users are not necessarily, and often not generally, expert users (some may be students or academics) and supporting workflow, underpinned by a coherent administrative practice, is essential to prevent the system as a whole becoming bloated or disorganised beyond the point of reasonable recovery. We note also that this chapter concentrates primarily on scholarly literature, being one of the main uses of institutional repositories currently, and there will be additional factors to consider if designing procedures for other materials such as administrative documents or institutional records.

The technology upon which any repository product is based should have some support for workflow and archive administration. The issues examined here will help in defining the sorts of features you may require from your software as well as the organisational arrangements with which a new service such as this will need to integrate. We will discuss several configurations for your workflow and administration practices, and you should be able to see which of these are appropriate for your situation and which will need modification. There should be enough information and guidance in this chapter to facilitate the adaptation of the examples to your local requirements without too much complication.

What workflow and administration mean for the institutional repository

When considering how to manage an institutional repository it is good to examine how we might structure the administrative tasks so as to produce individual modules, or workflow steps, which then allow for a standardised treatment of the relevant elements of the system. This is the essence of developing workflow and is often best achieved at a relatively abstract level, where the actual administrative tasks are only discussed very generally. In this section we will examine the sorts of workflows that might need to be developed and distinguish them from the actual administrative tasks which underlie the ultimate management.

An institutional repository will have some or all of the following features which will need administering:

1. One or more ingest procedures for acquiring content from the content creators.

2. One or more ingest procedures for acquiring content from an intermediary, such as an administrator involved in mediated deposit.

3. A content verification procedure.

4. A cataloguing step in which metadata are verified and augmented where appropriate.

5. Short- and long-term storage and preservation procedures.

6. User and user group management.

7. Archive structure and content management.

8. Policies and authorisations.

These areas can be split, broadly, into four sections: submission (features 1 and 2), post-submission (features 3 and 4), preservation (feature 5) and structural management (features 6–8). We examine each of these sections and determine where the workflow and the administration are.

Submission

First, we should note that submission is workflow often entered into by one person alone. Therefore, the stages of the workflow are very close together and the process can be completed very quickly; the basic purpose of the workflow, by which control of the flow of tasks is maintained, remains valid.

The submission of any given item into an institutional repository can be defined by the content of the item itself. Most will consist of a combination of metadata and files, but there are other elements which should not be forgotten, including licensing (licence agreements should be stored with items to provide a persistent record of what was agreed by the depositor) and structural information (such as sequential file order or complex file relationships). It is possible to define three predominant components for creating a submission bound for an institutional repository, based on this content:

- metadata capture;
- file management;
- licence handling.

Metadata capture would cover the bundling of primarily descriptive and access metadata, while file management would include the upload (if in a web context) or delivery of the content as well as the supporting structural metadata. Finally licence handling would allow for the construction of rights metadata covering both item metadata and content files. Repository systems could treat each of these as one or more stages in an overarching submission workflow which could be typified by Figure 4.1.

The order of the illustrated workflow is effectively arbitrary. Although there is some degree of sense in making licensing the final stage, the first

Figure 4.1 Three stage submission workflow

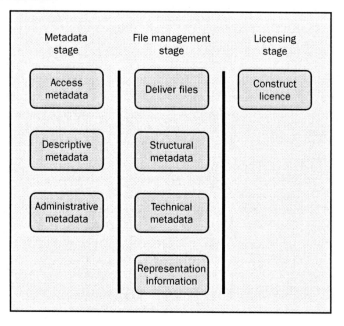

and second stages could easily be switched. Furthermore, depending on the complexity of the data being dealt with, each of these blocks could also be split into a number of subsections. For example, in our first workflow stage the administrative metadata might be primarily concerned with the location of the item within the structure of the archive; this might be best addressed by a single stage which allows for a potentially complex categorisation procedure.

The figure also includes references to some other types of activity that could be addressed as part of the submission process, especially in the second stage. Here we have included technical metadata and a representation of information components to the process. Both of these are included for later use in the preservation activities which may be undertaken with the repository, as discussed in the previous chapter. Meanwhile, administrative metadata, in the first stage, could refer to any number of local requirements for the management of items in the repository, such as the academic units in which authors work or the part of an internal document numbering scheme the submission represents.

It is worth nothing at this point that in some cases repository managers may wish to implement a number of alternative strategies which will impact on the workflow. Under certain circumstances it may be that the repository is only able to obtain or is only interested in the bibliographic details of a digital object (e.g. when copyright permission cannot be obtained for a journal article, but the repository would like to maintain a reference to the publisher version for completeness). Other circumstances may provide only a digital object with little or no accurate bibliographic data available (e.g. a retrospectively digitised item from a special collection); in this situation only minimal metadata may be associated with the item.

For the latter of the two above cases it is likely that the submission of the item will not be done by the author, but by a repository administrator. A similar situation may arise in advocacy strategies where the mediated submission of items on behalf of the creators may be a viable option. Thus, the workflow configuration will be different, and will especially contain a pre-submission workflow which needs to be defined. This is discussed again in Chapter 5, while an example is provided later in this chapter.

The workflow, therefore, is the framework within which all of the information is captured in a process called 'submission'. Each of the stages can be adequately and generally managed in software, such that all users of the system, be they content authors or administrators performing mediated submission, are able to create a Submission Information Package (SIP) for the repository. This is a concept which comes from the OAIS reference model, where the SIP is the original source of any asset that enters into the environment of the repository. Later this is converted into an Archival Information Package (AIP) and can then be delivered in the form of a Dissemination Information Package (DIP).

The workflow guides the process and the administrative requirements, as they can be loosely termed in this particular case, of providing the required information. Later in this chapter we will discus how users of all types are guided through the workflow step's administrative requirements, which is especially important in the case that users are non-expert, using 'how-to' and frequently asked question (FAQ) documentation.

Post-submission

Once a submission to the repository has been made it is necessary to perform a number of tasks before the item can be made public. These will be common tasks which are performed on many types of digital asset stored by an institution as well as some more specific tasks which arise from the very nature of the institutional repository. We are, through these processes, converting the provided SIP into an AIP. Although local institutional policy will have a strong bearing on post-submission workflow, the following are common requirements for the repository at this stage:

- submitter supplied metadata verification;
- addition of quality catalogue metadata (such as subject headings) and other value-added material;
- copyright and plagiarism checks;
- file verification (such as integrity and format checks) and content completeness;
- licence verification, and subsequent restriction application.

There is a lot of verification during the ingest procedure, which consists of both the submission and post-submission workflows. This means that it may be necessary to deliver or make the information available to a large number of distributed administrators such as the repository managers, collection administrators, and library cataloguers. As many people are involved it would follow that the workflow for this segment is going to be longer, although we should endeavour to keep the process as linear as possible in order to reduce complexity. Figure 4.2 shows how this workflow could be defined so that all verification and refinements can be done in a logical manner.

The sequence of these workflow steps is also relatively arbitrary. Nonetheless, a process like this may well provide the backbone to a fully

Figure 4.2 **Four stage post-submission workflow**

Metadata stage	File and content stage	Legal issues stage	Restrictions stage
Verify submitter metadata	Check file formats for preservation	Check item for copyright clearance	Check licence is acceptable
Insert value-added metadata	Check integrity of files	Plagiarism checks	Implement licence terms
	Check document completeness		

comprehensive post-submission workflow. As with other workflows presented in this chapter, each section may be split into subsections where appropriate and additional stages may be added for other local requirements, examples of which will be discussed shortly.

We have not discussed how the active workflow stage may change based on decisions made within this procedure. With verification stages we must allow for the possibility that items may fail to meet standards, and then understand how the workflow can deal with these eventualities. At this stage we are primarily concerned with understanding what are the nodes of the workflow and what they contain; once we know what activities need to take place and in approximately which order, we will be able to deal with the exact linkages and procedure flows.

Again, we anticipate that the elements of the workflow and the routes between the stages will be managed in software, but in this case we can expect our users to be expert, or at least informed, as we are dealing with the way in which the repository itself is managed. This allows us to employ internal documentation and training in a way which is not possible in the submission process. We are, therefore, able to demand of the users a higher degree of familiarity with the administrative tasks necessary at each stage.

Preservation

One objective of many repositories is to preserve its items in perpetuity. This means being able to provide access to the materials for all time, and to make it possible to read the contents of those same materials. Digital preservation, the subject area covering these activities, has been discussed in the previous chapter, but it is warranted here to bring up the techniques which fall under the scope of workflow and administration.

We have already seen that part of our submission workflow may contain stages which collect both technical metadata and representation information. Access to this information can make the preservation of the submitted materials much easier in the long term. Further, it is worth noting the recommendations of the OAIS reference model, which provides recommendations for best practices and workflow in all areas of any open archive that wishes to participate in digital preservation (CCSDS 650.0-B-1, 2002). Detailed discussion of this is outside the scope of this book, but an introduction is provided in the previous chapter. In this chapter we will aim to keep all our processes within the scope of this reference model, which is a standard to which a number of repository platforms are working to conform.

Structural

The structural management of a repository is an example of a situation where workflow is inappropriate. Procedures such as ingest engage participants in a well-defined set of activities happening in an often linear progression. Managing the structure of a repository, meanwhile, is a set of disparate, granular tasks which do not necessarily follow in order. The closest that we may find to a workflow is a set of small, independent tasks, which add up to a larger outcome. For example, setting up a user group to administer a section of the repository might require the following: create a user group, add users to the user group and attach policies to the user group. Each of these is a singular action which may occur in many other processes undertaken and are, therefore, not necessarily appropriate targets for managed workflow.

Instead, we would define a set of procedures and provide documentation on how to perform each one. Layered on top of this we would then need to have documentation to instruct the expert user which administrative tasks are required to be performed in what order to do certain operations. In the long term this sort of user will be able to determine the best way to perform any given procedure without reference to such top-level documentation, based on knowledge of the system and an understanding of how it fits together. Examples of structural management tasks and how best to perform them are provided later in this chapter.

Examples of workflow and administration

Building on the general guides developed in the first section we can now look at some example workflow and administration configurations for an institutional repository. We will introduce straightforward and complex submission workflow for different content types, as well as a couple of post-submission workflows that could be appropriate, and a demonstration of how mediated submission might be handled. In an ideal situation, all of these workflows could be implemented to live together within one system to allow a highly flexible research gathering service. After this we will look at some atomised administration tasks and ways in which these can fit together to produce an overall administration guide for the system.

Simple submission workflow

Figure 4.3 shows a straightforward submission process for the repository, and is possibly the most basic realisation of the workflow steps shown in Figure 4.1. It shows each of the stages encapsulated in a single workflow step with the appropriate linkages between them. We begin by adding the metadata record for the item, then proceed to upload content files, finally agreeing to some licence conditions for the archive. As previously noted, the first two stages here could be switched, and indeed in some configurations it may be appropriate to allow the start point to access both the metadata and the file stages simultaneously rather than linearly.

An alternative way of organising this to remove the linearity of the previous configuration might be to allow the user to access each step in whichever order they choose and then finish the submission once all stages have been completed, as shown in Figure 4.4.

Figure 4.3 A simple realisation of the three stage submission workflow

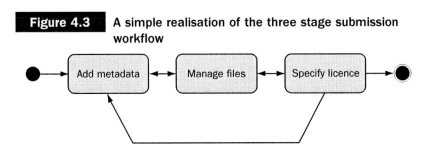

Figure 4.4 Alternative realisation of the simple three stage submission workflow

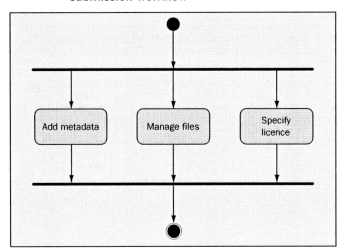

Complex submission workflow

Figure 4.5 shows a much more complex submission workflow, which is effectively an extension of the one shown in Figure 4.3. It takes each of the components of the three workflow steps in the previous example and provides a more complete management of each part. This may not always be necessary, but a repository attempting to cover all aspects in preparation for digital preservation may well wish to implement these stages.

Initially we collect the item's administrative information in the context of the archive; as previously noted this may contain information such as the user's academic unit or position. The next stage is the straightforward metadata capture process, which will in general be purely access or descriptive metadata.

Figure 4.5 A complex submission workflow

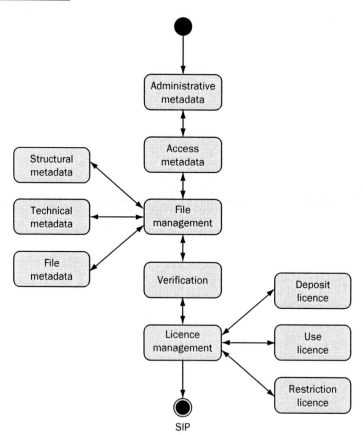

Following this we encounter the complex file content workflows: metadata for each file is captured, and we have included the option for technical metadata. Technical metadata may well not be user-entered, but may be a hidden system workflow step which attempts to extract from the given file the information it will need to aid long-term preservation, and to attach any available representation information. Given the need to manage arbitrarily many files, we then include a stage which allows the submitter to provide structural metadata, helping us understand how the item should be interpreted, or at least how the files involved relate to one another.

Once this set has completed we can move on to a user-friendly *verification* stage, where the user may check all the stages in one place to ensure that they are satisfactory, and finally to the licence specification as in the previous figure. In this case we have broken the licence into three segments: deposit licence, use licence and restriction licence. The user will have to agree to a deposit agreement for the repository (permission to store and preserve), provide a use licence (terms under which people will be able to use the item), and determine if they will apply a restriction licence (potentially temporal licence restricting use).

Each of these stages is held in a linear chain which is only accessible to the user as they proceed through the workflow, but, as before, are retrospectively available once the user has passed through each stage. Note that retrospective linking treats each of the stages on the main trunk as a single stage, even if it has an internal structure. As in the simple example, this could also be reorganised to allow simultaneous access to each of the nodes and then a final confirmation stage to complete the submission, as shown in Figure 4.6.

Post-submission workflow example 1: journal articles

The workflow illustrated in Figure 4.7 shows how you may manage a pre- or post-print journal article in post-submission. We start with a departmental administrator verifying that the submission is warranted for their departments (as some departments may have different policies regarding which of their materials should be held in the repository). Once the submission has been validated it can be delivered to the repository managers who can verify the content for copyright and so forth before determining that the material is fit for entry in the repository. Finally the item is sent to the cataloguer who can enhance the

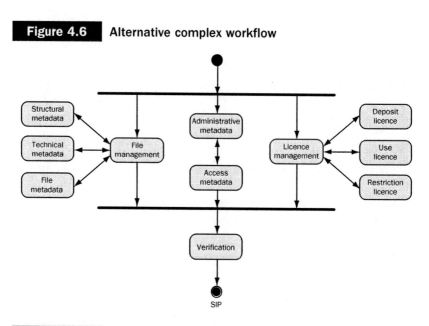

Figure 4.6 Alternative complex workflow

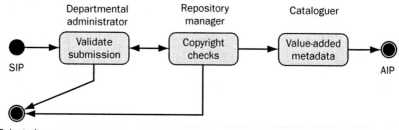

Figure 4.7 Basic journal article post-submission workflow

metadata and add subject headings if necessary; it is worth noting that once the item reaches the final metadata step it cannot be returned to previous steps, as it has already been cleared for accessing the repository, and no changes made in the final step can alter this.

Post-submission workflow example 2: electronic theses deposit

Assuming that an e-thesis has been fully marked and approved, the workflow illustrated in Figure 4.8 may be appropriate for post-submission.

In this instance we are not only attempting to deposit the e-thesis in the repository, but also to generate a print thesis for deposit in the

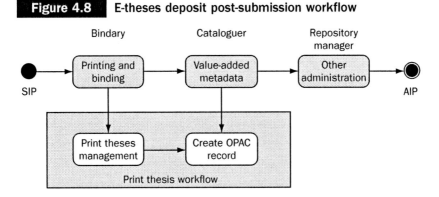

Figure 4.8 E-theses deposit post-submission workflow

institutional collection. For this reason the first stage of the process is *printing and binding* where the electronic copy can be used as the authoritative version from which all print versions should be derived. It is worth noting that this point interfaces with another (separate) workflow in the form of the print thesis management; these systems will need to live in harmony, and the second stage of this workflow will also need to interface with that same system. The print theses management system will handle the bound copies of the thesis generated in our first workflow step in the usual way.

Once a copy has been printed and injected into its own workflow the e-thesis moves on to the second stage where a cataloguer can verify, correct and augment the metadata. From this enhanced record a library OPAC record may be generated which also injects into the print theses management workflow, replacing or enhancing a stage where this information is manually input by cataloguers.

Finally the thesis will make its way to the repository managers who may perform important tasks such as copyright verification. Note that none of these workflow steps allow for backtracking as each is independent, and the thesis *must* reach the repository as this is a part of institutional records.

Mediated submission example

As discussed in Chapter 5, sometimes a mediated submission model is appropriate for obtaining content for the institutional repository. In these cases the workflow is quite different, as fewer parties need to be involved throughout the full document ingest lifecycle. Figure 4.9

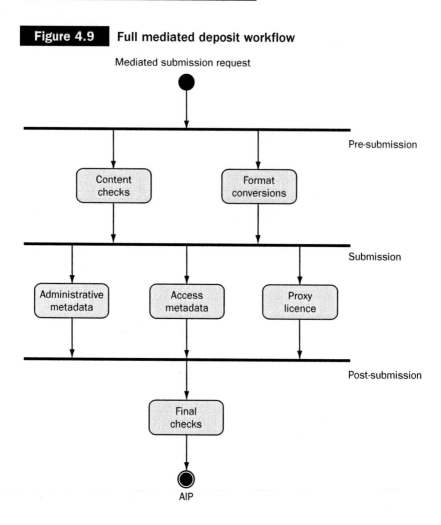

Figure 4.9 Full mediated deposit workflow

demonstrates how three main workflow segments can be defined which each contain tasks which lead to the object's deposit in the archive.

The first thing to note is that we now have a *pre-submission* workflow, which deals with what the mediator will have to do once the request for deposit has been made, but before the item can actually be entered into the submission process. What effectively happens here is that for convenience, greater likelihood that the item will reach the archive and to save on unnecessary work, some of the workflow processes previously dealt with in *post-submission* are shifted forward. Now we can perform the content checking (such as integrity and copyright) early on to save disappointment later. We can also pre-prepare the content for submission by transforming file formats and so forth.

Submission, therefore, mostly contains work revolving around managing the metadata, as we are already in possession of the files (although your software may still require a file management process). The usual administrative and access metadata for the item is necessary, which can be more challenging to obtain using a mediated model, and there is an alternative *proxy licence* which is granted on behalf of the author by the depositor.

As this workflow is usually entered into by a repository manager, there is not such a great need for extensive *post-submission* stages. We have included a *final checks* stage to provide quality assurance of the content of the repository, and this would generally be performed by a different administrator to those who have been involved in this workflow so far.

Administration example 1: collection structuring

One perpetual requirement of the repository, but hopefully one which requires minimal intervention once set up, is the structure of your internal data. Many repository systems support the concept of research collections, which allows them in many ways to mirror the storage and classification of traditional library and museum holdings. Other repositories may support the classification of the item in its metadata, possibly through the use of a controlled vocabulary. Either way, the choice of exactly how to structure or consistently classify your repository will be dependent on institutional requirements as well as the structures supported by the software. Here we will use the term *collection* to indicate either a repository level container for items or an item level controlled classification name. Some common structures for all types of data are:

- *Flat*: each collection is independent of all others, and sits as a peer alongside them.
- *One-to-many hierarchy*: each collection can be a parent of an arbitrary number of collections and a child of one collection, allowing for an ever refining classification of the contents. This is similar to the way that a traditional computer directory structure is laid out. For example: Biological Sciences > Cell and Molecular Biology > Internal Reports.
- *Many-to-many hierarchy*: each collection can be the parent and child of an arbitrary number of other collections, allowing for complex categorisation patterns. These can be very difficult to use and manage.

For the two types of hierarchy we will also qualitatively define the following two terms:

- *Shallow hierarchy*: the hierarchy cannot be followed down too far before reaching the bottom. The depth at which you may consider a shallow hierarchy to become a deep hierarchy will depend on whether you are using a one-to-many or a many-to-many relationship model. The latter will become complex much faster and thus a shallow hierarchy will probably mean two or perhaps three levels, while the former may tolerate three or perhaps four.

- *Deep hierarchy*: the hierarchy can be followed down a long way, and to arbitrary depth. These are difficult to navigate in some circumstances although they can provide a rich classification scheme, especially in a many-to-many model.

We will assume, for the purposes of this example, that your repository supports a one-to-many hierarchy, and look at the best ways of dealing with this. A many-to-many hierarchy can be simplified to a one-to-many hierarchy trivially, and a flat hierarchy can still draw on some of the techniques we use here, especially when working with a shallow one-to-many hierarchy. When administering, it is necessary to adhere to a set of standards, as there is no workflow to enforce the order. In the case of collection management this means having a standard structure for the repository and standard naming schemes. These allow any other administrator to take up the role at any point and continue to operate without an appreciable lag during the learning curve.

When choosing repository structure, there are two requirements to meet. The first is the needs of the users (often academics) who will be depositing material. Their needs will be of accuracy of description of the content and the ease with which they can determine the appropriate place to deposit material. The second is that of the users discovering material (also often academics). Their needs will be of simplicity of use and ease of understanding; accuracy of categorisation would be secondary as much material is discovered via a search rather than a browse approach.

While we cannot propose a solution which is guaranteed to meet your institutional needs, we can suggest some general guidelines which will result in a manageable and usable hierarchy of collections. For example, Figure 4.10 shows a collection hierarchy which has many levels, and is *not* a structure we would advise. This is due to the complexity of navigating it, and the inconsistency of the collection names. In a web context, such a structure can be very hard both to present and use; this

Figure 4.10   An over-complicated collection structure

- Edinburgh University Library
  - Digital Library Division
    - ➤ Information Systems
      - Technical Papers
      - Working Papers
      - Journal Articles
  - Special Collections
    - ➤ PhD Theses
    - ➤ Cartography Collection
- University of Edinburgh
  - College of Science and Engineering
    - ➤ School of Physics
      - Astronomy and Astrophysics
        - ○ Data Sets
        - ○ Journal Articles
    - ➤ School of Biology
      - Institute for Cell and Molecular Biology
        - ○ PhD and Masters
        - ○ Journal Articles
      - Institute of Evolutionary Biology
        - ○ Theses and Dissertations
        - ○ Journal Articles
  - College of Arts and Humanities
    - ➤ ...
  - College of Medicine and Veterinary Medicine
    - ➤ ...

would certainly count as a *deep hierarchy*. An additional problem with this lies with how the context of your environment, as you navigate this hierarchy, is difficult to maintain. The collection names do not provide all of the information, and the entire parent tree is required to understand where you are. If this is unavailable or is extremely long, this adds difficulties to using this sort of layout.

Instead of this, we would advocate a much simpler, broader collection structure, where the contents of each collection will ultimately be greater in number than if a highly specific classification structure is used. The shallower the hierarchy, the easier it will be for users to navigate to what they want, and the more descriptive the collection names the easier it will be to identify the contents. Consider Figure 4.11, showing a genuinely shallow (two tier) organisation which should be easier to use than that of Figure 4.10.

This collection structure represents basically the same information as the one in Figure 4.10, but instead groups all content types into a purely origin-based hierarchy. Remember that full item metadata should also be

Figure 4.11 A two-tier collection structure

- University Library
  - Digital Library Division
  - Special Collections
- School of Physics
  - Astronomy and Astrophysics
  - Condensed Matter
- School of Biology
  - Institute for Cell and Molecular Biology
  - Institute of Evolutionary Biology
- School of Education
  - Teaching and Learning

stored in the repository, so there is no need for a full taxonomy at the collection level, only a guide to the content. If you wish to apply some degree of separation between content types then there are two ways to go about it. The first is similar to that employed by Figure 4.10, where collections for individual content types are stored inside a parent collection; the other is to have two separate collection structures for each content type. The decision on which to use may be down to personal preference, although we would prefer the latter option. Figures 4.12 and 4.13 illustrate these different approaches.

In addition, content listings, when viewing a collection, could be used as an indicator of the item type, negating the need for additional collection structures. A sophisticated software solution would have a range of filtering and display tools which could make the life of the researcher easier, and move the job of accurately describing the contents of each collection away from the administrator and into the hands of the metadata creator (submitters and cataloguers, in many cases). In addition, as we are in the environment of the institutional repository, there is little doubt that the content is that of the institution. Thus, no specific reference to the name of the institution need be made in the collections; any metadata being harvested via, for example, OAI-PMH, would acquire the institution of origin as part of the metadata, and would not need to (and in many cases will not) respect local collection structuring.

While Figure 4.12 shows a hierarchy which would ultimately be shorter, Figure 4.13 employs a highly descriptive collection name at each level, allowing each one to be comprehensible in any context. Figure 4.12 requires appreciation of the entire tree in order to understand what you are looking at; the danger is that if you try to be even more

Figure 4.12 Three-tier content specific collection structure

- University Library
  - Digital Library Division
    - Technical Papers
    - Working Papers
    - Journal Articles
  - Special Collections
    - Technical Papers
    - Working Papers
    - Journal Articles
- School of Physics
  - Astronomy and Astrophysics
    - Technical Papers
    - Working Papers
    - Journal Articles
    - Theses and Dissertations
  - Condensed Matter
- School of Biology
  - Institute for Cell and Molecular Biology
    - Technical Papers
    - Working Papers
    - Journal Articles
    - Theses and Dissertations
  - Institute of Evolutionary Biology
- School of Education
  - Teaching and Learning
    - Masters Dissertations
    - Course Notes

descriptive then your collection names can become inconveniently long (especially for presentation in the user interface).

From an administrative point of view, what is particularly important is that a structure is chosen and adhered to throughout the life of the repository (or migrated as a whole where necessary). If we were implementing Figure 4.12, for example, we should ensure that our top-level collections represent approximately equal entities within the institution, our second-level collections doing likewise, and our

Figure 4.13 Two-tier content specific collection structure

- University Library
  - Digital Library Division
  - Special Collections
- School of Physics
  - Astronomy and Astorphysics
  - Condensed Matter
- School of Physics (Data Sets)
  - Astronomy and Astrophysics (Data Sets)
  - Condensed Matter (Data Sets)
- School of Biology
  - Institute for Cell and Molecular Biology
  - Institute of Evolutionary Biology
- School of Biology (Theses and Dissertations)
  - Institute for Cell and Molecular Biology (Theses and Dissertations)
- School of Education
  - Teaching and Learning

descriptive third level should contain collections named from a controlled vocabulary of content types. Holding to these should ensure that the repository structure is understandable, as a whole, by all users, no matter what their speciality. If implementing Figure 4.13, similar comments apply and the qualifiers indicating collection content type should be drawn from a similar controlled vocabulary. It is worth noting that the structure advocated by Figure 4.13 allows for 'catch-all' collections for material that does not fit into the specialised collections, in the form of non-content-specific collections such as *teaching and learning*, which Figure 4.12 does not do so naturally.

Administration example 2: naming conventions

In the previous examples, the names of the collections were similar across all versions of the example; this is not without intent. From a system point of view, the names of the collections is largely irrelevant, but from an administrator point of view, identification of the correct collection (and other system elements) is very important. Much time can be saved by having a well-designed structure which adheres to a comprehensive naming convention. Aside from the collections within your repository, other system entities that could benefit from good naming include user groups and policy groups. Meanwhile, standardising certain metadata elements across all items may be convenient (*controlled vocabulary*), based on certain pre-defined characteristics of the content (is it part of a series, or has it been submitted for a particular type of award?).

We must also bear in mind that if we are applying names which refer to parts of the institutional structure then the naming conventions employed should be flexible enough to deal with departments which can change or merge with others, as is relatively common.

Let us consider a small selection of collections in a shallow hierarchy containing different sorts of item and acted upon by some groups of users. We may represent this pictorially as in Figure 4.14.

We have two top-level collections and two second-level collections. The first is intended to hold postgraduate theses, while the second is for digitisations of fine art images. Postgraduate theses have certain pre-definable metadata requirements, such as the degree awarding body, the departmental name and the degree type: these are often defined by the institution responsible for the student, and should not be in the

Figure 4.14 System entities with administrator definable names

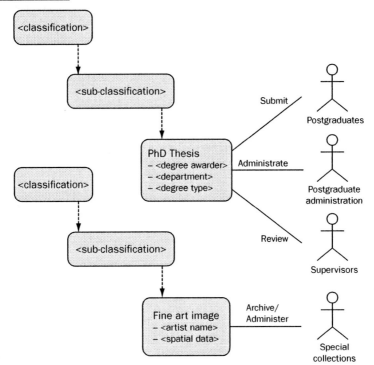

domain of the submitter to specify (*name authority*). Fine art images have similar sorts of requirements but, for the purposes of example, we only suggest two fields which may have naming conventions associated with them to demonstrate the concept. Here we have both the name of the artist and the spatial data; these are both special types of naming convention, because they are not necessarily a controlled vocabulary, but instead should be populated according to a particular layout (*standard form*). Acting on each of these types of material are interested user groups. Postgraduate theses are submitted by the student, administered by the faculty administration and reviewed by the supervisor. Fine art images have a much smaller administrative group associated with them consisting primarily of librarians.

Each of these components should have a naming convention associated with it, and Figure 4.15 demonstrates how this could be employed in a situation where the collections are structured based on the subject area interested in the enclosed material, and the subcollections are specific to the enclosed media types.

Figure 4.15   **Naming conventions implemented**

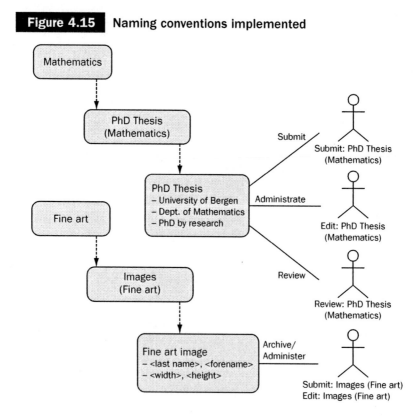

Each of the entities now has a name of a particular form. These are:

- *Top level collection*: the name of the subject area, often specified by an adopted classification system.
- *Second level collection*: the content type, as defined by the naming convention, including the name of the parent collection for out-of-context identification <content type> (<parent collection>).
- *Name authority metadata*: the content chosen from a controlled vocabulary, often specified at an institutional level. This is common practice in cataloguing.
- *Standard form metadata*: the form of the content is pre-defined, while the content is not. This ensures consistency across the metadata and aids search and browse. This is common practice in cataloguing.
- *User groups*: a description of the group and the name of the collection it acts upon. This highly focused user group model is advocated for its ease of administration, and accuracy of the names that can be applied to them. In this particular model, groups exist to bind a group of users with a single activity. For example, users who can all submit to collection A. If the same group of users could also submit to collection B, this model would have a separate group to which they also belong, rather than modifying the group policy to submit to both collections. This is an example of implementing a one-to-many mapping between roles and users, as opposed to a many-to-many mapping which can be hard to manage (and name effectively).

You will doubtless encounter other system entities which will be free for you to name, and should ensure that a naming convention is adhered to in all cases. Documentation is also essential, and should contain templates for generating new names as and when they are necessary. For example, the naming convention used in Figure 4.13 could be described thus:

- Top level: <school / department> [(<content type>)]
- Second level: <working group> [(<content type>)]

Here < and > denote variable text which should be replaced with the content described therein, while [and] denote an optional parameter.

Documentation

Documentation of all these processes is important and on the occasions when it is needed, it is invaluable. Good documentation will take the user step-by-step through the work that they need to do, and allow administrators to manage the system effectively. The documentation should define in advance the notation forms that it will use, and describe them clearly with examples. Here are some key components that your documentation should include:

- *Workflow*: the workflows, ideally with diagrams to support, should be described in full.

- *Responsibilities*: the responsibilities of the administrators involved in any stage of the process should be described in as much detail as is possible.

- *Collection structuring*: the generalised repository structure should be explained, along with examples (as in the first administration example).

- *Naming conventions*: general naming structures for all administrator controlled elements should be provided (as in the second administration example) along with examples.

- *Specific topics*: item types or actions which need special requirements should be outlined and the additional information provided.

- *Troubleshooting*: any problems encountered during use of a system should be documented, along with an appropriate workaround or solution.

Making this documentation easily available, for example, by posting it online, and embedding it within the system itself, will make management of the service considerably easier.

Administration in the context of the end user

It is not necessarily obvious that the end users of a system may also play a role in its administration, but there are at least three ways that this could be the case:

- The end user also provides material for the repository. This may be the case for postgraduate theses or journal articles, where the student and the academic respectively both supply material to the repository and simultaneously use its contents in their own work.

- The end user is provided with a customisable environment. This may occur if your choice of system has a home page for each user, which may have a customisable interface or workspace.

- The concept of administration includes the way in which users interact with the materials in the repository in order to fulfil their larger research goals. This could include managing lists of interesting materials for use later or performing very advanced search and filter procedures on the repository.

Users have their own administration to do, which is often viewed as normal use of the system. Nonetheless, online systems are reaching a level of complexity which can often greatly surpass actions which are simply 'obvious'. A good system will make administration by both professionals and end users as easy as possible, but supplying the latter group with additional documentation is sometimes unavoidable. It is for this reason that the concept of the *how-to* exists.

The how-to and its sibling the FAQ are relatively old and well tested ways of conveying discrete chunks of information to the user, and are also useful to administrators. Repository systems with a degree of complexity should contain these sorts of documents, often as part of the software package, but it is important that localisation of these documents is done before any system is rolled out as a service. The how-to should be similar, in concept at least, to the troubleshooting section of the main administrative documentation; it should primarily detail common tasks that users may need to undertake, such as submitting a document to the archive or managing their RSS feeds from the archive. The FAQ meanwhile should contain genuine frequently asked questions and their answers; it is usually of little value to create a list of questions that administrators *think* people might ask. Often feedback from the FAQ can lead to further improvements of both the system, and the service.

Although we cannot, and should not, impose hard administrative tasks such as employing naming conventions on end users, we must be aware that administration and workflow provide sets of procedures which help us achieve some goal within the system. These go beyond the scope of ensuring the system is functioning correctly and is fully maintained and extend into the realm of the end user, and increasingly so with the flexibility of modern systems.

Conclusion

As we have seen, the workflow and administration procedures which support the repository are essential to its effective sustainability as a service, just as they are in many others. Much time should be devoted to understanding how the repository fits into the institution and how it can be tailored to meet with people's needs and expectations. Changing working practices is a difficult process, as you will see throughout the course of this book, and one approach is to try and tailor the working practices of the repository to the ones that already exist in real life.

With well-written documentation the administration of the system can easily be devolved to small groups of individuals with specialist knowledge, and workflow can keep these disparate parts joined together such that information should not get lost or forgotten along the way. In addition, do not forget that the purpose of creating a comprehensive support structure and associated documentation is to make the use of the system by all much easier. Hence, using the documentation and tools should not be a difficult task if they are created properly.

There are many choices that you will need to make when designing your repository support which we cannot cover here; they will all be decisions that are unique to your situation. You may, for example, wish to pursue a many-to-many collection hierarchy, or go one stage further and maintain two or more entirely separate one-to-many hierarchies which represent the same underlying data. Or you may wish to reverse the direction of the user group to action mapping that we have suggested and instead map defined groups of users to multiple activities. Whatever choices have to be made at an institution, this chapter has introduced the main options and considerations to allow an informed decision.

Note

1. Much of what is contained in this chapter is based on experience and experimentation. Nonetheless, the OAIS reference model (CCSDS, 2002) has provided a basis for much of the work, while a number of papers cited here have been consulted to aid our understanding of workflow. There are also many useful presentations available at the erpanet website from the Budapest workshop on digital preservation workflow (erpanet, 2004). Other works instrumental in the creation of this chapter include Brunwin (1994), Lau et al. (2003), and the Workflow Management Coalition Handbook (Fischer, 2002).

5

Advocacy

An empty institutional repository is analogous to a library with empty bookshelves. Even though a lot of time, money and effort has been spent in setting up the optimal technological infrastructure, the success of the initiative will be ultimately measured by the usefulness to users, and thus, by proxy, the depth and richness of the body of content contained within. Discounting architects and other building professionals, who in their right mind would want to visit a library with no books?[1]

As institutional repositories are increasingly being adopted by universities and other organisations to manage and disseminate their digital research output, digital librarians and information professionals are cumulatively discovering that author 'self-archiving' is the exception and not the rule; content does not always automatically flow into the archives. Consequently, a number of studies have been carried out to investigate academic working practices (Foster and Gibbons, 2005) and current Internet use (Andrew, 2003; Hey, 2004).

It has been necessary for institutional early adopters to augment their modest repository content by developing and testing a number of content recruitment strategies which engage academic staff directly. These practical strategies have predominately been targeted at types of research output, for example, e-prints (Mackie, 2004), and electronic theses and dissertations (Jones and Andrew, 2005). Successful strategies include targeting departments with ready content (the 'low-hanging fruit' approach), seeking high-value exemplary or historical content for positive public relations (the 'digital baby-seal' approach), or a mediated-deposit service (the 'cradle-to-grave' approach).

Although not completely understood, it is nonetheless appreciated and well-documented that at the conception of a beneficial innovation a lot of hard work is required before widespread adoption. This chapter aims to draw together current thinking and experiences, and present ideas for the reader to take away and develop their own coherent strategy to help ensure critical take-up by their own community. In the context of further and higher education institutions, one size does not fit all, and the advice and ideas presented here should be taken as a starting point to be nurtured and developed further.

The process of advocacy and content recruitment for institutional repositories draws a striking parallel to the theoretical framework described by the diffusion scholarship field of behaviour science, first described and synthesised by Rogers (1962). A number of early adopters of institutional repositories have found it useful to draw relevant elements of the diffusion of innovation theory to design a robust programme of advocacy and content recruitment. We present here the basic concepts of innovation diffusion and apply them to the institutional repository scenario. The theoretical framework for this model was originally synthesised and developed by Everett Rogers in his seminal book *Diffusion of Innovations*. For a more in-depth and critical analysis of this area of behavioural science it is highly recommended that the interested reader should refer to the original text.

We conclude the chapter by combining the theoretical model with observations from real-life case-studies, which help to highlight a number of successful strategies for content recruitment. Finally we suggest some practical advice in how to engage in useful dialogue with academic staff to address their concerns.

Diffusion of innovation applied to institutional repositories

The adoption of new inventions by individuals and the sequential transfer through to widespread use by communities is not as straightforward a process as you would first imagine. Although counterintuitive, many innovations, although highly advantageous often take a long time to come to fruition, while some unlucky innovations are discarded altogether. The study of this fickle process has been the pursuit of diffusion scholars for several decades. Since the 1960s diffusion scholarship has endeavoured to describe a theoretical framework based on real-life case study observations. This framework is commonly referred to as the *diffusion of innovation* theory.

The theory of diffusion of innovation describes the manner in which a new technological concept, product or process, migrates from creation to use. Furthermore, diffusion theory suggests that this innovation is communicated through particular channels, over time, among the members of a social system. By understanding the particular characteristics of the social structure and the possible types of communication we can help to speed up the rate of adoption by developing a targeted methodology.

Another useful way of thinking about diffusion is that it is a type of social change, as defined by the process of alteration which occurs in the structure and function of a social system. Rogers (1995) makes the observation that when new ideas are invented, diffused, and are subsequently adopted or rejected, this can lead to certain dramatic consequences and social change. Although institutional repositories share a similar social change agenda to the open access movement, it is worth making a distinction between the two causes.

Each diffusion system displays four common elements that can be identified and analysed. These common elements have been described as follows:

- innovation;
- social system;
- time;
- communication channels.

The strength of using diffusion theory to analyse a specific condition is its power as a descriptive tool, to describe and understand the multifarious processes involved. Critically, diffusion studies are less strong in their explanatory power, and caution should be applied when predicting potential outcomes. However, if we are mindful of the scope of the theory, then diffusion studies will help us describe the nature of the advocacy problem and provide us with extremely useful pointers towards workable solutions.

Innovation characteristics

Before we start describing the process of diffusion, it is important to understand the distinct characteristics of the innovation which have a direct influence on the flow of communication. Specifically it is important to analyse the characteristics of the innovation as perceived by individuals as this will ultimately determine the rate of adoption across the given social group. Behaviour scientists suggest that how an individual perceives and subsequently reacts to an innovation depends on a number of critical factors, including:

- the *relative advantage* of adopting the new technology;
- the *compatibility* with existing work practices and ethics;
- the *complexity* involved in actually using the innovation;
- the *trialability*, or the degree to which it can be experimented with;
- the *observability* and visibility of the results.

In order to effectively sell the 'institutional repository' concept to academic staff it may be useful for us to think in the context of these terms. To illustrate this point, we will now consider the example of an institutional repository being used by academic staff to manage, store and disseminate research output (e.g. e-prints). There are immediately clear benefits for everyone involved, the primary *relative advantage* being the removal of price and permission barriers to research literature; secondly, increased visibility for the author; and thirdly, other intangible assets, such as increased institutional prestige and generally enhanced research productivity and progress for society. Even though these benefits are extremely laudable, it is actually the degree to which the institutional repository is perceived to be better than what it supersedes that is the important factor in whether it is adopted by academic staff. Rather than being left to form their own opinions, or worse, having their attitudes shaped by misguided counsel, it is critically important that academic staff are guided towards understanding the relative benefits offered by using institutional repositories.

Closely related to the previous point is the *compatibility* and consistency with existing academic values, past experiences and needs. To partly paraphrase the words of the Budapest Open Access Initiative, the institutional repository is compatible with, and has grown out of the scholarly tradition of willingly giving away the fruits of academic labour for the sake of inquiry and the advancement of knowledge. The institutional repository addresses current academic needs on a number of levels. If we briefly enter the mindset of a typical researcher: *as an author I want my research papers to be read and cited. In short, for the sake of my academic career I need my research to have professional visibility and the maximum possible impact.* The preliminary data support the view that open access articles have a greater visibility and thus potential impact (Lawrence, 2001; Harnad et al., 2004). Heading back into the academic perspective, however, this time as a reader of scholarly or scientific literature: *I want to be able to access anything that is relevant to my research. As subject areas are increasingly becoming more interdisciplinary I require access to a greater pool of literature.* It is well documented that no single library can afford a subscription to every possible journal, rendering much of the research literature inaccessible to many readers. By design, networked open access repositories lower these access barriers and offer the widest possible dissemination of a scholar's work (Johnson, 2002).

If we now consider the *complexity* involved for a researcher using an institutional repository for the first time we find there are a number of small barriers to overcome. New ideas that are simple to understand are adopted more quickly than counterparts that require the adopter to develop new skills and understandings. Surveys of Internet use (discussed in more detail later this chapter) indicate that a good proportion of academic staff do already use web pages to disseminate material, however, even though this is not normal working practice across the entire campus, most repository platforms are extremely simple to use. The complexity is not derived from actual use of the system but from secondary concerns. Experience has shown that some academics still view the Internet with a fair share of scepticism, but more importantly most have a poor general understanding of basic information science concepts, for example, metadata, and an even worse comprehension of the legal framework. This last point is entirely understandable as early adopters of technological innovations commonly work and exist in the legal gap between policy and actual use, created by the constantly evolving technological landscape. So, the problem of complexity is not predominately one of physical use, but rather a poor comprehension of various issues, including copyright and other concerns.

The beauty of an online repository platform is that the *trialability*, or the degree to which it can be experimented with by academic staff is extensive. New ideas that can be tried with minimum fuss will generally be adopted more quickly than products that are not accessible. The underlying rationale is that an innovation that is trialable represents less uncertainty to the individual who is considering it for adoption (Rogers, 1995). If we make the assumption that academics have unrestricted access to the Internet, once initially alerted to the service then they are free to experiment with the product in their own time. No special hardware is needed, no software is needed to be installed, and very little help is required in navigating through the repository. The critical factor is thus raising awareness of the repository service to ensure critical buy-in from academics to trial the product (see the section on raising awareness, later in this chapter).

Finally, the last important characteristic is the *observability*, or visibility of the impact that institutional repositories can have on research dissemination. This is a major factor to be considered as diffusion scholars indicate that the rate of adoption is directly related to the perceived observability. It seems like common sense, but anything we can do to help improve the visibility of results within the academic community will speed the uptake of repository use. This is already happening in a formal and less formal basis, through a number of different communication channels. A number of studies to assess the impact of open access to research literature have been, or are being, carried out (e.g. Lawrence, 2001). These results are conveyed to the academic community via the traditional, well-established reporting mechanisms, such as peer-reviewed journal articles and conference papers. These methods are important as they ensure formal acceptance within academia, but in themselves do not deliver wholesale widespread coverage across all subject areas. There are as yet no communication channels available that can give us this kind of coverage. It could be argued that to ensure a greater coverage a more personal and informal approach is also required, fostered by institutional support. It is relatively simple to capture online usage data, either direct from the repository software or the indirectly from the webserver on which the service is hosted. A number of institutions are now collecting this data and making it publicly available to boost support for their institutional repositories (see below).

In conclusion, we find that the physical and social characteristics of institutional repositories should make them amenable to adoption by the academic community, however, the observed diffusion has generally been slower than expected. It is apparent that a number of other critical factors must also be considered.

Social system: adopter categories

Within any institution there are going to be a wide range of attitudes towards the adoption of new innovations from academic members. In the terminology of diffusion scholars, the academic staff would comprise the social system. To help analyse the process of diffusion more closely, behaviour scientists have found it useful to refer to groups within the social system with similar attitudes as adopter categories. This classification is based upon the relative timing of adoption. These different adopter categories are commonly divided by behaviour scientists into five separate groups as follows:

- innovators;
- early adopters;
- early majority;
- late majority;
- laggards.

Within the context of an academic institution the *innovators* group can be described as the venturesome researchers who already understand the benefits of using repositories or similar structures. These scholars and scientists would already be self-archiving their research output in subject-based repositories, for example, the arXiv physics repository which has now been in existence for over a decade.

The *early adopter* group would usually be composed of liberal-thinking, technologically savvy academics, with a great enthusiasm for participating in new endeavours. Although the early adopter group is among the first to adopt and integrate digital media into their working practices, they are generally not information professionals. This has potentially serious implications because international standards and intellectual property rights are not strictly adhered to. To illustrate this point many academics who would fall into the early adopter category are already putting their research material online in personal or departmental web pages. In doing so they are not complying with international copyright laws and potentially putting themselves or their institutions at risk.

In our experience, an *early majority* group is usually comprised of an academic unit led by an opinion leader (see next section) who possesses a favourable view of repositories. The term 'academic unit' is meant here as scale independent; the group could consist of only a small research lab led by one principal investigator, or it could be an entire school whose research output could consist of hundreds of peer-reviewed papers per year. What does matter is that the opinion leader has considerable influence over the behaviour of the other members of the academic unit.

Unfortunately for change advocates, most academic staff within a higher education institute would fall into the *late majority* group. The problem described in simple terms is not that the members of this group are opposed to the idea of repositories; in fact most would be broadly supportive, but rather that there is a fundamental lack of awareness of the service, and also critically a lack enthusiasm. A common viewpoint that we have encountered in academics is that while they broadly understand most of the issues and the altruistic benefits that repositories promise to deliver to themselves as authors and readers, the fact of the matter is that they are currently unwilling to change their working practices to fit with our ideals. The specific details and reasons for this may be multifarious, but until repositories are accepted into the wider social context as part of the normal research process, individual academics will be reluctant to use them. Thus we may consider this to be mainly a social problem. We will touch upon this subject again in the concluding comments of the chapter.

In our scenario the final adopter category to be convinced to use repositories would generally comprise not only the technologically sceptical academics, but also the extremely cautious, who may be put off by technical or legal misconceptions. It is tempting to think these *laggards* commonly are the more senior academics who are close to retiring age. However, it is worth noting that there are always exceptions to the rule, and not all retiring professors should be considered as laggards! Some institutions have found that the more senior academic staff wish to preserve a legacy collection of work for posterity, thus, given the right conditions, they can often be early adopters of institutional repositories.

Change agency: change agents and opinion leaders

The role of the predominant social system, in other words the different adopter categories of academics, describes only half of the people involved in the process of repository adoption. The other major role in the innovation process is that of the change agency. The change agency can be described as the group that is actively engaged in promoting the new innovation. In our chosen scenario of institutional repositories this is a somewhat complicated concept as there are a large number of positive stakeholders involved at different scales of granularity; from international organisations, e.g. SPARC/SPARC Europe, national organisations, e.g. CURL, funding agencies, e.g. JISC and individual institutions, e.g. universities. As we are investigating practical, hands-on advocacy, for the purpose of this study we will only consider the process of diffusion from within a university, or a similar higher education institution setting. Even then this microcosm is full of complexity, which can be broken down into the following sets of people:

- opinion leaders;
- change agents;
- change aides.

In simple terms, an opinion leader is someone who exerts influence over the social system, who could either be from the social system or the change agency. We have already discussed the importance of opinion leaders in charge of an academic unit (see previous section). This kind of influence is critically important in tipping the balance in favour of academic staff using institutional repositories. Similarly, a strong opinion leader is needed in the change agency itself. Most successful repositories have strong support from the senior management level of the change agency, which is normally the library and information service sector. The effect is two-fold, in that an influential opinion leader in charge of the change agency can help bring in much needed resources, critically staffing time, and also help with the introduction of institutional policy change.

The critical position in the innovation adoption process is the role of the change agent. The change agent operates in a role mediating between the change agency and the relevant social system, which is in our case the university and its academic staff. Rogers (1995) specifically suggests that the change agent positively influences innovation decisions within the social system by carrying out these important following functions:

- developing a need for change within the academic community;
- establish an information-exchange relationship between parties;
- diagnose potential problems which will inhibit adoption;
- create intent to change in the academic community;
- translate this intent into action;
- stabilise adoption and prevent discontinuance; and
- shift reliance from the change agent to self-reliance.

Each institution needs to identify and recruit someone to fit this role, either from short-term project funding, internal secondment, or by creating a new position within the organisation's structure. In the early stages, institutional repositories have been commonly developed as projects to show the proof-of-concept before being developed into a full production service. Consequently the role of the change agent is often taken up by project staff. This role of *agent provocateur* needs someone with non-traditional librarian qualities and skill-sets, and who is comfortable and able to engage with academics on their own terms. A knowledge of academic working practices, alongside a good understanding of information systems is essential.

The central role of the change agent can be supplemented with change aides, who complement the change agent, by having a pre-existing knowledge and relationship with clients. The change aide may have less technological competence with the innovation, but their established relationship with the client means that they are already a trusted intermediary, thus will have to spend less time investing in building relationships. This point should not be overlooked as in a large institution the effect of one change agent may not be able to reach all constituents of the community. A change agent will also have a detailed knowledge of the correct communication channels to take within the community to achieve maximum dissemination of their information. A good example of a change aide would be a subject or liaison librarian.

The innovation–decision process

The third major element in the diffusion process is time. A set number of stages are passed before any technological innovation is widely accepted and used. Behaviour science researchers have described and defined these theoretical stages as follows:

- knowledge;
- persuasion;
- decision;
- implementation;
- confirmation.

Collectively, the process through which a decision-making unit passes from first knowledge of an innovation, through these stages towards a decision to adopt or reject the new idea, and beyond, has been termed the *innovation–decision process*.

The innovation–decision process begins with *knowledge*, or exposure to the innovation's existence, and understanding of its functions by the adopter community. During the *persuasion* phase, aided by the change agency, the members of the community form a favourable attitude towards the innovation. The *decision* step is characterised by widespread commitment to its adoption, with actual widespread use of the innovation occurring during the *implementation* phase. Reinforcement based on positive outcomes typifies the final *confirmation* stage.

The innovation–decision process is a sequence of events along which each individual has to pass. If we now consider the same chain of events for a large organisation, although a lot more complex, it can be superficially similar. In strictly hierarchical and rigid organisations, for example, governmental bodies and commercial entities, this may not be apt. A number of studies (e.g. Zaltman et al., 1973) specify the distinct aspects of innovation within such an organisational structure. However, in a free-thinking organisation like a university, where informal patterns of behaviour are predominant, the overall behaviour can be likened to that of an individual.

It has been observed that in any given organisation, the intent of bureaucratic policy is to depersonalise human relationships by standardising and formalising them (Rogers and Agarwala-Rogers, 1976). It is primarily this function that drives organisational behaviour away from that of an individual. However, when the organisational intent is as broad as a university's, generally speaking, to provide teaching and research in all areas of human endeavour, then we find that the responsibility for organisational behaviour is devolved largely to smaller defined research-specific groups, often led by strong personalities. This, coupled with academic freedom, which largely lifts the confining structures associated with other organisations, fundamentally means that individuals predominantly define the organisation behaviour through their informal practices, norms and social relationships.

A practical hierarchy of effects: the advocacy process in brief

The rationale behind using the diffusion of innovation theory to look at the adoption of institutional repositories is to be able to systematically analyse the advocacy process, parts of which can be otherwise overlooked. The theoretical framework we have just discussed can help plan and implement a practical advocacy strategy. We now move from the theoretical and consider some real-life processes that occur during the dissemination and adoption of institutional repositories within universities.

| Figure 5.1 | 'Ripple-diagram' showing the relationship between (1) stages in the innovation–decision process (after Rogers, 1995), (2) the practical hierarchy of effects (adapted from McGuire, 1989), and (3) the dominant social-system of repository use |

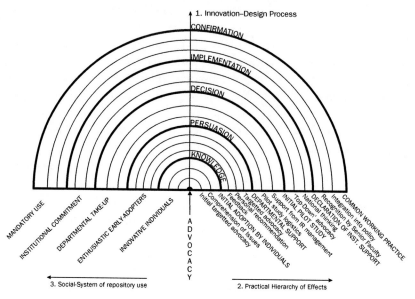

Figure 5.1 shows the relationship between the theoretical stages in the innovation–decision process, the practical hierarchy of events, and adopter categories. The figure takes the form of a series of concentric semi-circles nesting within one another. If we consider the advocacy programme to start at the centre-point of the circle, then the effects of the change agency will spread outwards like ripples as the ideas propagate through the social system. The five theoretical stages of the innovation–design process (1) are represented on the figure by the bolder 'ripples', which also correspond to the adopter categories (2). In this figure these ripples also represent the individual watersheds when members of the different adopter categories start to deposit items into the institutional repository. The minor interstitial ripples represent significant events occurring in the practical hierarchy of events (3). The hierarchy of events presented here are adapted from the theoretical work of McGuire (1989), but brought into context using a sequence of events from experiences shared by repository early adopters. Specific techniques and procedures are discussed in the next section.

The inception of the advocacy programme brings about the *knowledge* step in the innovation–decision process. The primary aim is to disseminate as widely as possible, with special attention given towards academic staff who would fall into the *innovators* adopter category. This initial targeted information exchange leads towards comprehension of the various issues. This step is relatively rapid as the target group is likely to be already amenable to adoption. The end of the knowledge phase is characterised by the initial adoption and use of the repository by individual academics.

The second step is the *persuasion* of the academic community. With some real clients using the repository it is now possible to solicit valuable feedback to improve the service. Additionally, an open dialogue with the initial repository users is important to determine common anxieties that the academics may have. The reassurance that is offered now is critically important because personal recommendation is an underused but significant communication channel used by academics. The major aim of this stage is to escalate the adoption process by moving from targeting individuals to academic units. Once again the term 'academic unit' is mean to be taken as scale independent. The initial adopters are usually willing to help the change agency by identifying the correct channels to approach opinion leaders, with the aim of soliciting overall departmental support. As discussed previously, the support of an opinion leader within the academic unit is critical to win over the hearts and minds of the rest of the group. With an opinion leader becoming an *early adopter* of the repository it becomes much easier to encourage the rest of the unit to participate.

Before a firm *decision* is made by the academic unit to fully endorse the repository, a proof-of-concept pilot study is highly recommended. Initially the pilot study logistics will have to be arranged. At this stage it is recommended to bring on board support members of staff from the academic unit, for example, secretarial staff or computing officers. These support staff members should be considered as change aides, and are extremely valuable because of the local knowledge they possess about the academic unit. At this stage, the repository may still be seen as confusing by both academic and support staff; thus it is important to offer as much support and encouragement as possible. This may take the form of staff training, help with item deposition, or general help advocacy within the academic unit. It is important to remain flexible to meet the specific needs of the client, as each academic unit will have their own strengths, weaknesses and agenda.

The *implementation* of a pilot study provides an excellent showcase to promote the repository to other academic units. This is important because it instantly adds academic credibility to the project, in a similar manner to a peer-review process. With advocacy progress occurring so far at the grass-roots level, this is the right time for the change agency to think about initiating a top-down advocacy approach, to work towards a declaration of institutional support, for example, signing up to the Berlin Open Access Declaration. A major focus of the top-down advocacy approach has been to lobby for support at the highest levels of the university's senior management. To this end, an opinion leader of considerable influence is required from the change agency. In addition, it may be beneficial to link up nationally to form strategic partnerships to boost not only the agenda of the institutional repository movement, but also the visibility and prestige of the institutions and nations involved. Much coordination is required to achieve this win-win situation.

At the time of writing, many early adopter institutions have reached the beginning of the *confirmation* step, however, it looks like the course of events described in Figure 5.1 will be likely. In general, we are already beginning to achieve widespread recognition from senior academic members, which is the first step towards integration into formal institutional policy. With such a policy recommending deposition of research material into the repository then the service will naturally become part of the common working practice of the university. Mandatory deposition is a large step to take, and whether this is achievable depends on the type of material. The institutions taking this step have started with collections of material produced and owned by their own members, for example, electronic theses and dissertations, before even thinking of moving on to more complex items such as teaching and learning objects, or published journal articles, which may or may not be viable.

Communication channels and innovation decisions

Now that we have described a basic framework for an advocacy programme based on theoretical and practical experiences, it would be useful to focus attention on the act of communication itself and how this can affect the decision-making process. With a large number of options available, communication between the social system and change agency can be a complex process. Broadly speaking, thinking about the communication process can be simplified greatly if we divide the types of communication channels into a number of discrete categories depending on their nature. Commonly, behavioural scientists distinguish communication channels and sources respectively as:

- interpersonal or mass media; or
- local or cosmopolitan sources.

An interpersonal communication channel implies that a pre-existing relationship exists between the individuals involved and that any information exchange is intimate, either face-to-face or similar. Alternatively, no prior social contact is required for a mass media communication channel and any information exchange predominantly uses technology as a proxy for personal action. In the special circumstances of our scenario we would consider the use of telephone as an interpersonal channel, and e-mail as both an interpersonal channel as a mass media communication channel depending on the specific context (e.g. personal mail or distribution lists).

A number of well-noted generalisations have been recognised by other diffusion studies, however, the following observations are particularly relevant for our own scenario:

- mass media channels are relatively more important at the knowledge step; whereas,
- interpersonal channels are considered more important at the persuasion step;
- local channels are relatively more important at the persuasion stage;
- mass media channels are proportionately more important than interpersonal channels for late-stage adopters.

With this in mind, it is now useful to consider how the innovation decisions are actually made by academic staff. In general, these decisions can be described using the terminology constructed by diffusion scholars:

- optional;
- collective; or
- authority-based.

In the *optional* decision the choice to accept or decline the innovation is made on an individual basis, so each member of the community has a real opportunity to adopt or reject the idea. Where the decision is reached by a general consensus among the members of the community then the decision is said to have been made on a *collective* basis. The final distinction of decision making is when the process is *authority-based*. Here the individual has little or no influence in the decision, which is imposed by people higher up the management structure. The role of the individual is to implement the required changes needed to facilitate the adoption of the innovation. Rogers (1995) made the observation that the fastest rate of adoption results from authority decisions; however, these decisions may be circumvented by individuals during the implementation stage. Because of the need for consultation and organisation, optional decisions usually are made more rapidly than collective decisions.

Figure 5.2 is similar to the previous 'ripple' diagram, in that the advocacy process is represented by concentric half-rings emanating from the central starting point. Once again one of the axes represents the adopter categories of the depositing academic staff (1). This time, however, the other axis represents the how the *innovation decision* is made (2). Overlain are details of an example campaign, derived from the

Figure 5.2   'Ripple-diagram' showing the relationship between (1) adopter category (after Rogers, 1995), (2) innovation decisions (after Rogers, 1995), and (3) example of a successful advocacy campaign leading to adoption of repository use in normal academic working practice

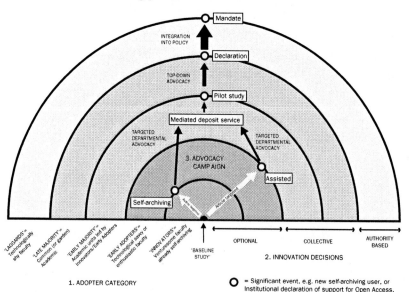

original advocacy plan at the University of Edinburgh (primarily discussed in the next section), which highlights some of the most common content recruitment techniques used (3).

In the hierarchy of events we suggest here (Figure 5.1 (3)) the actual type of innovation decision taken by members of the social system changes as the adoption process progresses. Initially at the knowledge step the decision is definitely *optional*. Similarly at the *persuasion* stage the decision remains in the hands of the individual. However, by the time the *decision* step is reached we have found that the process of adoption is made on a *collective* basis. If we follow the logical hierarchy of events that is currently being played out then the *confirmation* step will end with the decision to adopt being *authority-based*. This is already happening for some types of research output, for example, electronic theses and dissertations.

Practical advocacy strategies for content recruitment

So far we have discussed a theoretical framework of diffusion, with brief details of a real-life case study to propose a loose model for repository advocacy. Next we would like to fill out this process with some real-life strategies used by early adopter institutions. The 'ripple diagram' in Figure 5.2 shows an example advocacy campaign based on the theoretical model in Figure 5.1. Discussion of the implementation of such a campaign can be found in Chapter 7.

Baseline survey

Prior to the implementation of an advocacy plan, a scoping survey of research material already held on departmental and personal web pages in the institutional web domain would be beneficial for a number of reasons:

- it would help the change agency to understand scholarly use of the Internet across different subject areas;
- it would aid the initial population of the repositories by identifying ready material to ingest;
- to identify willing scholarly contributors who would form the *innovator* and *early adopter* categories; and

- such a survey would provide an invaluable baseline from which progress of the projects can be measured during any subsequent evaluation process.

The real benefit of this exercise is to identify members of academic staff that would become the *early adopters* of the institutional repository. Specifically it is worth looking for individuals who are *opinion leaders* in their academic sphere of influence, who would be able to work alongside the change agency in promoting the institutional repository concept. These individuals are important to find because their input is critical for both the early and later stages of the advocacy programme (as detailed subsequently).

Initial awareness

At the same time as the baseline scoping survey is being carried out, it is advantageous to proceed with a number of strategies to raise awareness of the institutional repository across the campus. Some of these efforts will prove to be more successful than others. Bearing in mind that mass media channels are reportedly more important at the knowledge step (see earlier) it is initially best to use as many mass media communication channels as are available. Practically, this could consist of using print and electronic media to disseminate information about the repository service to a broad general audience, for example, using university websites and newsletters. To draw the reader's attention the change agency could specifically deposit a number of items with historical or exemplary status. Content from famous alumni, or significant pieces of ground-breaking research would be ideal to promote the repository in a favourable light. In addition, it is recommended to ask senior figures from within the university, for example, the Principal or Provost, to add content to the repository.

During the course of any advocacy campaign it is required to not only raise awareness of the repository service, but also to explain and promote the rationale behind it. To facilitate such a discussion with academic staff it may be necessary to provide education about the open access movement, copyright in digital materials and other related issues. With this aim in mind, many early adopters of repositories have organised university-wide seminars. Some experiences of organising such an event are described in the case study in Chapter 7. A slightly different, and arguably more effective, strategy is to give more focused presentations tailored to suit individual academic units.

This second strategy of targeted departmental seminars can be initiated through contact with academic staff members identified as potential *early adopters* by our baseline survey. Contact should be made with the aim of building potential close relationships between the library and departments. With this link it should be possible for the change agency to be invited to give presentations at suitable pre-established forums, for example, departmental lunchtime seminars or committee meetings. Being invited along to a such a venue means that the change agency is more efficient in spreading awareness because an attentive audience is guaranteed for less organisational effort – the host department makes all the advertising and hosting effort. Another significant source of academic contact, important for building these meaningful linkages can be through unsolicited correspondence from academic staff, who had initially heard of the repository service from the initial awareness activities and other peer-to-peer communication.

Targeted content recruitment

Alongside raising the general awareness and presence of the institutional repository with academics, it is important to gather content and start to fill those empty shelves. Instead of waiting for academics to start 'self-archiving', a targeted content recruitment strategy yields instant results. As shown in Figure 5.2, this can practically take the form of two main strands: targeting authors with content, and targeting the content directly. Experience of contacting authors is further discussed in Chapter 7.

A large amount of material can immediately be made available to the repository team from this targeted content recruitment drive; however, complications can arise. Upon investigation of the journal self-archiving policies it might occur that a significant proportion of this content cannot be deposited into the repository in its current form due to prohibitive restrictions. Consequently, a second content recruitment strategy should be developed in tandem. It may be beneficial to identify content that is freely available to be placed in our repository, thus it is recommended to source content from publishers with self-archiving friendly policies ('green' journals). These journals can be identified from the original ROMEO project copyright transfer agreement analysis reports and web pages (Gadd et al., 2003), and subsequently from the updated database hosted by the SHERPA project. Open access ('gold') journals can be targeted; however, there are some fundamental moral issues with this approach. The primary objective of an institutional repository should be to open up access to research, followed by other secondary benefits. Gold journals already make their material open access, so any inclusion of this material in repositories would effectively be duplication of effort. It would be better to direct all efforts towards making new research freely available.

An additional criterion for journal selection should be the journal impact factor. A common misconception by academics, circulated and repeated by various publishers is that the quality of material to be found online in repositories is in some way inferior and of lower quality of that to be found in traditional print journals. To demonstrate that this is clearly not the case, the change agency can decide to specifically target content from the more respected and illustrious 'green' journals with the highest impact factors. Authors who have published in these journals can be identified from subscription bibliographic databases (e.g. Thompson ISI's Web of Knowledge service, *www.isinet.com/*). Due to the volume and the desire to gather the most useful research it may be worth concentrating on the most recently published journal articles.

A similar strategy of targeting high quality research has been successfully deployed by the Digital Academic Repositories (DARE) programme in the Netherlands. One of the initial aims of DARE was to set up a working institutional repository for every single Dutch university. This objective was achieved at the beginning of 2004. To significantly boost content the DARE programme launched the 'Cream of Science' initiative. In a concerted effort, over 25,000 publications by 200 of the leading Dutch scientists and researchers were added to the DARE repository network. Such a high-profile show of support for open access by the country's top scientists and researchers has significantly helped to boost the awareness and credibility both nationally and internationally. For more information about this initiative, the reader is referred to the DARE website (*www.DAREnet.nl*).

Such a national initiative, where the top researchers are hand-picked, may not be appropriate for all countries, especially where highly competitive research reporting mechanisms are used as a basis for funding allocation and distribution. For example, in the UK the Research Assessment Exercise (RAE) is held every seven years. Every single academic unit will be asked to submit their best research to be assessed by an independent panel of experts. With funding, reputations and personal careers dependent on submissions to the RAE, this process creates a highly competitive and defensive environment for research. It may not be appropriate to effectively pass value judgments of any kind on scientists and researchers prior to such an exercise.

Mediated deposit

The programme of targeted content recruitment formed the basis for developing the workflow for the mediated deposit service. Our own experience, similarly backed up with a number of important independent studies (e.g. Swan and Brown 2004a,b), has shown that although many academics are sympathetic to self-archiving, actually translating this sentiment into positive action and content requires someone to take the initiative. In practice, the general uncertainty regarding actual mechanisms and consequences of self-archiving means that this initiative is not intuitively taken up by the average academic (if there is such a thing). Thus, it is up to the change agency to lead by example and help authors deposit their material in repositories.

Many of the leading content repositories have developed this line of thinking into offering a mediated deposit service for authors. The level of service offered will depend on a number of factors, including the scope and available resources. At its most basic level a mediated deposit service will act as a simple ingest conduit for content. More sophisticated services will layer value-added services on top, for example, copyright clearance, file format conversion or metadata enhancement. These value-added services may, or may not, have the potential to recoup costs if fully investigated.

A more detailed investigation of the workflow required to run a mediated deposit service is shown in the case study in Chapter 7. This model is based around a core service where the author passes to the library an electronic copy of the item to be placed in the repository. Before the item appears online a member of the project staff will check the copyright status of the work, convert any file formats that are preferred not to archive to supported formats wherever possible, and submit the item to the relevant collection with the relevant metadata. This mediated submission is generally warmly welcomed for all types of research materials as many students and academics are too busy to spend time learning and using a new service, and need help to archive their research output into repositories.

Pilot projects

Once contact has been established and a good number of early adopters are depositing items into the repository, by either self-archiving or by proxy, it is time to escalate the innovation–decision process to the next stage by inviting an early majority group to participate. Quite often one of the early adopters is an influential member of an academic unit, for example, a departmental head, and can be considered an opinion leader.

One problem commonly encountered by change agents is a lack of familiarity with the working practices of different subject areas; more importantly, however, is a major problem with enforcement. It is one thing to persuade someone of the benefits of self-archiving, but to actually put it into practice requires persistence and tact. On the one hand you have to do so much to raise awareness, but not so much to put people off. The lack of a prior personal relationship and familiarity can make this difficult, which is where the backing of an opinion leader is extremely valuable. An opinion leader has the ability to enforce decisions, something which ultimately the change agent cannot do.

The next natural step in any advocacy campaign is to work with an opinion leader, either in a formal or informal basis, to help lead the members of their academic unit from inaction to become the early majority. Leading with a pilot project is a great way to do this, which can act as proof-of-concept. Examples of pilot projects which have successfully engaged the academic community include:

- Creation of a new online report series, or transferring and then expanding an established report series online, e.g. the publications database for the School of Electronics and Computer Science at the University of Southampton (*http://eprints.ecs.soton.ac.uk/*).

- Recent departmental journal publication lists, with access to full-text where applicable, e.g. the Scottish Universities Environmental Research Centre (SUERC) publications hosted in the Glasgow e-prints service (*http://eprints.gla.ac.uk/view/faculties/suerc.html*).

- School or departmental theses and dissertations collection, e.g. the School of Informatics theses and dissertation community in the Edinburgh Research Archive (*http://www.era.lib.ed.ac.uk/handle/1842/306*).

- Conference paper series, either for a recent conference or retrospectively added, e.g. the Modern Languages Publications Archive hosted by the University of Nottingham (*http://mlpa.nottingham.ac.uk/*).

Feedback

An important part of the process that helps to reinforce the behaviour and awareness we are trying to promote is to actively show the benefits that self-archiving can deliver through feedback mechanisms. The online environment presents an exciting opportunity to exploit a host of automatically gathered statistics, collected either by the host web servers or the repository software itself.

The access statistics presented by the University of Queensland repository service ePrintsUQ (*http://eprint.uq.edu.au/*) is a good example of how to present this kind of data. Here the data can be accessed from the front page of the site and is available to browse by author, or by looking at the top 50 items or authors.

More detailed access and service statistics are offered by the Edinburgh Research Archive (*http://www.era.lib.ed.ac.uk/statistics*). Available to view are monthly breakdowns and the running total of statistics such as item views and bitstream downloads; the number and specific keywords searches users have carried out on the repository; the repository content volume and type; as well as the most accessed items. This information is not only valuable to the change agents as good publicity, but can be used to see how the repository is being used. We have found this information can also be valuable for senior management to accurately keep up to date with progress of the development of the repository.

This information can be creatively used to reinforce the benefits of the repository with the users. Instead of passively disseminating this information to users who may stumble across the site, it may be worth developing systems to actively target depositing authors by directing them to the statistics. Even if resources are not available to develop automated e-mail systems it may be worth considering a more 'low-tech' approach. It would not take too much effort to identify the top authors and send them personalised e-mails telling them how often people are accessing their material. The rationale behind this is to show and impress how well used the online material is. By appealing to author vanity in this way we are hoping that the good word is spread further through contact with their peers. This approach assumes that the content is actually being downloaded and used in large enough quantities to be impressive!

Declaration of institutional support

The next step in the advocacy process is to intensify the awareness of the repository through institutional or national channels by seeking the support of senior management. Formal backing of this nature helps not only with spreading awareness, but also with allocation of resources to the repository project. With this kind of backing it becomes easier to appropriate funds, especially if the 'put the money where your mouth is' argument is used.

A common approach for institutions to take is to create a departmental or university-wide policy supporting self-archiving and the open access movement in general. Many institutions have forged ahead and taken the initiative to recommend that their staff deposit their research in a suitable repository. The wording of each policy varies considerably, however a typical policy is to strongly request the authors to deposit a copy of all published and refereed articles in the host institutional repository. This falls short of a full mandate which some consider would be difficult to implement in a single institution without the full backing of the wider academic community, including research councils and learned societies. The policies also have significant loopholes which could be used to extricate unwilling authors from depositing their research; for example, documents that contain material obtained under a clause of confidentiality or are intended for commercialisation (e.g. books), are often exempt from the policy.

At the time of writing only a few institutions worldwide have taken such a lead and implemented a broad self-archiving policy. Most of these institutions are European, with a handful of North American and Australian organisations. For a more up-to-date list the reader is referred to the eprints.org Registry of Institutional OA Self-Archiving Policies.

These local developments have been influenced, developed in conjunction with, and supported by the Berlin Declaration on Open Access to Knowledge in the Sciences and Humanities. This declaration, along with the Budapest Open Access Initiative and the Bethesda Statement on Open Access Publishing, has helped to form the central hub of the open movement. Together they have drawn together a cross-disciplinary community, worked to express a terminology and common language, and worked to define the aims and objectives of the open access movement, all while nurturing a growing international awareness of the periphery issues and central goals.

Even though the Three B's (Berlin, Bethseda and Budapest) are the most high-profile initiatives of this kind, other national initiatives exist. This is well illustrated by the Scottish Open Access Declaration and the Finnish Government's decision to support open access publishing.

In summary, the creation of an institutional, or even departmental, policy of self-archiving is a purposeful statement of intent and a useful step in the right direction towards our final destination. To achieve something worthwhile, however, it is an act which needs to be followed with a lot of hard work. It is very easy to relax the pressure after successfully lobbying for an institutional declaration of support; however, turning broad intent into action is something for which we must continually strive.

Mandatory submission

Closely related to an institutional declaration of support, but significantly different, is the question of mandatory submission of material to a digital repository. This is an important issue at the time of writing as a number of major national funding bodies have investigated, developed and have implemented or are considering a mandate to make research funded under the tenet of their sponsorship openly accessible and freely accessible to the general public. As this is a rapidly changing environment we are not going to delve into the details of specific research council policies, as any premature analysis will be based on speculation and conjecture however well-meaning it sets out to be. Conversely, it is extremely worthwhile to investigate and comment upon the underlying rationale behind such a mandate. The most persuasive argument for mandating deposition of publicly-funded research in repositories, aside from the highly laudable aims of opening up access, is that both the available published data and theoretical behavioural science studies suggest that it is the quickest and surest way to do so.

If we think back to how individual innovation decisions are actually made, these decisions may be optional, collective, or authority-based. In the majority of case studies it has been proven time and time again that the fastest rate of adoption stems from authority decisions (Rogers, 1995). Certainly these types of decision have the ability to provide the greatest widespread impact in the shortest amount of time. During the course of this chapter we have seen how the decision process during the adoption of institutional repositories by the academic community initially can be considered as a continuum; the process starting with optional decisions made by individuals, before moving through to collective decisions taken by academic units. If we are serious about rapidly achieving self-archiving as a normal working practice in the academic community, the next logical step is to consider making an authority-based decision and mandate the deposition of research outcomes in institutional repositories.

Before moving away from our theoretical framework we can see that from the handful of universities and institutions that have progressed to the decision and implementation stages in the innovation–design process, that there is something missing to bring the late majority and laggards into the self-archiving fold. Certainly awareness is an issue, and important studies in this area point to this being a key factor. The following quote from Swan and Brown's 2005 study into author self-archiving habits suitably illustrates this point:

> There is still a substantial proportion of authors unaware of the possibility of providing open access to their work by self-archiving. Of the authors who have not yet self-archived any articles, 71 per cent remain unaware of the option. (Swan and Brown, 2005)

We should, however, consider that the process of raising awareness by itself might not be enough. Open access advocates have been actively pursuing this strategy for over a decade, and although it has been pointed out that there has been steady growth throughout this time, there is no indication that continuation of this strategy will accelerate this process any further. Many of the most experienced open access advocates have indicated that another trigger factor is needed to expedite the growth of self-archiving, and that trigger factor is for their employers and/or funders to have a policy requiring it (Harnad et al., 2004). Further to this point, supporting studies have shown that the vast majority of authors indicated that they would self-archive willingly if their employer, or funding body required them to do so (Swan and Brown, 2004a,b).

Generally it is much easier to make an authority decision and mandate submission of material that is created within and owned wholly by the institution or its authors. This is in part due to the fact that the decisions are more easily delivered and implemented with fewer parties involved. Examples of types of material that may be suitable for such a mandate are student theses and dissertations (particularly doctoral and masters theses), teaching and learning objects created for classes, project outcomes and documentation.

We will briefly consider the case of electronic doctoral theses. One of the major sources of inspiration and technical/cultural help for setting up an electronic theses programme is the Networked Digital Library of Theses and Dissertations (NDLTD), an international organisation dedicated to promoting the adoption, creation, use, dissemination and preservation of electronic theses. At the annual International Symposium on Electronic Theses and Dissertations organised by the NDLTD, a recurring theme strongly advocated by all the successful institutions is the need to mandate the electronic submission of doctorate theses. This step seems to be critical in achieving success. For more information in all areas of electronic theses the interested reader is referred to the organisation's website.

Conclusion

We have presented in this chapter a theoretical framework for an advocacy campaign to follow. A case study of implementation of the advocacy strategy presented here is discussed further in Chapter 7. Although we have concentrated almost exclusively on recruiting peer-reviewed journal articles, the methodology should broadly be applicable for a wide range of content. On a first examination of the problem of content recruitment, it is apparent that this is a complex situation depending on a number of factors and it can be extremely daunting to know where to start. However, if the situation is broken down and analysed in smaller pieces then a coherent strategy can be formulated.

Individual-blame or system-blame?

It is fitting to end this chapter with a word of caution. All too often the inaction of individuals is blamed for the slow take-up of new ideas, and the institutional repository concept is no exception.

We can fall into the trap of blaming the late adopters for not being innovative because they are stubborn or resistant to change. If care is not taken then this can become a self-fulfilling prophecy as attention is lavished upon the more enthusiastic members because we are reluctant to waste time on less-fruitful avenues. This can lead to an entrenchment of position which is to the benefit of nobody. In the long term, any advocacy campaign must be inclusive and cater for the more reluctant academics among us.

The diffusion of new technology is always dependent upon a complex array of often interacting circumstances. It is useful to frame these circumstances into individual- or system-related causes. Individual-blame is defined as the tendency to hold an individual responsible for their problems, rather than the system of which the individual is part, whereas system-blame is the converse situation (Caplan and Nelson, 1973). Diffusion research scholars have often highlighted that there is often a degree of individual-blame bias in place from the start. For the case of institutional repositories there are a number of reasons why this should happen. As we are trapped in the inertia of the current scholarly communication system it may feel like it is impossible to change the system-blame factors. In contrast, the individual-blame variables may seem more immediately responsive; thus it is natural for us to target them more readily. Many minor factors underlying our particular problem may be individual in nature; for example, concerns in extra workload or plagiarism, and any solution will have to embrace these points. But, any solutions that are limited in nature to individual intervention will not be effective in addressing the larger social problems. We must move away from defining the self-archiving problem in terms of individual blame and address the wider social aspects of system-blame by following such paths as seeking institution support.

Note

1. The inspiration behind much of this chapter, in particular the theoretical framework for the advocacy model has come from Everett Rogers' seminal book *Diffusion of Innovations* (1962, 1995).

6

Intellectual property

Although many different stakeholders within the academic community, from individual researchers through to institutional administration, have vested interests in setting up institutional repositories, the main impetus and drive so far has been from the academic library community. There seems to be a number of reasons for this, primarily related to funding opportunities, advances in the field of digital librarianship and the close fit with the long-standing tradition and experience that libraries have with stewardship of scholarly materials. This casual observation of ownership, although not backed up with hard evidence, does have a number of important implications. Traditionally the role of the library within the academic institution has mainly been collection management and access of external material. The key word to note here is *external*, which in this context means any content that is brought in either through purchase, subscription or other mechanisms. New digital library systems are subtly changing this relationship, by providing the means to capture *locally* produced material; for example, teaching and learning objects, journal pre-prints and e-theses, and publishing them on the Web, either for free or with appropriate restrictions. Acting in this new role of publisher poses a number of potential problems, especially with regards to legal and moral obligations. The aim of this chapter is to thus discuss some of these complications, focusing on how to best protect the copyright of all parties involved (which is not always the author) and any third parties whose content is included in material deposited in an institutional repository. This is balanced against discussion of how to grant appropriate re-use rights and responsibilities for end users and institutions alike. It is not the intention to provide a detailed analysis and review of copyright law with respect to electronic information, as this is better done elsewhere (e.g. Oppenheim, 1999). In addition, the specific copyright legislation implemented in each country could make this of limited use to the international reader. We begin by steering the reader towards identifying and characterising risks, before suggesting some commonly adopted solutions. Specific legal solutions or wording are not described or given, however, examples of good practice are offered as a guide to adopt.

Stakeholders and their interests

When considering how to manage the various intellectual property rights and responsibilities that come with running a repository, the intuitive place to start is to examine the needs of each of the main stakeholder groups involved in the creation and dissemination of scholarly works created at the university. The main stakeholders in this area can be summarised as:

- author;
- institution;
- funder;
- publisher;
- user;
- library;
- general public;

Each of these groups has a number of key issues and criteria which need to be considered prior to and during repository implementation. Some key initiatives have previously summarised and documented the interests of these groups; these are presented in Table 6.1. The most influential group to be working in this area is the Zwolle group, a steering committee set up by a number of national funding bodies after an initial working conference on copyright ownership in higher education held in Zwolle, the Netherlands, in 2001. The Zwolle group's objectives have been to investigate and promote balanced approaches to the management of rights, and they have produced a number of important resources which are available online (Zwolle Group, 2001); including the Zwolle principles, stakeholder analysis (reproduced here) and revised publisher agreements.

Table 6.1 Stakeholder interests in the creation and dissemination of scholarly materials (adapted from Zwolle Group, 2001)

	Author	Institution	Funder	Publisher	User	Library	Public Interest
Instructional uses	Use of content in author's teaching	Use of content in course and curriculum planning			Use of content in teaching and course planning	Accessibility and delivery for teaching through reserves and other systems	
	Use in teaching at new institution	Use in teaching after author has left institution		Publication for instructional markets			
Research uses	Use of content in author's research		Use of content in further research		Use of content in own research		
Future reuse	Reuse of content in future publications and other projects	Extract and reuse staff contributions in similar works		Derivative products; licensing alternative media	'Re-engineer' of works for new needs		
	Exercise of fair use	Exercise of fair use			Exercise of fair use	Exercise of fair use	Exercise of fair use

Table 6.1 Stakeholder interests in the creation and dissemination of scholarly materials (adapted from Zwolle Group, 2001) (cont'd)

	Author	Institution	Funder	Publisher	User	Library	Public Interest
Intangible rewards	Academic freedom; moral rights		Acknowledgment on work				
	Recognition; academic rewards	Name on work; name off work; reputation		Journal title recognition			
	Right to choose to publish/not publish		Input into publication timing (e.g. patent issues)				
Financial issues		Recover expenses		Recover expenses			
	Share of any revenue			Optimise revenue			
		Optimise class enrolments and revenues based on the materials			Affordable acquisition and uses	Affordable acquisition and uses	

Table 6.1 Stakeholder interests in the creation and dissemination of scholarly materials (adapted from Zwolle Group, 2001) (cont'd)

	Author	Institution	Funder	Publisher	User	Library	Public Interest
	Liability/indemnity exposure	Liability/indemnity exposure		Liability/indemnity exposure (e.g. in sublicences)		Protection against liability/indemnity exposure	
Access issues	Sharing with peers	Wide dissemination	Maximising readership	Maximising readership	Easy access from any location	Interlibrary loan	Maximum access
	Long-term preservation and accessibility	Long-term preservation and accessibility	Long-term preservation and accessibility	Continuous database development; long-term preservation	Long-term preservation and accessibility	Storage, preservation, archiving; migration to new media	Long-term preservation and accessibility
						Access standards (international)	
Quality issues	Peer review; editorial contributions	Peer review		Editorial and other added value	Quality control or evaluation	Quality control	
	Integrity of work	Integrity of work	Integrity of work	Integrity of work	Integrity of work	Integrity of work	Integrity of work
Administrative issues	Effective rights management					Effective rights management	

From interests to issues

The importance of this exercise is summed up in a direct quote:

> ...This effort to identify stakeholders and their interests is a crucial step toward the development of policies or agreements that seek to assure to the stakeholders the ability to use and manage the works in fulfilment of their most important interests. (Zwolle Group, 2001)

Table 6.1 lists the broad range of interests for each group, and as such is a good starting point. However, we need to focus on specific points for it to be of use. In any legal sense, the main stakeholders we need to consider are the authors/end users of scholarly material and the library or institution, if appropriate, in the role as repository managers. Secondary consideration is needed to protect publishers' rights. Following this, we can expand some of the generic points from the table into more specific areas, as detailed below.

Access issues

- Securing the rights for the storage of digital media. In particular we need to allow for long-term preservation, which might require specific acts such as future migration to new media.
- Develop appropriate access and workflows to protect sensitive materials; for example, embargoed doctorate theses.
- Ensure compliance with local regulations which may have implications for access to content; for example, freedom of information (FOI) legislation.

Reuse issues

- Develop and implement appropriate reuse rights for repository content.
- Investigation of digital rights management for sensitive materials.
- Exercise of fair use.

Quality issues/intangible rewards

- Protection of the archived works integrity through risk mitigation and other mechanisms.
- Ensure the recognition of author and moral rights to the works.

Financial issues

- Develop robust protection against liability/indemnity exposure.
- Work with publishers to ensure all copyright holders' rights are respected.

Institution as publisher

In addition to the issues raised from the analysis of stakeholder interests, we have previously noted that librarianship is entering new territory with the adoption of repository management. The lack of previous experience in acting in this new role of publisher of locally produced material opens up the host institution to a whole array of risks and issues, some of which they will not be prepared for. In particular, we should be aware of:

- the need to secure distribution rights to publish material online;
- the risk of copyright infringement; either accidental or otherwise, for example, inclusion of third-party content or direct plagiarism;
- infringement of other intellectual property rights, for example, database right;
- the risk of defamation; either inadvertently or otherwise;
- liability for provision of inaccurate information;
- contravention of particular local laws;
- compliance with data protection regulations;
- accidental/premature disclosure of confidential info, findings.

It is worth expanding on some of these points in a little more detail. Through copyright, the author of an intellectual creation gains rights which enable them to control the use of their work. Primarily, authors hold the exclusive right to control how their work is used. Copyright will be infringed by anyone who reproduces, adapts or distributes the work without the prior consent of the author. Primarily this has a number of important practical implications for repository managers. First, we need to secure the right to deposit material into the repository from the copyright holder. When dealing with published material, the situation rapidly gets complicated, as the primary author in most cases has signed over some of their rights to the publisher in order to get their work accepted, for example, in academic journals or textbooks. As authors of scholarly material have become more copyright savvy, a recent trend is for publishers to offer exclusive distribution clauses in place of the copyright transfer agreement. This essentially has the same end-effect to tightly control distribution of the work. A number of exceptions are permitted by law under the 'fair dealing' defence ('fair use' in the USA). Although there is no precise definition of 'fair dealing' and interpretation is ultimately decided by the courts, it essentially allows limited copying without permission provided it is fair and the commercial interests of the rights holder are not damaged. Publishing whole works online in repositories is definitely not protected under this defence.

Even if permission from the copyright holder is granted to place material online there is a secondary risk of infringement, whether it is malicious in nature or unintended. The often cited fear of plagiarism is actually more of a red herring. Although freely accessible material online is more likely to be read and used, there is the presumption that it will be easier to reuse content, in whole or in part, and pass it off as original work without the usual academic citing conventions. Even though such use is yet to be fully analysed, when best practices (discussed later in this chapter) are followed in conjunction with plagiarism detection software, these risks should be at worst manageable – but in reality they are much more likely to be negligible. A more relevant risk to repository managers is that of inadvertent dissemination of copyright material held by a third party. Often scholarly works, for example, doctorate theses, are composite pieces of research that comprise many strands, usually building upon and quoting previous research, or including diagrams, pictures or music produced by other creators. It is conceivable that a large work of this type may be submitted to a repository with the full permission of the primary copyright holder, but without the full clearance of content held within.

When publishing and widely distributing content, there is always an ambient risk of defamation. How the application of libel law transfers to the online environment has been keenly observed by the legal community. In summary, the owners and/or operators of networked computers can be deemed liable for defamatory material which they write and publish on the network, or receive from third parties and cause to be published on the network. Thus, by extrapolation the host institution would be held liable for defamatory material submitted to a repository. It may be useful to consider this statement a little more closely. One of the most important issues is whether the institutional repository would be considered in court as a:

- common carrier (absolute immunity);
- distributor (not subject to liability unless they have specific knowledge); or
- publisher (liable for what they choose to publish).

Common carriers, including telecommunications, are seen as a conduit that passively allow for the transmission of data and, therefore, are not responsible for the nature, or character of that data. However, the situation for carriers has become more complicated if we inspect the case of Internet service providers (ISPs). The original stance has been that the position of an ISP equated with that of the traditional telecommunications carrier, but recent advances in the law on defamation on the Internet show an increasing trend towards imposing greater liability on ISPs (Hayes, 2003).

Distributors, such as booksellers, news vendors and libraries, generally have no liability for libel unless they are found to be negligent and have reasonably known of the defamatory nature of the work. Publishers, such as newspapers, magazines and broadcasters, are responsible and liable for everything that they produce, post and broadcast. Their liability is grounded in the fact that they can edit what they wish to include and exclude from their publication, and with this editorial control comes increased liability. Whether repositories are considered distributors or publishers will critically depend on this amount of editorial control. Either way repository managers should consider the implications carefully and develop robust policies to counteract this risk (discussed later in this chapter).

In addition to regulatory concerns, we should be aware of more practical concerns. Easy access to full-text content can lead to the situation where widespread accidental, or premature disclosure of confidential or sensitive material can occur. Depositors can remain naive about the full extent of disclosure they are making by placing works online in repositories. For some content, like pre-prints and electronic theses and dissertations, it may not be advisable to reveal too much practical and intellectual detail at a pre-publication stage. It makes the most practical sense if the final decision is made by the author, who must be made aware of the issues involved. Mistakes are, however, made and it may be necessary to periodically withdraw items.

Risk mitigation

With the main legal risks and issues identified, it is now worth investigating some current best practices, workflows, policies and procedures being used to protect and indemnify repositories and the authors. As ever, please remember that the information provided in this book is for guidance and should not be considered as legal advice.

Licences

Ownership rights issues arise both with incoming content, known as upstream rights, and also with outgoing content at the other end, known as downstream rights. Licences are an excellent way to manage this process legally, by providing a framework to systematically allocate and identify rights. Such agreements should ideally be comprehensively gathered at source from the original owner so rights can effectively be passed down the management chain through the institution to the end user with minimal effort. In all cases an agreement from the depositor, henceforth called a *deposit licence*, is required to cover the special requirements necessary to store, organise and manage repository content. At the time of deposition it is useful to gather the terms and conditions of use that are acceptable to the creator in a separate reuse licence. This makes subsequent rights management much more straightforward and helps to manage expectations. A comprehensive deposit and end-users licence agreement should cover a number of core topics, including a depositor's declaration, the repository's rights and responsibilities and the re-use terms and conditions. The following sections discuss the individual elements required for each of these agreements before a suitable licence is constructed.

Access and distribution rights

The depositing author needs to grant to the host repository a number of permissions and conditions with respect to online access to their work. Many of the current deposit licences in use ask the author to grant the repository the non-exclusive right to carry out these additional acts and distribute copies of their work via the Internet. A non-exclusive licence does not compromise the author's rights like an exclusive licence or transfer of copyright would. This is normally implemented in conjunction with a declaration from the depositor. The main function of this depositor's declaration is to ensure that the depositor is the copyright owner, or if by proxy, has the permission of author/copyright holder to deposit. Equally important is to determine whether the author has sought and gained permission to include any subsidiary material owned by third-party copyright holders.

A number of licences also make it clear from the start that any work deposited will be available to a wide variety of people and institutions. As not all readers of scholarly information are human, the author also needs to be aware that readers may include automated agents, for example, web indexing robots, or automated text processing and data mining methods.

Digital preservation

Even though individual requirements may differ between institutions, the majority of working institutional repositories insert clauses into the deposit licence to allow for future acts of digital preservation to be carried out. Without focusing too deeply on the specific issues involved a number of recommendations have been made. In a report jointly commissioned in the UK by Resource, the Arts and Humanities Data Service (AHDS) and the Joint Information Systems Committee (JISC), it is advised that any deposit licence for digital materials must consider the following clauses to allow for future digital preservation efforts (Jones and Beagrie, 2001):

- permissions needed for copying for the purposes of preservation;
- permissions needed for future migration of content to new formats for the purposes of preservation;
- permissions needed for emulation for the purposes of preservation.

Metadata and item removal

The next significant part of the deposit licence is to determine the access, distribution, removal and ownership rights to any catalogue or metadata records associated with the item. Metadata is structured information that describes, explains, locates, or otherwise makes it easier to retrieve, use or manage an information resource (NISO Press, 2004). For some items the repository may need the right to incorporate metadata into public access catalogues and to determine protocols for the removal of such records from the catalogues should the need arise. Similarly a clause defining the circumstances for item withdrawal would be beneficial to prevent future liability of hosting unwanted material, for example, defamatory or accidentally disclosed confidential material.

Among the working institutional repositories it is common practice to routinely enhance simple bibliographic records to provide higher quality metadata to enable the improved search and retrieval of documents to occur. Examples of metadata enhancement could include the assignment of Library of Congress subject headings, or the application of rights management information in the metadata. Such enhancements usually require the dedicated time of a specialised metadata editor and are often labour-intensive activities. The host repository may, or may not, wish to claim copyright in any additional data created during the submission and subsequent archiving of the work.

Liability

It is also desirable for the host institution of a repository to protect itself legally in case of any future dispute as to the repository content. The deposit licence should clearly indicate that the repository is not responsible for any mistakes, omissions or infringements in the deposited work. Furthermore, in the event of a breach of intellectual property rights, or other laws including defamation, the repository should indicate that it is not under any obligation to take legal action on behalf of the original author, or other rights holders, or to accept liability for any legal action arising from any such breaches.

Reuse licence

A reuse, or end-user licence, agreement is important to clearly define the rights of end users to downloaded material, for example, reproduction and access, and to remind end users of any restrictions placed on the item. The deposition of work within an institutional repository does imply that an author wants to grant generous use rights to the reader; however, it does not mean that the author wants to give away all of their rights to the work. As a minimum, authors will want to retain their moral rights of attribution and to object to derogatory treatment. Where appropriate, other authors may find it appealing to reserve the right to approve commercial reuse of the work. These interests can be communicated though the adoption of an appropriate licence, such as an attribution/non-commercial/share-alike creative commons licence. This is more effective when used in conjunction with the prominent display of notices alerting users to the terms and conditions of use (discussed later in this chapter).

Confidentiality and freedom of information

In exceptional circumstances, it may be necessary for authors to restrict access to the online copy of their work, for a limited period or indefinitely. Restrictions are commonly considered when the work is concerned with topics that are politically, commercially or industrially sensitive.

Not all repository content will be affected by this issue; however, for the small subset that is affected it may have important legal and regulatory implications. The doctoral thesis is an example of a type of literature that may be treated as confidential in its lifetime. A recent discussion paper by the UK Council for Graduate Education (Powell and Green, 2005) gives an accurate analysis of the state of play for confidentiality of PhD theses in the UK. The report observed that there is an almost universal policy to have regulations in place to permit confidentiality of the PhD thesis after the examination process is complete. However, it is notable that very few candidates actually apply for a restriction. For the year 2003/2004 only 118 applications were reported by 37 of the 64 institutions involved in the report (Powell and Green, 2005). It is worth noting that the institutional adoption of electronic theses and dissertations may substantially increase general thesis reference and use, thus it is likely the incidences of restrictions will increase, partly to protect sensitive data sets from the public domain while the author formally publishes their work, either in a journal article or monograph.

We have identified that complications arise with FOI legislation when an author wants to restrict access their work, even if the restriction is just a short-term one. The Freedom of Information Act 2000 in the UK, and other similar international FOI legislation, gives a right of access to any information held by an institution, unless an exemption applies, regardless of who owns the intellectual property rights in that information. This means that anyone has the right to see the information held in any format in any part of the university, unless refusing access can be justified in terms of an FOI exemption. It is not sufficient for the author to indicate that they want to restrict an item; they must also explain the reason for that restriction in terms of an FOI exemption.

Regarding scholarly materials, a number of possible exemptions may apply under the legislation including where: (a) the material is due for publication, or the author is actively seeking to publish this material; (b) the release of the material would prejudice substantially the commercial interests of any person, or (c) the material includes information that was obtained under a promise of confidentiality.

Of course the exact terms of the FOI legislation will depend on the jurisdiction of the country in which the repository is based, thus the reader is advised to check their own circumstances carefully. If a request is received for restricted material it will be necessary for the institution to have appropriate supporting information to enable it to decide whether or not the request can be lawfully refused. If the restricted material does not have the appropriate information then the host repository is likely to be obliged to release the information to the requester. Any deposit licence which offers an option to restrict material should indicate that supporting exemption wording is required from any depositor who expects the repository to withhold the material when a request to release it is received.

Website best practices

Aside from creating and implementing a comprehensive deposit licence system, a number of ancillary steps can and should be taken with regard to online access. The approach to adopt is one of maximum visibility so that readers can be informed clearly of the terms and conditions of use placed upon the work by authors or other stakeholders. Because the responsibility to observe and follow the use/reuse criteria rests with the users, and not with the repository itself, these notices should be of a simple design, which can be easily understood and preferably requiring some degree of interaction with the reader, for example, tick boxes or a click-through licence.

It is important to make sure everybody is clear about what steps have been taken to ensure rights are protected, what steps will be taken in the event of a breach of rights, and the general terms and conditions of use of the works. The prominent display of this information can be achieved through several approaches, used singly or in combination:

- upfront display;
- on download; or
- cover sheet.

The upfront display of legal information is excellent for static web pages where access to content is predominantly through the front main page. An exemplary example of this approach implemented is the Archaeology Data Service catalogue (Figure 6.1). Before access to the service is allowed the reader is referred to the terms and conditions of use which are prominently displayed. The reader is then invited to use the service only if they accept the conditions of use by clicking on a clearly defined button which takes them to the main catalogue. If they decline to accept the conditions they are taken back to the home page of the host service.

Figure 6.1   Screenshot of the entry page to the Archaeology Data Service catalogue (*http://ads.ahds.ac.uk/catalogue/*)

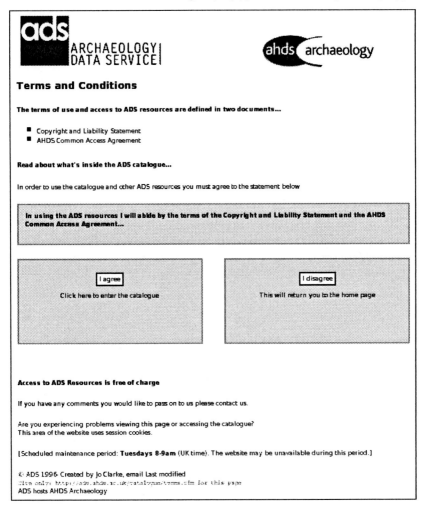

The terms and conditions of use are comprehensive and contained within two separate documents accessed from the front page, probably to keep the design clean and simple for users to navigate. The copyright and liability statement and the common access agreement approach aims to cover all the issues raised previously, plus a few more specific to that service.

This upfront display of terms and conditions is not always suitable, particularly when access to repositories is unpredictable. Often the point of entry for repositories is direct to the article and not via the front page. This can occur from automatic indexing of the repository by search engine services, which allows the contents of the repository to be visible and accessible from external services. Additionally it is common for repositories to give individual items a persistent identifier which users can cite to gain permanent direct access.

Bypassing the front pages of repositories can mean the item is not seen in the context in which it which it was originally intended. Often any copyright/liability statements or access agreements are not seen by the reader. In this scenario it may be desirable for the repository to force the reader to view this supporting information through confrontation. Some approaches present the reader with a click-through acceptance prior to download; another includes a cover sheet on the item. The advantage of the latter approach is that the presence of supporting information is permanent.

The final best practice we would recommend is to develop a take-down policy. Repository administrators should safeguard against liability claims for defamatory or other disputed material by clearly indicating on the repository website that reasonable care has been taken to prevent such occurrences and that any work will be removed if it is found to violate any copyright or other rights of any person. The right to do this should be indicated in any deposit licences. The favoured model to deter instances of Internet-based infringement of intellectual property rights, in both Europe and North America, appears to be 'notice and take down' procedures. To back up this, all repositories should have clear guidelines in place to fast-track the removal of illegal, infringing or defamatory content from the service.

Retaining rights

We have noted that the major difficulties with clearing permissions arise when dealing with materials that are not owned by the submitting author. Generally speaking, where possible we would advocate that authors should retain as much of their rights as possible. To illustrate this point we will briefly focus on a particular case study of academic publishing.

Copyright ownership initially rests with the author

Traditionally there has been a lack of clarity regarding the question of ownership of scholarly materials produced by universities. Although the situation will be slightly different between countries, the legislation is generally clear that where an employee creates a work in the course of employment, then subject to contrary agreements, ownership belongs to the employing institution. Historically the custom and practice that universities have adopted is not to assert copyright ownership over scholarly materials, but rather to grant favourable conditions to its authors under the sobriquet of 'academic freedom'.

Copyright transfer to publisher

We find that all exploitation rights to the work are then fully given away by authors as part of the copyright transfer agreements routinely signed to publish in academic journals. A number of studies have focused on this activity, particularly investigating specific areas, e.g. the impact of copyright ownership on academic author self-archiving (Gadd et al., 2003b), implications for open access literature (Hoorn and van der Graaf, 2005) or authors' expectations of how they want to use/reuse academic literature (Gadd et al., 2003c).

Severe restriction of use

By assigning copyright for the right to publish in the journal of choice, the author/institution will find that important reuse rights are severely restricted, including:

- reproduction of parts of the work for commercial purposes, for example, inclusion in textbooks, or e-learning programmes;
- republication or redistribution of the entire article, for example, self-archiving in an institutional repository, or photocopying/scanning article for inclusion in a course reserve list.

The impact of transferring copyright in journal articles and the subsequent loss of rights is manifold, and has serious resourcing and financial implications for institutions. Each year, higher education institutes in the UK alone spend a significant budget on copyright permissions for journal articles, either through blanket agreements with organisations such as the Copyright Licensing Agency, or on one-off permission agreements with individual publishers. Although accurate data are not readily available, a conservative estimate would place this figure easily into the realm of seven figures. One of the oft-quoted reasons for assigning copyright to publishers is that they are best suited to look after the subsequent copyright management. However, author studies show the exact opposite is wanted. In an international survey commissioned by the UK's JISC and the Netherlands' SURF funding organisations, only a minority of authors (10 per cent) thought that the publisher should handle permission requests to reuse the article (Hoorn and van der Graaf, 2005). In summary, allowing publishers to manage the copyright certainly does make things a lot easier for individuals, i.e. they have to do nothing. However, it does not make it any easier for institutions when they want to reuse whole works for teaching, learning and other endeavours. Additionally the costs of doing so can be prohibitive and are generally not passed onto the original creators.

Retaining rights

The logical conclusion to solve the majority of these reuse problems is not to create the bottleneck restriction in the first place. By granting appropriate rights at the time of creation then all parties can benefit. The traditional copyright transfer agreements do not currently allow the range of activities that all parties wish to engage in. A number of initiatives have investigated what constituent elements a mutually beneficial agreement should have. As it is not the purpose to re-establish these points in detail the reader is referred back to the original studies (see Clark, 2005; or Friend, 2003)

We would recommend that an appropriate agreement should offer the follow stakeholders the following points:

- *Publishers*: retain the exclusive right to distribute the final 'as-published' version. This would be the definitive typeset PDF version available from the journal website.

- *Institutions*: retain the right to incorporate part or whole works into teaching and learning objects, or to distribute works in whole or in part for the purposes of teaching, for example, course reserve lists.

- *Authors*: retain the right to mount the final peer-reviewed article, not necessarily the 'as-published' version, in an institutional/subject repository, or departmental intranet.

Conclusion

In summary, we have presented a succinct appraisal of the various intellectual property issues that arise with the distribution of academic literature through digital media. As these issues have arisen, the early adopters of institutional repositories and other electronic scholarly fora have had to be adaptable and implement practical strategies; some of the most successful have been discussed here.

It is recommended that a robust and practical licensing scheme, as discussed here and in Chapter 4, is implemented as soon as possible. Deposit and end-user agreements perform an essential role in determining the respective rights and responsibilities that users and institutions hosting digital repositories need through creating a formal legal framework by which each party can abide. Other risk mitigation and intellectual property management steps to be considered should include website best practices, such as the prominent display of copyright notices, or click-through licences. Finally, we recommend that authors should review the academic norm of copyright transfer agreements for journal publication and aim for the retention of some rights to create a mutually beneficial environment for all concerned with the production, dissemination and use of academic literature.

7

Case study: The Edinburgh Research Archive

Introduction[1]

Theses alive: a project history

Until relatively recently, there has been minimal interest from the UK in e-theses, and a very select few institutions have been developing these capacities. To encourage the disclosure and sharing of content, the Joint Information Systems Committee (JISC) initiated the Focus on Access to Institutional Resources (FAIR) programme in late 2002. The purpose of this programme was to investigate the sharing of digital institutional assets, including e-theses, and to gather intelligence about and increase understanding of the technical, organisational and cultural challenges of these processes. Under this programme Edinburgh University Library (EUL) obtained funding for the Theses Alive project which began to work on a prototype for a national e-theses promotion and management concept at the end of 2002. This project worked alongside related projects Data-providers for Academic E-content and the Disclosure of Assets for Learning, Understanding and Scholarship (DAEDALUS), based at Glasgow University Library, and Electronic Theses, based at the Robert Gordon University Library. At the same time EUL was involved in the SHERPA project led by the University of Nottingham, which was primarily concerned with the creation, population and management of several e-print repositories in partner institutions in the UK. The synergy between these related projects has helped to reinforce and support each other through collaboration and shared experience, ultimately aiding the development of the Edinburgh Research Archive (ERA).

The drive for the proposal of the Theses Alive project came from the original e-theses investigations carried out at the Science and Engineering

Library, Learning and Information Centre (SELLIC) at the University of Edinburgh. The SELLIC team presented a report to the UK Theses Online Group (UTOG) in late 2001 on the results of a doctoral theses digitisation project. The report concluded that universities were moving into a digitally networked environment which had the potential to transform the current system for providing access to theses by making them open access online.

Under the Theses Alive remit to investigate the technological and cultural issues involved for UK higher education institutions wishing to attain e-theses capability, the following general objectives were proposed:

- to develop a digital theses submission system for use by interested universities;

- to develop a standards compliant digital infrastructure to enable e-theses to be published online (with a subobjective that 500 e-theses exist within the UK segment of the Networked Digital Library of Theses and Dissertations (NDLTD) within two years);

- to develop and support a metadata schema for the UK higher education e-theses environment;

- to test the value of a national support service for e-theses creation and management in the UK;

- to produce a 'checklist approach' institutional guide to adopting and managing e-theses;

- to work with other e-theses developments internationally, and in particular to assist the research aims of other JISC FAIR programme projects.

Throughout the course of the project a wealth of activities whose significance had not initially been fully realised were addressed. These included areas such as:

- advocacy; not only of the service, but of the concept of open access;

- licensing, copyright and other intellectual property issues;

- open source software development, maintenance and dissemination;

- post-production service administration and continued technical support.

In order to achieve these results a core team of three staff at EUL was formed, consisting of a project director, a project officer and an information systems developer. The project investigated two main strands: technical development and advocacy/liaison. Each of these was primarily investigated by the information systems developer and the project officer respectively, under management from the project director. Each strand was, however, closely related to the other, making feedback essential to shape the development of the work packages in each strand.

Preliminary decision making

Beyond the project proposal's suggestions and recommendations there were some minor additional decisions to be made before work could start in earnest, concerning the software development process. The first was to take the route of open source software (OSS) to provide the basis for the resulting e-theses management system. This decision was influenced by two main points:

1. It is desirable, when following the ethos of open access, to endorse OSS, as both have highly related objectives.
2. The JISC recommend the use of OSS wherever possible in funded projects.

There are also general advantages in using OSS, including zero cost of acquisition, the ability to use and adapt to meet local requirements and the freedom to distribute modifications.

The subsequent decision from here was which packages to adopt for evaluation for the repository. As the appendices demonstrate, there are now many packages which may provide the functionality, and it was not feasible (or possible at the time) to evaluate all options. We therefore chose between two likely packages, knowing that the DAEDALUS project was evaluating two packages, with one package being common between projects. This would provide us with the opportunity to compare three packages before making a final decision.

Development

This section discusses the many issues encountered during the development process of a combined e-theses and e-print repository which ultimately became ERA. Much of what is described in the following subsections happened concurrently across the project, and there is a great deal of interaction between each of these areas.

Software evaluation and development

Initially the project carried out a broad review of current open source digital repository packages available, and an in-depth evaluation of two packages. It was felt that a formal evaluation of the most commonly used platforms would provide the most robust approach and eventually yield the most comprehensive and meaningful results. These results could then feed back into the design process for developing a system suitable for use in the UK context.

The comparison, carried out as per the evaluation guidelines outlined in Chapter 3, looked at some of the common elements between the packages and drew conclusions on which was best in each field. In addition, it looked at how difficult it would be to modify each of the packages to provide an e-theses service for the UK. This analysis was considered alongside the medium-term future of each of the packages as they are developed as well as the scope for expansion that each package had within the library and the university as a whole.

A direct comparison of the software was difficult because of the differing focal points of their functionality and design philosophies. The main part of the study considered elements particularly relevant to e-theses as well as essential requirements such as security and administration. For example, in the area of metadata collection we were particularly interested whether the data collected was sufficient and relevant, or more importantly extensible or flexible in any way. We compared the metadata handling features of the system particularly in light of the complications we were expecting to encounter during schema development. We also looked at the support for the OAI-PMH protocol, via which exposure of data was an essential requirement and part of the initial project proposal. Holding material in a digital repository confers on the host institution some responsibility with regard to long-term care, thus another factor to consider was the preservation focus of the package and the stability of its storage layer.

With the e-theses functionality evaluated, we then gave consideration to more general features of the software, such as its ease of customisation, the configuration options available to the system administrators, and the general design methodology employed. In addition we were interested in the community surrounding the software, as this can often be an indicator of the likely longevity of the package, especially in an open source arena.

We arrived at a situation where one package had the features we wanted in some form, but was not at a stage of development where we would be happy deploying a service on it, while the other was a solid package with much of the groundwork for e-theses in place, but no specific functionality. Therefore we could ask the question defined in Chapter 3 in two ways:

1. How hard would it be to add the required functionality to Package A to make it support e-theses for the UK?
2. How hard would it be to add the additional support features to Package B to make it acceptable for institutional usage?

After considering the feedback from the DAEDALUS project regarding the third package and after several months of testing and evaluation we decided to build ERA using the DSpace software (see Appendix C for more details). The reasons for this were, at the time, as follows:

- metadata capture and storage techniques were relatively flexible;
- support for OAI-PMH was at the most recent version;
- the storage system was geared towards digital preservation, although at the time there were still no clear procedures;
- the underlying application design and implementation was of a reasonably high quality, supporting good internal authentication and authorisation procedures;
- the administrative interface was relatively mature, and provided many features;
- the community surrounding it was already strong and showing signs of growth which gave us confidence in its future;
- feedback from Glasgow suggested there was no specific way in which DSpace and their other evaluated package could be defined as better than the other.

Nonetheless, it lacked some of the functionality we were interested in and immediate support for the metadata schema which we were in the process of developing. Therefore, taking more from the evaluation than we first anticipated, we used our other package to help us define the work that we needed to undertake. The feature list that we then defined was:

- support for multiple metadata capture processes (submission procedures);
- enable capture of UK e-theses metadata;

- allow for rapid identification of content types within the repository;
- apply multi-part licences to the e-thesis;
- apply 'physical' restrictions to e-theses where necessary;
- a collaborative workspace where supervisors and students could observe and work on a submission;
- an annotation tool, to allow supervisors to leave comments for students.

The next challenge we faced was the best way to implement these changes to DSpace, which required developing or adopting a methodology for third-party software developments. We chose to write and maintain our own 'add-on' to the system, which would require installation onto an existing repository. We chose this method over writing our changes directly into a local copy of the source code or committing our changes to the central source code repository for a number of reasons (Jones and Andrew, 2005):

- our developments were not necessarily of interest to the whole repository community;
- the development model for DSpace at the time was not easily compatible with simply writing our changes back to the main code-base;
- our developments were UK focused, and we did not anticipate them moving at the same speed or in the same direction as the main DSpace development process.

For these reasons we created our own online source code repository, and were free to choose our own development model. Naturally it was necessary for us to always work from the most recent ('bleeding-edge') version of the DSpace source, and we employed a lightweight and iterative development cycle, which is easily to implement for a small product within a small development environment. We broke up the software into components as defined by the requirements stated above, and began by developing what we considered to be the most useful functionality first, taking into account the current state of developments outside the software process, such as the metadata schema.

The result of this development work was named the Tapir (Theses Alive Plugin for Institutional Repositories), and was free to download as a self-contained add-on to the core DSpace code. Subsequent download and use of this software by institutions all over the globe resulted in quality feedback which in turn was fed back into the iterative development cycle for further advancement of the software.

At the end of the project, Tapir offered many of the features originally specified (although some fell by the wayside due to other developments in the area or lack of interest in the functionality). Some of the features were found to have uses outside of the e-theses sphere of interest, and a subset of features have also now found their way back into the main source distribution of DSpace.

Metadata schema development

A primary aim of the project was to work with other e-theses developments both internationally and with the research teams of other e-theses projects in the UK. As part of this objective we participated in the creation of a recommended UK e-theses core metadata set. Led by the Robert Gordon University, working with representatives from the University of Edinburgh, the University of Glasgow and the British Library, this set was created in preliminary form and sent out to interested parties for comment. Feedback from this consultation then resulted in further refinements to the metadata set, which is now maintained by the Robert Gordon University (see Copeland et al., 2005).

As a guiding principle, we felt it was necessary to ensure that we coordinated activities with other initiatives and projects to produce meaningful outputs and results. Where international standards were already available and in common use (e.g. the OAI-PMH) we would try to adopt and support the concepts and implementations of these protocols. We examined potential metadata sets that may be able to support e-theses: the default DSpace Dublin Core registry configuration; the Electronic Theses Dissertations Metadata Schema (ETD-MS) from Virginia Tech and the NDLTD, and the Theses and Dissertations Markup Document Type Definition (TDM DTD). With the aim to 'genericise' metadata creation processes for UK e-theses we drew on the recommendations by these various schemas to produce the final set.

The recommended UK e-theses metadata set, therefore, supports the elements that are common to all UK theses, with suggested additional options for classification of holdings using various common classification schemes. As an advantage, it is easily represented in an *element.qualifier* style in which qualified Dublin Core can be expressed, and by obeying pure Dublin Core basic element definitions can be reduced from its full form to that which can be natively transported via OAI-PMH without major data loss.

As DSpace effectively supports any metadata in the *element.qualifier* form, and will compress this data into the standard Dublin Core elements for exposure via OAI-PMH, it was relatively straightforward to implement this schema as part of the Tapir software. Using the submission software the students insert their own metadata, which is subsequently quality-controlled by the library, and thus automatically compliant with the requirements defined at this stage of the project.

Simultaneously the University of Nottingham provided us with the core metadata set that the SHERPA project intended to work with across the institutional repositories with which it was involved. This could also be represented in an *element.qualifier* style, so it was straightforward to see that we would be able to support both metadata sets within DSpace and were able to provide a dual submission interface to deal with each set.

Policy and procedure development

Alongside the technology strand of the project, there were also many administrative and managerial policies and procedures to investigate, define and develop. The software for the research archive would allow for the collection of e-theses metadata and e-print metadata and the additional tools required to manage them. It was, therefore, also simultaneously necessary to investigate how the repository would be looked after and fit into day-to-day working of the institution so that feedback could be passed to the technical strand.

The first form of this feedback was to suggest that in addition to creating an e-thesis archive under the guidance of the Theses Alive project, it would be advantageous to support within the same environment e-prints, and potentially other types of research materials. We found that there was a strong endorsement from academic staff and students alike to support the inclusion of e-theses in an institutional repository with other research outputs. With a firm decision made to house the content together it was then possible to look at the implications for the service and how it would be managed. It was at this stage that a firm advocacy strategy was developed and put into action. More details of the planning, form and implementation of the advocacy campaign are discussed in Chapter 5.

As previously mentioned in Chapter 5 we felt it would be beneficial to perform a baseline survey of research material already held on departmental and personal web pages in the University of Edinburgh domain. A systematic approach was taken, whereby each departmental and staff web page was visited and the content of self-archived material was noted. The survey looked at each college in turn, searching for content at each level of the hierarchy, down through the school and to individual levels. During the period of this survey over 2,500 staff web pages were visited.

Initially the survey began with documenting formal research material (post-prints, pre-prints and e-theses) within the science and engineering domain, but when other colleges within the institution were examined it became apparent that the type of material available online varied considerably between subjects. To represent these different research cultures other content such as book chapters, conference and working papers was also considered when compiling the data.

Considering the wide-ranging self-archiving trends between academic colleges, and even within schools, there appeared to be a direct correlation between willingness to post-material online and the existence of subject-based repositories. In the small variations from this rule we would argue that some subject repositories (such as the Los Alamos ArXiv for high-energy physics) have become so successful at capturing and making persistently available a very high proportion of the output in their domains that academics trust it as their 'natural' repository for self-archived material. So it appears that where there is a pre-existing culture of self-archiving e-prints in subject repositories, scholars are more likely to post research material on their own web pages until such time as the subject repositories become trusted for their comprehensiveness and persistence. As personal web pages tend to be ephemeral, the long-term preservation of the research material held on them is extremely doubtful. We were, therefore, proposing to provide a more stable platform for effective collaboration, dissemination and preservation of research.

This scoping study (for more details see Andrew, 2003) proved to be extremely valuable and provided evidence that there was already a substantial corpus of research material available from personal and departmental web pages in the Edinburgh domain. It was extremely encouraging to see that such an unexpectedly high volume of research material (over 1,000 peer-reviewed journal articles) were available in this manner. Originally we planned to contact the pre-existing self-archiving authors to gather initial content for the repository (as described in Chapter 5). Unfortunately a high proportion of the material was published on the Internet with no consideration to intellectual property rights. In practice this meant that we, as responsible repository owners, were not in a position to take all of this content.

It was also identified fairly early on that academics were interested in maintaining at least some distance between e-theses and research papers, suggesting that in some situations the former were 'research training' and not necessarily up to research standard. This then fed back into our repository design by introducing a requirement that all content types are rapidly identifiable.

We also successfully defined the requirements of the relationship between thesis authors and supervisors. The requirement was to allow supervisors to observe the work of students, to make changes, suggestions or comments prior to submission of the thesis. By proposing a collaborative workspace wherein items in the process of being authored could appear in both the supervisors' and student's private areas, we were able to define how an e-thesis repository and an e-print repository could be natural partners. As a unified workspace could contain both the supervisors' students work and also their own academic works, we could reduce the number of systems necessary for authors to use, lowering barriers to adoption. Allowing annotation of items in this workspace would also enable us to support online, recorded communication between students and supervisors, and increase the likelihood that academics may also wish to use the system for peer-to-peer collaboration.

One aspect of the survey demonstrated the lack of consistency in dealing with copyright in intellectual property issues. Some academics responded to these uncertainties by not self-archiving any material at all; others used general disclaimers which may or may not be effective; a minority posted material online which is arguably in breach of copyright agreements. Most, however, took the middle line of only posting papers from sympathetic publishers who allow some form of self-archiving. It is apparent that if institutional repositories are going to work, then this general confusion over copyright and intellectual property rights (IPR) issues must be addressed at the source.

It has, therefore, been necessary to investigate the effects of IPR and other legal implications (e.g. the Freedom of Information (Scotland) Act 2002) which arise when publishing research material online. These unforeseen problems have proved to be a significant barrier to the progress of the project and the development of repository programmes in general.

As previously mentioned in Chapter 6, there exist some genuine concerns about the premature release of research material in PhD theses, which raises the need for some items in ERA to remain confidential. The e-theses solutions developed by the Theses Alive project (for example Andrew, 2004) have proved to be very valuable to the higher education community. In practical terms for e-theses, we considered two main issues:

- the range of parties involved: the submitter, the institution and the end-user,
- that the restrictions placed on an e-thesis are not necessarily absolute; they may have time or domain dependencies.

In order to address these points we defined six scenarios where restrictions could be applied to an e-thesis such that it could be stored within the repository:

1. *No restriction*: the item is not restricted from access in any way.
2. *Domain restricted for one year*: the item is restricted only to users within the institutional domain for one year.
3. *Domain restricted for two years*: the item is restricted only to users within the institutional domain for two years.
4. *Withheld for one year*: the item is restricted from all users including the author for one year.
5. *Withheld for two years*: the item is restricted from all users including the author for two years.
6. *Permanently withheld*: the item is restricted from all users including the author for all time.

Thus, we defined a three-part licence which would allow for a comprehensive treatment of this problem. The licence is split into a deposit licence, a use licence, and a restriction policy. The deposit licence primarily gives the rights to the repository to hold the material in perpetuity, and to transform and migrate that work as and when necessary in order to meet the requirements of digital preservation without changing content wherever possible. We have also selected a creative commons (CC) licence under which the theses can be used; the authors are required to agree to this, as we felt this would make the material sufficiently open access to be of use, without compromising the author's rights. The version of this licence that is in use is an attribution, non-commercial, share-alike licence, which implies that any derived works must attribute the author of the thesis, and must also share that derived work under the same licence, with no commercial use of the item allowed. Of course any of the terms and conditions can be renegotiated at any point with the author if they are not deemed suitable in the future. Finally, the submitter is prompted to select the desired scope of restriction and provide appropriate FOI exemption wording specified during the submission process. Figure 7.1 shows how this licence is constructed.

While it was necessary to investigate these separate issues for e-theses, IPR concerns for e-prints are primarily based around the publisher's policy regarding self-archiving. Later in this chapter we discuss the processes that must be followed when depositing an item into the repository to ensure the intellectual property rights are not breached. At this stage we note that there are generally no restrictions applied to e-prints in ERA because any items we are legally permitted to deposit are not affected by the Freedom of Information Act and prior publication issues in the same way that e-theses are. Instead we require the submitter to confirm to the repository that the author is the sole copyright holder, or that they have permission to archive the item in a public space. A more comprehensive discussion of the other deposit licence criteria that we considered vitally important can be found in Chapter 6.

The next issue to be addressed was that of how to the brand the repository service. The initial plan was to integrate the service seamlessly into the university library web presence, and to provide smooth transitional navigation between the two systems. Throughout the course of the policy development, though, it became understood that branding ERA as a library service may discourage potential users or departments from endorsing the service, and for that reason the design coupling between the systems was weakened; a derived but unique branding for the service was, therefore, proposed and deployed. It was also decided early on to refrain from using potentially confusing nomenclature and to

Figure 7.1   **Three-part licence construction**

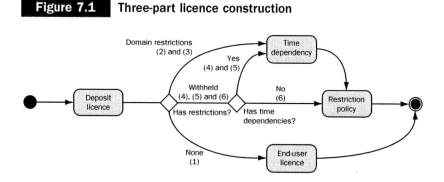

use generic terms that the academic community would feel comfortable with. Although the Library decided to use the DSpace platform as the basis for the repository, all references to DSpace were removed. DSpace as a software product is well known in the Information Science and Digital Library communities, however, in the wider academic community it is relatively obscure. A generic service name like the *Edinburgh Research Archive* has a more instantaneous recognition of function than any associations that DSpace or e-prints would confer. An additional rationale to adopt a neutral nomenclature is that any efforts to develop a strong brand would not be wasted if at a future date the underlying repository platform was changed. There were also issues concerned with how the contents of the repository would be surfaced within existing and future university systems. A great deal of work was in progress with other projects to provide portal-like access to many resources including the institutional repository, so the need for specific product branding was reduced further on the grounds that ultimately the service may be invisible to many users.

Other outputs of this process of policy development include best practice guidelines for institutions wishing to adopt electronic theses, and the authoring of extensive management and administrative procedures which will be discussed in more detail later in this chapter.

Deployment

One initial aim within the project plan was to work with a set number of additional higher education institutions to help test and develop the proposed e-theses management system; the project officer would arrange and liaise with a number of pilot institutions taking delivery of the project software, to gather feedback about the system and to help provide installation and end-user support. As the project progressed it became apparent that a national e-theses support service was not entirely appropriate at the time. Although it is necessary to help institutions build repositories and appropriate policies, it was felt that other types of support such as student support or mediated deposit would be best offered by the local institution where embedded staff would have detailed knowledge of current working practices. This was a common theme through all feedback from the initial partner institutions during site visits.

With the software side of the project approaching maturity we moved on to provide a pilot e-thesis service within the University of Edinburgh.

As a proof-of-concept we worked closely with two schools within the university: the School of Informatics and the School of Geosciences. During the pilot phase we hoped to refine our e-thesis service from the combined experiences of users and administrators alike, before expanding to cover the university as a whole. At the same time we hoped to assist our partner institutions in setting up similar e-theses repositories by providing technical and advocacy support.

The two pilot schools were chosen to represent as fully as possible a wide range of disciplines, which could have an impact on the types of material submitted. The School of Informatics, to some extent, already had a culture of producing e-theses, but lacked an effective method of online dissemination. The School of Geosciences, however, had no previous experience creating or publishing e-theses, but were willing to embark on the pilot. To encourage submission we felt that incentive was needed, particularly for the geoscience students; to meet these aims we arranged for the project to pay for one hard-bound copy of a thesis for every electronic version submitted during the pilot.

Typical theses from geosciences include features that could be problematic to represent electronically; for example, large fold-out inclusions, high diagrammatical content and large auxiliary data sets. By including these types of thesis, the pilot study hoped to directly asses the impact on students and the repository itself. A significant component of this part of the pilot was dedicated to providing end-user support for postgraduate students and supervisors via telephone and web-based technologies. During this time 20 students completed their doctorate theses and submitted an electronic version.

The School of Informatics study was more concentrated on investigating and developing a sustainable strategy for high-volume ingest; this included topics such as providing efficient workflow and format conversion. During the pilot phase the project gathered 136 theses retrospectively and obtained 11 theses submitted electronically.

Developing such a system in isolation is, of course, unwise, and throughout the lifetime of the project it was necessary and desirable to disseminate findings as well as to interact heavily with other researchers in the field. From these interchanges we found that many institutions had achieved successful e-theses programmes by mandating at a top-level the electronic submission of theses and dissertations, especially in the USA. This persuaded us to pursue a strategy of persistent lobbying for postgraduate degree regulation change at the highest level to mandate that students submit their theses in both electronic and print forms. The successful adoption of this policy has been a crucial moment in the development of ERA, and mandatory submission of e-theses will start to take effect around 2008/9. Changing university regulations is a notoriously slow process, and plenty of time should be allocated if pursuing this course. In addition, the postgraduate studies committee has been encouraged to regard the electronic copy as the authoritative version ('golden copy'). Printed copies can then be derived from the electronic version and bound by the library. If successful, then electronic theses submission may become the default, even before electronic deposit is mandated by regulations. A decision was made to develop a mediated deposit service and provide e-thesis creation support. In practice this consisted of providing guidance for postgraduates and supervisors on suitable file formats, scanning resolutions, conversion and system administration. This user support service was successfully piloted, and mediated deposit has become a formalised method of obtaining repository content of both e-theses and other research types, as will be discussed later in this chapter.

With the pilot study complete, and a small collection of content in the form of e-theses, e-prints, technical reports, conference papers and related research material, ERA went live in October 2003. The next stage in the advocacy process was to raise general awareness through internal publicity. To raise the general awareness of repositories and other open access issues we decided that an appropriate action would be to hold a seminar. We arranged such a meeting and sent invitations to every single academic staff member in the university. The only practical way to do this was via e-mail, and distributed leaflets.

Careful consideration was given to the relative timing and the venue itself. To attract the maximum number of staff we held the seminar in late summer, when most faculty have no teaching obligations and were not likely to be on vacation. For ease of access the venue itself was situated in a central location. To widen the appeal, and to prevent our endeavours from appearing too parochial, a number of speakers from external organisations were invited to give presentations. Senior management were also invited to lend their support to the initiative. Despite our best intentions the event was only modestly attended by members of the academic community. We felt that this lower than expected turn out was in part due to the reluctance of faculty taking time out from their schedule to travel to a central venue to listen to presentations in which they may only be marginally interested. Learning from this experience we decided that any subsequent advocacy seminars would be better placed if we held the event in their own environment (Chapter 5).

Following the advocacy plan we developed, the next stage was targeted content recruitment (Chapter 5). Academics identified from the initial baseline survey (Chapter 5) with significant content (ten items or more) already online in personal or departmental web pages were invited to deposit their content into the repository. Due to the scale of content, the faculty members were initially approached via e-mail. Figure 7.2 shows the scale and range of responses from one targeted content recruitment project at the University of Edinburgh.

During this particular targeted content recruitment drive, made during the summer of 2003, 96 individual academics from the subject areas of science and engineering were contacted initially by e-mail. Subsequently we had a response from 30 individuals (a response rate of 31 per cent). Part of this lower than expected turn-out was due to the timing of the project – five academics were away on vacation or research. From the remaining respondents, 19 were happy to self-archive some of their material immediately, whereas nine were more cautious. After explaining the aims of the project and soothing concerns they were also happy to deposit material. Only two academics were strongly opposed to being involved in the study from the start. Interestingly, one of these academics later changed their opinion and was actively involved in a departmental pilot study (Chapter 5) after the involvement of an opinion leader.

The actual responses from academics made interesting reading and broadly fell into four categories. Examples 1–5 taken from real-life subsequent correspondence with academics illustrate these points:

Figure 7.2   Pie chart showing the range of response from academics at the University of Edinburgh with content already online in personal web pages who were invited to deposit material in the institutional repository

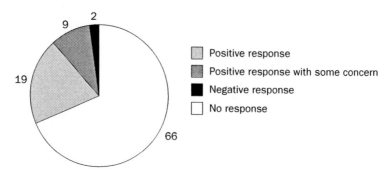

- Broadly welcoming:
  - 'This seems like a worthwhile endeavour and, yes, I am interested in having my research work in such a repository.'
- Concerned about extra workload involved:
  - 'You can include my papers as long as I don't have to do more than sign the permissions. Some of the departmental archives take a ridiculous amount of staff time to populate.'
  - 'My only reservation about using a centralised repository would be ease of use. Right now I send PS and PDF files to a public area with unix commands and I don't have to worry about passwords, formats or anything. I can change versions in an instant (I know this is horrifying to an archivist).'
- Concerned about copyright:
  - 'One thing though, I'm sure there are potential copyright issues … I think I would like more information on that side of things before I get involved with a more formal repository. I think one is unlikely to raise too much ire by having PDFs on a personal web page, but I could imagine journals being a bit more touchy about copyrighted material on a more official university website … This difference may seem trivial but sleeping dogs and all that!'
- Unwilling to participate:
  - 'No, not at present. There is already a world-wide archive of research papers in physics that is used extensively.'

These quotes seem to encapsulate a whole range of common reactions by academic staff towards institutional repositories. Familiarity with these points can help to formulate responses which will aid in content recruitment.

Administration

Providing ERA as a service is similar to providing any other institutional web resource, and the administration of these services can often be as challenging as the technical support requirements. When deciding how to administer ERA we had to determine how much effort would be put into areas such as metadata verification, administering policies for users, setting up research collections, correcting post-submission errors, and defining the archive structure.

Various solutions have been found to these problems and detailed documentation has been produced to deal with almost every part of standard service maintenance. Tasks which fall outside the normal bounds of library and administrative work are dealt with by a group of individuals with the relevant knowledge and experience. These tasks include decision making with regard to the state and development of the system as well as liaising with academic departments. An informal ERA Management Group (EMG) has been set up in order to deal with these broader issues and will be discussed later in this chapter.

As discussed in Chapter 4, there are many areas of the system which need to be soundly administered in order to run a service which does not get out of control. This section introduces some of the actual administrative decisions and processes used to operate ERA with a reasonable degree of success.

An important goal for the repository was to define a relatively static collection structure and have this map onto the institutional organisation as easily as possible. We define a community as a collection which may only contain other communities and collections in a DSpace context, and, therefore, these are used to create a shallow hierarchy within which the university's research will be categorised. A community maps directly in most cases onto a single recognisable academic unit such as the School. The collection, then, maps onto any internal subsection of the community, including working groups, institutes or centres. For example, the informatics community contains the Centre for Intelligent Systems and their Applications, Department of Artificial Intelligence and the Institute for Adaptive and Neural Computation. Naturally, this relationship of communities and collections to academic units does not always hold, and we leave it to the administrator to use their own discretion in unusual cases.

In terms of how research types should be distributed among the collections we faced a number of decisions regarding how best to reflect this in the hierarchy. After trying a number of configurations, and taking into account comments from academics regarding the perceived necessity to separate e-theses from other forms of research output, we decided use separate community and collection structures to deal with the different types of content. Extending this idea to be more generic we allow the communities and collections to have special designations attached to them to define their function beyond that of being affiliated with a particular academic unit. A particular case of this is that we define a community and its collections as being designated only for theses and dissertations.

To control all of the configurable system elements, we developed systematic naming conventions to which administrators must adhere. We identified two system elements to which this needed to apply: research collections/communities and user groups. The objective was to create name structures for each of these which allowed the purpose and likely content to be known quickly and easily, and for like elements to be easily found together in various browse contexts.

For communities the naming convention is defined (logically) in almost the same was as the community itself is defined; that is, by the academic unit to which it belongs, with an associated element which allows the administrator to define a special designation for the content. Thus the following general statement defines how they should be named: '<school to which community belongs> (<special designation>)'.

Therefore we would name the *theses and dissertations* designated *informatics* collection as simply: 'Informatics (Theses and Dissertations)'.

Similarly, the convention for collections is defined in the same way as the collection itself is defined, as being that of the subsection to which it belongs and the associated special designation, thus: '<group to which community belongs> (<special designation>)'.

Therefore we would name the *theses and dissertations* designated *Institute for Stem Cell Research* collection as: 'Institute for Stem Cell Research (ISCR) (Theses and Dissertations)'.

A similar methodology is used for naming user groups. We identified four primary user types: workflow administrators, theses supervisors, content submitters, and collection administrators. Each of these user types performs a specific role in the administration of ERA, and each will, therefore, have similar system policies associated with them. These policies can be effectively managed if applied to general groups of users, rather than on an individual basis (as is common in many computer systems), and we can make it easy to identify the relevant group at all stages by having sensible naming conventions. The general form for all these group names is: '<group prefix>: <associated system entity>'.

By having group prefixes associated with each group type, and a target entity of each group's policy, we can quickly identify who is working with what. We are simultaneously enforcing a very rigid 'one group, one purpose' model which can result in a large number of groups, but all of which are easy to manage. The prefixes we have chosen are:

- WF (<stage number>): A workflow group for the numbered stage in the process (there are three available stages in the workflow);
- SU: A supervisor group;
- IN: A submitter group;
- AD: A collection administrator group.

Therefore, the following group names would be allowable:

- *WF(1): Institute for Cell and Molecular Biology (ICMB)* – The first workflow group for the Institute of Cell and Molecular Biology.
- *WF(3): Accounting and Business Method (Theses and Dissertations)* – The third workflow group for the Theses and Dissertations designated Accounting and Business Method group.
- *SU: student@myu.ac.uk* – The supervisor group for the student with e-mail address *student@myu.ac.uk*
- *IN: Atmospheric and Environmental Science* – The submitter group for the contributors who can submit to the Atmospheric and Environmental Science collection.
- *AD: Celtic and Scottish Studies* – The collection administrator group for the Celtic and Scottish Studies group.

Each of these user groupings allows for a set of users with a defined purpose to be allocated the relevant system policies to permit their actions, or be referenced by other areas of the system to be allocated certain types of functionality. The workflow system, for example, is integrally linked to the workflow groups, in more than just pure policy (although this is also required to be correctly configured). Each workflow group has a set of defined actions associated with it such that it can be presented with the relevant options at the relevant stage of a submission's passing through the system. The first stage contains options to merely accept or reject the submission; the second has the additional option to edit the metadata and file content of the item; the third stage implies that the item is destined for the repository and permits only metadata and file management and ultimate acceptance for archiving.

The ERA is specifically aimed at handling research split into two broad categories: e-theses and all other research output. For this purpose there are several abstract pre- and post-submission workflow models defined which are implemented on a case-by-case basis for material as it is submitted into a collection. Each collection is associated with an implementation of one of these workflows, based upon the special

Figure 7.3 E-theses submission workflow

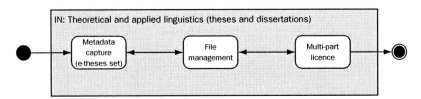

designation given to it, or the route via which it will be placed into the archive. The workflow diagrams in this chapter use examples of possible naming conventions for further clarity.

Figure 7.3 shows the submission workflow for an e-thesis. First, the metadata fulfilling the recommended UK e-theses requirements is collected from the submitter. These data include some information which is pre-populated by ERA, and unchangeable by the submitter, such as the host institution and department under which the work has been produced. Second, the files for the thesis are collected. Finally, the student must agree to a three-part licence which covers the rights of ERA to hold a copy of the thesis, the rights that the user gives to the users of the online version, and the Freedom of Information (Scotland) Act 2002 disclaimer associated with the restriction type (if any) that they define at this point. This multi-part licence is then constructed as explained earlier in this chapter.

Restriction of theses is only acceptable provided that one of the FOI exemptions is met, and the licensing stage also allows the submitter to choose which restriction option they require and also to provide a reason for this. The system then builds a large multi-part licence which is stored in the archive alongside the rest of the item (see Figure 7.1).

Figure 7.4 shows the submission workflow for all other types of research output. First, the metadata compliant with the recommendations from the SHERPA project is collected. Second, the files are uploaded. Third, the submitter needs only to agree to a deposit licence to allow ERA the rights

Figure 7.4 Other research material submission workflow

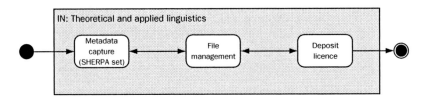

Figure 7.5   E-theses post-submission workflow 1

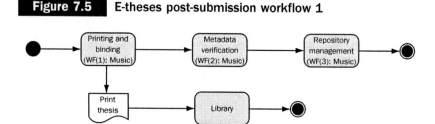

it needs to hold the material in perpetuity, and perform migrations and transformation as with the e-thesis. This is because the copyright situation is often more clear-cut at this stage for the material, insomuch as it is usually controlled by the journal publisher (as much of the contents are e-prints). There are also no FOI issues as the material is published and available anyway.

Figure 7.5 shows one workflow configuration for an e-theses collection in ERA. Once the post-submission stage of ingest has begun the thesis can go straight to the bindery, from where copies of the thesis can be produced and bound. In liaison with the student, this department can produce the requisite number of print theses as required by regulations as well as guarantee that the 'golden copy' (i.e. the electronic version), is identical to the print versions (a common issue with e-theses) by the very fact that the print is derived in a controlled way from the electronic. Once this has been done and the library has taken delivery of the print versions, the e-thesis moves on to the second stage, which contains collection librarians who will be responsible for ensuring the quality of the metadata and performing the final checks before the thesis is allowed to irrevocably reach the archive. Once value-added metadata has been inserted (e.g. the application of standard classification schemes such as Library of Congress Subject Headers where appropriate) and the quality of the submitter-authored metadata has been verified then the thesis can move on to the final stage. Here, the repository administrators get a final opportunity to ensure that any necessary restrictions have been applied and that the copy is in a fit state to be archived, performing any necessary additions to the contained files along the way (e.g. inserting copies in standardised formats).

Figure 7.6 shows an alternative workflow configuration which is currently not in everyday use, but exists should changes in the way people rely on ERA as a support service require it. Here, once the post-submission workflow begins, the first point of contact is the college office, which ensures that the thesis is intended and ready for submission

Figure 7.6 E-theses post-submission workflow 2

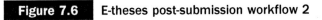

and that all relevant paperwork has been done in advance. If the thesis is ready to go ahead it can then be presented to the examiners of the work, to ensure that no corrections are outstanding or necessary and that the thesis has indeed been accepted for award. With these checks complete it is then finally up to the collections librarians to ensure the quality of the metadata, add additional catalogue information where necessary, and confirm that the thesis is in a fit state to archive.

Figure 7.7 shows the much simpler workflow required to support the post-submission phases of all other research output from the university. Only two stages are required for this sort of material. First, a school administrator has the opportunity to confirm the validity and authenticity of submissions; that is, that they are appropriate for the collection to which they have been submitted. Second, collections librarians will be responsible for ensuring the quality of the metadata, as before, and verifying that the submission is in a fit state to enter the archive. Note that the group names for the two existent workflow stages correspond to parts two and three. This is because our three workflow stage types in DSpace support different activities, and these groups are associated to those specific roles: accept/edit/reject and edit/reject respectively.

All these workflows and naming conventions along with how-to and troubleshooting guides and full administration procedures have all been gathered together into a single ERA Administration Guide. This documentation acts as a single reference point for all administrators, ensuring that there is consistency throughout and that long-term maintenance is possible. As an added bonus, the documentation acts as a set of extremely detailed use-cases against which new versions can be tested for functionality and suitability for purpose.

In the early stages of ERA's life we also offered a mediated submission service; this service has brought with it its own workflow procedures

Figure 7.7 Other research material post-submission workflow

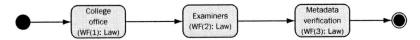

which override the previously discussed ones. The reasons for this, and the resulting related workflow issues are discussed in the next section.

Management

Beyond the procedural administrative requirements of the whole ERA system (which includes the people involved in its running and maintenance) there are data management issues which need to be looked at more closely and defined carefully. As previously mentioned, tasks which fall outside the normal sphere of library and administrative work are dealt with by the ERA Management Group (EMG). The tasks addressed here include the state of the development of the system as well as liaising with academic departments and handling mediated submission. It administers which institutional units are represented in the repository, obtains content, influences university regulations and implements functional requirements.

To manage the requests of various natures to the EMG we employ the university call management system (CMS) which is used for logging, tracking and reporting on the interactions involved in resolving support requests. The policy is that any task which takes more than a few minutes to administer in ERA should be entered into the CMS (note that this excludes requests purely regarding the underlying software packages, which are addressed directly to the development community). Other requests may not necessarily be directed to the CMS initially, but may lead to a call being opened. For example, if an e-mail is received asking '*Why is ERA not registered with harvester X?*' then a call would be opened in the CMS: '*Register ERA with harvester X*'.

We have defined a set of protocol tags which are attached to each call that is opened in the ERA CMS. These are placed in the short description of the request to ensure that efficient searching and querying of the open calls can take place. Effectively this is further use of good naming conventions for improved usability. These tags are as follows:

- *[FEATURE]*: high-level, non-technical feature request or suggestion for ERA. These should be requests which are not directly about the nature of the underlying software, and will be followed up by a member of the EMG.

- *[DEPOSIT]*: anything relating to the submission of items to the repository, including copyright issues. The aim is to answer each of these requests within seven days of receipt.

- *[ADMIN]*: any administrative task to be performed on the system. This includes user authorisations, group management, community or collection configuration and so forth. This will primarily be addressed by the ERA system administrator.

- *[FOI]*: Freedom of Information (Scotland) Act 2002 invocations. By law requests for information should be completed within 20 days. During this time advice is sought from the local FOI adviser.

- *[ENQUIRY]*: any information request which is not FOI related, such as requests for advice regarding issues including as copyright or best practice. The aim is to answer each of these requests within seven days of receipt

- *[!]*: the request is urgent and should be dealt with immediately. This enhances other requests on this list.

So, for example, you may find the following in the CMS: '*[ENQUIRY][!] Legal question over copyright content*'.

We aimed to provide a general information and user support service for submissions. This partly took the form of the mediated deposit service, which in practice consisted of providing guidance for postgraduate students, supervisors and academics on suitable file format types, scanning resolutions, and format conversion. This service has been warmly welcomed by students and academics alike. The submitter passes to EUL an electronic copy of the item to be placed in the repository and a member of the EMG checks the copyright status of the work, converts file formats as necessary and submits the item to the relevant collection with the relevant metadata.

This sort of service comes with quite a large administrative overhead, and the long-term sustainability is a question that should be considered by repository managers before implementing. For our situation, ERA is considered a core library service and features prominently in the University of Edinburgh's knowledge management strategy (Hayes, 2004). Given that the task of actually submitting on behalf of another is not too complex, documentation describing the process has been developed, with the design to delegate the work to sectors of the library, which although not necessarily specialists in institutional repositories, already have complementary working practices, for example, cataloguing staff.

Once a call for mediated deposit comes in there are two possible strands that should be followed: *journal articles* and *theses and dissertations*. The following sections cover each of these strands in some detail.

Journal articles and other research material

Figure 7.8 shows the process for mediating the deposit of a journal article.

First, the item submitter needs to be sufficiently satisfied that the caller is a genuine member of the University of Edinburgh. For brevity, the recommended way of doing this is to check the university web pages and staff lists for the caller and to ensure they are using a recognised internal e-mail address. Next it is necessary to perform a check on the item being submitted. If the item is sent by e-mail then care should be taken to ensure that it is virus free and uncorrupted, and that any description of the item in the e-mail corresponds to the attached file. In some cases no file is sent, and only a reference to the electronic object is provided (often

Figure 7.8   Mediated submission of journal articles

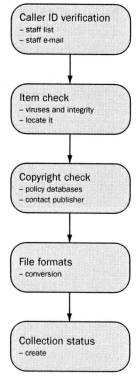

Mediated submission request

Caller ID verification
– staff list
– staff e-mail

Item check
– viruses and integrity
– locate it

Copyright check
– policy databases
– contact publisher

File formats
– conversion

Collection status
– create

Proceed with submission

in the form of a link to an online journal), and in these cases some effort needs to go into obtaining the item. In other circumstances it may be necessary to assist in the digitisation of a print-only resource.

In terms of whether a particular offer of submission is valid, the general policy is that if an academic thinks the material is worth putting online then it will be accepted. The rationale behind this ethos is to disseminate the university's research as widely as possible. As a member of academic staff has already been subject to a form of peer review during the job interview and selection process we automatically assign them a trusted contributor status.

The copyright check is perhaps one of the most important stages of the deposit process. By placing content online EUL is acting in the eyes of British law as a publisher, and thus can be found liable if the content disseminated is defamatory, libellous or breaching copyright or licensing terms. While some materials, such as e-theses or unpublished manuscripts do not carry such risks for the repository, the situation is more complex when we want to archive previously published materials. Often authors pass their copyright over to the publishers, or assign a non-exclusive licence, which prohibits further distribution by other parties.

For journal articles we use the following sites to find a summary of permissions that are normally given as part of each publisher's copyright agreement:

- SHERPA Romeo database: *http://www.sherpa.ac.uk/romeo.php*;
- EPrints Romeo database: *http://romeo.eprints.org/*.

Searching through these databases should quickly give you the copyright information required. Commonly, we have found that journal articles are subject to the following archive conditions set out by publishers:

- self-archiving not formally supported;
- self-archiving of pre-print permitted;
- self-archiving of post-print permitted;
  - author's own version of accepted paper;
  - publisher's version;
- self-archiving of pre-print and post-print permitted.

Additional terms and conditions for self-archiving are defined by publishers, particularly with regards to where e-prints are permitted to be deposited. To makes things clear for depositing authors we regard ERA as:

- a non-profit, non-commercial, institutional, open-access e-print server;
- *not* an author's personal website, departmental web page or password-protected site.

Sometimes we find that publishers are not listed in either of the databases cited, or we may be dealing with other types of content such as book chapters or conference proceedings. If this is the case, then direct contact with the publisher is required. We have devised a standard form letter which can be sent to the publisher by post and e-mail, requesting permission to use the item. If the response is positive we can go on to archive the item.

Regarding file formats, we prefer to archive PDF files above other proprietary formats, partly due to longevity and prolonged ease of access. If a file is received that is not PDF then it is converted using the appropriate tools. Most local PCs are installed with software to do this, however, sometimes more unusual file formats such as PostScript, LaTeX (or related device independent files) are supplied. If this happens then there are additional tools available for the repository staff to convert these files to PDF. When the item is archived, the source files and the PDF are archived together to provide the most options in future digital preservation efforts.

Finally, before an item is submitted it is necessary to check to which community and collection the item belongs. This is determined primarily by which academic unit the author is part of, and secondarily by item type. Theses and dissertations have specially designated collections, as discussed earlier, and need to be placed in the corresponding collection. If no community or collection exists for the item it must be created as per the ERA Administration Guide, otherwise the mediated submitter can proceed with inserting the item into the relevant collection and have it made available within ERA within a very short time.

Theses and dissertations

Figure 7.9 shows how the mediated submission process currently occurs for an e-thesis. This is effectively a subset of the steps required to archive journal articles, which we will recap here.

Figure 7.9   Mediated submission of e-theses

Mediated submission request

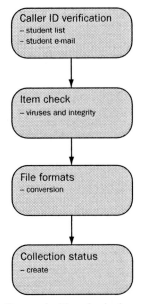

Proceed with submission

Again, it is necessary to verify the authenticity of the caller, and student lists (especially those documenting postgraduates in their final year) can be used in conjunction with verifying that the e-mail address is internally recognised. The items in these cases are usually delivered via e-mail or directly on CD to the EMG and the normal integrity checks are performed on the files. It is extremely unlikely that a print copy will need to be digitised. Note that there is no copyright verification stage, because in general the thesis is original and unpublished work. In unusual circumstances, such as thesis by research publication some action may need to be taken. As usual, conversion to PDF is ideal, although given the nature of some e-theses this is not always possible, but steps are taken to ensure that formats which meet basic preservation requirements are used. Finally, similar checks to before are carried out to ensure that the relevant collection exists for the item (taking care to adhere to the special designation requirements of the archive structure), and then the item can be submitted.

Conclusion

Through involvement with other JISC FAIR-programme funded projects we were able to develop and launch ERA within a year and a half. The repository now contains full-text e-theses, book chapters, journal pre-prints and post-prints as well as a small number of technical reports and conference papers. We have investigated and implemented revised thesis rules and regulations for the University of Edinburgh to permit and encourage e-theses. Similarly we have updated the thesis submission and management workflow to take advantage of the benefits that adopting e-theses creates. We have also delivered a report on IPR and e-theses commissioned by the JISC Legal Service to advise on the legal implications of this sort of work. Template use and deposit licences have been developed, along with advice on the FOI implications. At the same time a huge amount of community support for theses sorts of activities has been achieved via the dissemination of project findings.

For institutions worldwide one of the most recognisable outputs of the project was the development of the Tapir, which is now partly included in the general DSpace release. Meanwhile the creation of the UK e-theses core metadata set, along with our collaborating institutions has formed a good basis for further e-theses classification, storage and access. In addition, a major impact has been the provision of open access status to selected research and thesis literature; this toll-free access to students and academics is available constantly without the physical lending restrictions that are traditionally associated with published literature. In addition to the core project aims we have also addressed a number of critical side issues. The resolution of these issues, in particular IPR, proved to be of paramount importance, not just for project completion but also for the wider community.

The knock-on effects of this work confer dynamic impacts on the teaching, learning and research communities. There is an opportunity for enhanced teaching and learning in that source material such as book chapters and research articles are increasingly being made public through this repository and others like it.

The technical and cultural expertise garnered through developing and implementing ERA has been invaluable, and has been disseminated in various forms to the higher education information and library services community. This book has been one of our contributions to the community in the hope that the hard-won lessons we have learned will make this process for other institutions a much more enriched and enlightened one.

Note

1. This chapter is comprised primarily of the findings of the Theses Alive and SHERPA projects. Cited here are many of the articles and reports that were produced during this time. In addition, many project documents and presentations were consulted that were written during the project. Most of these resources can be found in one form or another on the Theses Alive project website: *http://www.thesesalive.ac.uk/*. Of particular importance are Andrew (2004a,b), Jones (2004a–f) and MacColl (2002a,b) and the contribution by Glasgow University Library (Nixon, 2003).

Appendix

There are many packages available upon which to base an institutional repository, some open source, some service based and others the product of pure in-house development. This appendix introduces package profiles from six of the major open source platforms available, provided by their communities:

- Archimède;
- CDSware;
- DSpace;
- EPrints.org;
- Fedora;
- OPUS.

Appendix A
Archimède

Programming languages	Java
Native languages	French, English, Spanish (internationalised)
Required software	J2SDK 1.4.1+, mySQL (or any database supported by Jakarta Torque). J2EE Servlet 2.3+ container (ex. Tomcat 4+), ANT
Online resources	Main installation: *http://archimede.bibl.ulaval.ca/* Software: *http://www.bibl.ulaval.ca/archimede/index.en.html*
Code licence	GPL
Available as	Source code and standalone binary
Components included	Web interface, LIUS indexing framework, storage layer, OAI-interface

Archimède is an institutional repository software designed to preserve and disseminate the scholarly publications of Université Laval research communities. The system is built around autoregulated communities, allowing them to upload their publications with the appropriate description (metadata) in a very convivial and secure interface. Furthermore, it includes a user-level authentication, strong indexation features, and it is OAI compatible.

Around 2002, the development team made an analysis of available open source software solutions and decided to create their own customised application. This does not mean that the other solutions were not good, but the products did not, at this time, have all the features that were needed. The principal reasons that led Université Laval to design and develop their own system are as follows:

- as a francophone university, Université Laval needed a repository offering a French interface;

- a good indexation module fitted to handle multiple documents formats and offering the possibility to perform a search through 'full-text' and metadata at the same time was needed;

- the new system had to be compatible with the Windows environment as well as Linux (because when we conceived the system we only had Windows servers in our infrastructure).

A comparison of the different open source repositories (including Archimède) is available on the SOROS foundation website in the *OSI Guide to IR Software 3rd edn (http://www.soros.org/openaccess/pdf/ OSI_Guide_to_IR_Software_v3.pdf)*.

As a starting point for the development of the Université Laval Institutional Repository, the development team selected a panoply of open source softwares and frameworks; they did not try to reinvent the wheel. This approach has led to an effective development in a short amount of time, thanks to the open source community.

The main features of the system are as follows:

- A security module with five users types, each one with their privileges and restrictions.

- A module for uploading several documents at the same time with a form to enter the metadata. All 'deposits' are hosted in virtual folders with access restrictions.

- An OAI data provider with Dublin Core metadata element set.

- A selective dissemination of information (SDI) feature, to keep users informed about novelties.

- i18n: Following the principle of internationalisation, we have made Archimède very flexible, allowing the addition of any language support very easily. The system already comes with three language options (French, English and Spanish). All the elements of the interface can be easily customised because they are independent from the code of the interface.

- Lucene Index Update and Search (LIUS): is an indexing framework based on the Apache Lucene Open Source project. It adds to Lucene many files format indexing capabilities, such as: MS Word, MS Excel, MS PowerPoint, RTF, PDF, XML, HTML, TXT, Open Office suite and JavaBeans. LIUS allows mixed-indexing, carrying out in the same occurrence the full-text and metadata, thus making a very effective search tool.

- Browsing system: Archimède features a browsing system by research communities, collections, titles, creators, etc.

- Portability: Archimède is a web-based application entirely developed in Java language (J2EE) (OS independent). Thus, for an institution wishing to implement the system there is no obligation to buy a particular server or to learn a new operating system. Archimède will work with the existing infrastructure.

The application is entirely developed according to the MVC pattern (model – controller – view) using the Struts framework. Thus, Archimède is divided into three distinctive parts, each one performing a specific task. The *model* is the logics of the application, it manages the data and the functionalities using JavaBeans and data object pattern (DAO). The *view* is the user-side of the application. The *controller* is the synchroniser between the *model* and the *view*: it catches the inputs of the user and sends them to the *model* that will perform the operations, before the result is sent back to the *view*. This way of breaking the application into distinctive parts makes the maintenance and updates of the system simpler, as well as allowing the addition of new features to Archimède.

Archimède is OAI compliant. It is compatible with the OAI-PMH 2 protocol to ensure dissemination of the metadata toward the 'data providers', allowing the spread of research, teaching and learning materials created by Université Laval's, teachers and researchers.

From the user point of view, Archimède offers multiple collections in which community members upload their contents and metadata, using the Dublin Core elements. These 'deposits' are secured by a user-level authentication and the users of the communities can choose between tree status for their documents: public (i.e. browsable by everyone), community (i.e. browsable by community members) or private (i.e. restricted to the users of the system). Several navigation mechanisms are provided: by research communities, collection, titles, creators, subject and dates. Furthermore, users may take advantage of both the simple search module and the advanced search module to find contents easily. Users can also subscribe to communities and collections and be informed of developments in two ways: via a personal web page and by e-mail. Community administrators can benefit from a workflow system if documents need approbation before being uploaded to the system.

As an institutional repository, Archimède serves research communities wishing to work in a collaborative environment and its indexation features make it a reliable tool to disseminate the outputs of scholarly research. Furthermore, it can be used in any situation requiring document management with research and indexation capabilities.

The development team has plan for future developments. First, a module supporting any metadata formats, responding to any specific needs regarding the document description, will be added. The possibility to integrate versioning support and a fully configurable workflow is also one of its concerns. Furthermore, the HTTP uploading module will be replaced by WebDAV.

The development team also plans to implement java portlet (JSR 168), and JAVA Content Repository for content management (JSR 170) and to integrate LDAP capabilities for institutional authenticating mechanism. The completion of those functionalities started in June 2005. With the incoming new version of Archimède, we are planning to put in place a community of developers around the project.

Archimède can be found at *http://archimede.bibl.ulaval.ca* and the packages can be obtained from *http://www.bibl.ulaval.ca/archimede/index.en.html*.

Rida Benjelloun and Dave Anderson, Université Laval Library.

Appendix B
CDSware: CERN document server

Programming languages	Python/PHP
Native languages	English (internationalised)
Required software	Linux/Unix, MySQL, Apache, GNU Autoconf, WML
Online resources	Flagship implementation: *http://cds.cem.ch/* Software: *http://cdsware.cem.ch* Mailing lists: *project-cdsware-announce@cem.ch*; *project-cdsware-users@cem.ch*
Code licence	GPL
Available as	Source
Components included	Web interface, storage layer, OAI-interface

In 1993 the CERN Preprint Server was developed to collect and disseminate all high energy physics (HEP) and HEP-related research documents. In 1996 it was further developed into the CERN Library server, using the same software to provide access to periodicals, books and most of the material kept in the library. In 2000, multimedia data, such as photos, posters, brochures and videos produced at CERN were integrated in a new version of the application, called the CERN Document Server Software: CDSware. This package was made OAI-compliant and widely distributed. It can be used either as a general document management solution, a library system or an institutional repository. It has been developed primarily at CERN, where the head architect and developers supervise many students from top European universities. Development is also carried out at the Ecole Polytechnique de Lausanne (*www.epfl.ch*) and in other institutes, such as the Réseau des Bibliothèques de Suisse Occidentale and the University of Geneva.

The installation can be done by any system administrator with Linux skills. The operation and configuration is primarily web-based, but there are some additional command-line functions to ease some tasks (for example, the job scheduler). There are a number of public installations that have customised their CDSware installation to fit their local requirements (see the list at: *http://cdsware.cern.ch/demo/*).

More than ten years of organic development, with validation by users and librarians and a performance driven design (more at: *http://cdsware.cern.ch:8000/hacking/*), has led to a software package intended to cope with very large collections (approximately 1 million records at CERN) with library-like functionality. The underlying idea is to combine the best of the library world with the best of the information retrieval world.

You can archive virtually any type of data with CDSware; for example, you can submit and store and search and stream MP3 files easily. You can also submit only the metadata, without attaching or linking any object at all to the record description. Other core features of CDSware include:

- search ranking: by full text download, by citations, or by journal impact factors;
- full-text indexing of content;
- use of MARC21 for internal metadata representation, which is less restrictive than Dublin Core and allows the coverage of more metadata standards; other metadata formats can be converted to this using packaged tools, and ready-to-be-used templates for DC are also included;
- internal custom indexing technology allows up to 3 million records with instantaneous reponse;
- modules are provided to support data- and service-provider OAI services.

The native language of the interface is English, but the use of a templating system simplifies the task of translating the software. Other currently existing translations are: Czech, German, Spanish, French, Italian, Norwegian, Portuguese, Russian, Slovenian and Swedish.

You can search and browse on any content field, and define global and local indexes on the fields you want. End users can run very simple and very complex (boolean expressions, regular expressions, etc.) queries.

This permits an interesting combination of metadata, full-text and citation search in the same query. For example, to get all documents written by *Lin* whose full-text files contain the words *Schwarzschild* and *AdS*, and who cite journal *Adv. Theor. Math. Phys*:

> author:lin fulltext:Schwarzschild fulltext:AdS reference:"Adv. Theor. Math. Phys."

Sorting and ranking are also provided in the native search. The default is to sort with most recent documents first but the end-user can decide to sort by any field, or to rank according to different criteria (word similarity, citations, downloaders, etc). Any query can be output in multiple formats: HTML brief, HTML detailed, MARC native format, Dublin Core, user defined. In addition, the OAI-PMH protocol is supported, and a direct use of the APIs is also possible.

Various workflow models are supported from a direct submission with no approval, to monitoring or requiring approval from authority. Each document type can be configured differently, with different fields, controls, associated functions and processes.

CDSware also has some versioning support for full-text files, similar to VMS OS. That is, every full-text file is stored by CDSware with automatically appended version number (e.g. 'file.pdf;13') and the numbers are automatically incremented for each file revision. At the current time, though, there is no versioning for metadata, however a similar approach to the full-text solution is being considered.

There is a user-role-action based access control system where user groups are simulated via roles. The collection/file access is done either by Apache access credentials or by CDS (or external, LDAP) login. The site access can also be restricted by IP (see: *http://cdsware.cern.ch:8000/admin/webaccess/guide.html*).

The CERN document format Conversion Server can be plugged into CDSware to convert all incoming files (Word, PPT, LaTeX, etc.) into PDF for long-term preservation. In addition, internal identifiers are persistent, and removing a record keeps the identifier attached to the information regarding its removal. Internal identifiers are also used as OAI identifiers and as well as in the URL to take a user directly to the detailed record.

In future versions there are many developments planned, some of the most interesting being:

- support for up to 30 million records;
- inverted submission process: document first, metadata extraction and validation afterwards;
- further developments in advanced search ranking.

J.-Y. Le Meur and Tibor Simko, CERN.

Appendix C
DSpace

Programming languages	Java/JSP
Native languages	English (internationalised)
Required software	Linux/Unix (or OS/X, Windows), PostgreSQL/Oracle, Java servlet container/webserver
Online resources	DSpace homepage: *http://www.dspace.org/* Project wiki: *http://wiki.dspace.org/* Software and mailing lists: *https://sourceforge.net/projects/dspace/*
Code licence	BSD
Available as	Source
Components included	Web interface, storage layer, web services

DSpace was originally created by a collaborative research and advanced development project between Hewlett Packard Labs and the MIT Libraries over a two and half year period from 2000 to 2002, under the HP-MIT Alliance.

Since that time, DSpace has evolved into a full-blown open source software project with an evolving governance model loosely based on that of the Apache Software Foundation. The current DSpace Project Committers who manage the code include staff from Cambridge University, University of Bergen, OCLC, University of Toronto, MIT, HP Labs, and the Australian National University.

In addition to the formal committers, many people have made significant contributions to DSpace. The list is long and growing, so for a current look at who has worked on DSpace, consult the project wiki (*http://wiki.dspace.org/*).

The DSpace open source software is a web-based digital asset management application written in Java and JSP, and employing a large number of third-party tools and applications in addition to the main DSpace code. These include PostgreSQL (or other relational database software), Apache and Tomcat (or other web server and Java application server), and numerous Java tools, as well as add-ons such as SRW (Search and Retrieval on the Web, a web service for remote search and retrieval of DSpace content) which contain other libraries like JZKit. The project documentation on the dspace.org website provides a more complete list and other information about how it all fits together.

The project provides free, open source code under the Berkley Software Distribution (BSD) licence, which allows for commercial applications of the software, although it is not guaranteed that all subcomponents of the application share the same licence so commercial implementations should be careful to review what is allowed and substitute other components as necessary. Individual DSpace sites can also choose to replace the default DSpace tools with commercial software (e.g. Oracle rather than PostgreSQL) if their implementation calls for it. DSpace runs on any computer platform that supports JVM, including all variations of Unix and Linux, Mac OSX, and Microsoft Windows. The project's site on SorceForge.net provides all the source code and everything needed to install DSpace, as well as extensive documentation to help adopters. Installation requires some systems administration expertise, but there is an active mailing list for support from other implementers and lots of documentation to help.

DSpace is a complete, breadth-first application that supports the development of an institutional repository service at a research-producing organisation, typically a research university but not limited to them. It has functionality to support:

- *deposit* of digital content and associated (Dublin Core) metadata into the repository by users (i.e. faculty or researchers of the organisation, or librarians on their behalf), following a customisable workflow that supports various policies with regard to review, approval, etc. by the owning community;

- *management* of the digital content in the repository over long periods of time, and preserve that content for digital file formats that the organisation has chosen to support (as specified in an internal format registry);

- *search/browse and retrieve* digital content via a simple web user interface, including some support for advanced searching of structured metadata, or full-text.

In addition, a number of web services are available to support interoperability with local client applications such as learning management systems or collaboration tools, including deposit, search, and retrieval of items in the repository. There are also a number of tools for batch loading, and support for all aspects of the Open Archives Initiative Protocol for Metadata Harvesting (OAI-PMH).

DSpace was created as a platform on which to build an institutional repository, but it is currently used for a variety of types of repositories where the set of functions described are needed, for example, as a learning object repository and a digital publishing platform. Using DSpace for these other purposes is not deprecated, and is, in fact, helping the community understand the requirements for organisational asset management which will, in turn, inform development of institutional repositories.

DSpace has access control functions to allow organisations to control who may deposit items into the repository, and to restrict public access to certain collections or individual items as necessary. While providing open access to digital research is a goal of many implementers, it is not a requirement of the platform. Licenses for deposit are required for every item, granting the repository managers the right to manage, preserve, and disseminate the content on behalf of the copyright holder. Creative commons licences are available for selection by depositors who wish to grant some of their copyrights to the public. Access control is managed either by logon ID and password or by PKI (X.509 certificates) by default. Other institutions have added support for LDAP, pubcookies, and other authentication mechanisms.

DSpace 1.0 and subsequent releases have maintained the breadth-first application design, but efforts have begun to evolve the system towards a new DSpace 2.0 design which will be more modular and more closely aligned to the OAIS framework for digital archives. As long-term preservation of digital content is one of the two major goals of the DSpace platform (with access to content as the other), this redesign will be important if we want to take advantage of new technologies such as the Data Grid and the Semantic Web. For DSpace to meet the growing needs of the many organisations that need to manage digital research assets for archival time frames, a practical, modular design that can easily be adapted to new organisations, new content types, and new service models is necessary.

One of the main distinguishing characteristics of the DSpace project today is the growing community of open source software developers surrounding it. In less than three years the system has evolved from a product under the tight control of a small number of developers to one which is being actively managed, debugged, and improved by a large number of developers from institutions all over the world. A few commercial implementations have emerged, and one company (Biomed Central in the UK) has developed a new commercial support service for institutional repositories that uses the DSpace system. As the developer community continues to grow and mature, the project continues to improve and expand in new directions. To get an accurate picture of what is happening please visit the DSpace website: *http://www.dspace.org/.*

MacKenzie Smith, MIT Libraries.

Appendix D
GNU EPrints archive software

Programming languages	Object-Oriented PERL
Native languages	English (internationalised)
Required software	Linux or other UNIX-like OS, Apache 1.3 or 2 as a web server, mod_perl, MySQL for storage, some perl modules (all freely available)
Online resources	Main installation at Southampton University: *http://eprints.soton.ac.uk/* Mailing lists: *http://software.eprints.org/mailist.php* Software: *http://software.eprints.org/*
Code licence	GPL
Available as	Source
Components included	Web interface, storage layer, OAI-interface

> The potential role of electronic networks in scientific publication, however, goes far beyond providing searchable electronic archives for electronic journals. The whole process of scholarly communication is currently undergoing a revolution comparable to the one occasioned by the invention of printing. (Harnad, 1990)

Although Harnad established a broad vision for EPrints, early software was limited in scope in order to deliver an initial repository capability in a reasonable time-frame to support a new open access model of disseminating research findings. The early releases of EPrints delivered a repository for research publications, providing a web-based archive system for storing documents and their associated metadata. To support a key goal of 'increasing the impact of research' the software provided a number of methods for accessing material, such as search (both the full-text and metadata) and by navigating predefined views such as subject taxonomy or by year of publication. The metadata was also made available to external search services via the OAI-PMH protocol.

More recent developments have extended the software's scope to support archiving of a wider range of supporting research materials, such as experimental data, images and other multimedia files. The ability to subscribe and receive notifications when material on specific topics is added to the archive and an RSS interface for integrating with websites and increasing research dissemination have been included.

Although EPrints is sufficiently general purpose to be used for many purposes (including teaching resources, museum exhibits and administrative materials) it is configured by default to act as and the archive of research materials which have been published/presented formally in seminars, conferences, symposia, journals, books, etc. It also supports the archive of pre-prints, theses and technical reports that have undergone various degrees of review but are not yet final. An e-print may contain significant drafts which track the revision process from initial submission to final accepted draft.

EPrints has been developed with a single purpose – to provide greater access to and utilisation of research, as well as offering a valuable mechanism for reporting and recording its impact. This focus is resulting in a unique software package that can be simply installed in a research organisation and be of immediate benefit.

It already has a growing international user base behind the software and new repositories are being established all the time. It is developed by a research organisation for the benefit of other research organisations. The active engagement of this community will ensure the software is developed to meet the needs and demands of the research community. Internationalisation has been a core part of the design. The default language is English but freely available third-party translations are available. These include Russian, Spanish, Hungarian and Japanese. Other known translations include Portuguese, German, French and Italian. Support for EPrints is currently provided via three EPrints mailing lists (see *http://software.eprints.org/maillist.php*): eprints-announce, eprints-underground, and eprints-tech. Archives of the lists are available online, and the developer plays an active role. There is also an EPrints wiki which contains how-to guides and third-party contributions including scripts, patches and translations (*http://wiki.eprints.org/w/*). Members of the community share solutions and ideas via the list and wiki.

The default configuration is suited to an institutional repository of a research organisation, but can be modified to any number of other purposes, from storing experimental datasets to MP3 files. A sensible simple and advanced search are configured by default, but it is easy to modify their parameters or add new searches. Periodically browse-by-year and browse-by-subject pages are regenerated. Latest additions are available as an HTML page or an RSS feed. Most HTML pages can be retrieved as an HTML fragment (without the normal site template). This is very useful integrating the information into your other websites. Latest e-prints can appear on your home page, a user's e-prints can appear on their homepage.

Most parts of the system can be customised if needed, which include:

- website template;
- all text on web pages;
- e-mail notification messages;
- citation styles;
- record summary pages;
- types of record;
- record metadata fields;
- default values for fields;
- validation rules;
- the subject hierarchy and search forms.

The EPrints system is designed in object-oriented PERL so it is possible to build simple scripts to search, read and modify the e-print and user records. Elements of the submission process which are not needed may be disabled. A default archive automatically acts as an OAI service provider, providing unqualified Dublin Core, but other formats can easily be added.

User registration is performed via a web page and e-mail confirmation. This can be disabled, and users created via a script. Many archives import their staff database. Users are authenticated via an encrypted password in their user record. This can be disabled, and an alternate password authentication scheme, such as LDAP, may be used.

The vision is to support the complete lifecycle of academic endeavour from concept through experimentation and evaluation to final publishing and for those interested in the research to be able to investigate and navigate the trail that lead up to the final presentation of results.

The School of Electronics and Computer Science at the University of Southampton has initiated a new investment programme to increase the capability and the industrial strength experience of the development team effort behind EPrints. It is also providing a programme of user community engagement to help people to get the best from EPrints.

Our development activities fall into three broad categories:

- active involvement with the user community to develop the features they request;
- working to support are greater degree the complete research creation path;
- increasing the impact of research by simple and effective open access to materials and providing a range of tools reporting and recording its impact.

Christopher Gutteridge, Southampton University.

Appendix E
Fedora

Programming languages	Java
Native languages	English (internationalised)
Required software	Apache Tomcat, Apache Axis, Xerces, Saxon, Schematron, MySQL and Mckoi relational database, support for Oracle 9i, Windows/UNIX/Linux/Solaris
Online resources	The Fedora development project website: *http://www.fedora.info/* The Fedora users' mailing list: *https://comm.nsdl.org/mailman/listinfo/fedora-users*
Code licence	Versions 1.0–2.0: Mozilla 1.1; Versions 2.1 and higer: Educational Community Licence
Available as	Source code, binary
Components included	Core object model

In 1997, the Flexible Extensible Digital Object and Repository Architecture (Fedora) began as a DARPA and National Science Foundation (NSF)-funded research project of Carl Lagoze and Sandy Payette at Cornell University's Digital Library Research Group. Two years later the University of Virginia Library's research and development group installed the research software version of Fedora and began experimenting with some of Virginia's digital collections. They re-interpreted the implementation and developed a prototype which provided strong evidence that the Fedora architecture could indeed be the foundation for a practical, scalable digital library system. In 2001 the University of Virginia Library and Cornell University collaborative development team received a grant of $1 million from the Andrew W. Mellon Foundation to enable the development of a sophisticated digital object repository system based on Fedora. Up until

2005, Fedora has passed through two major versions, and the Mellon Foundation awarded this project a $1.4 million three-year grant to continue refining and building on Fedora's functionality.

Digital content is not just documents, nor is it made up exclusively of the content from digital versions of currently owned non-digital content. Repository managers have two general categories of objects to cope with: conventional objects (e.g. books and other text objects, geospatial data, images, maps) and complex, compound, or dynamic objects (e.g. video, numeric data sets and their associated code books, timed audio).

As digital collections grow, and are made use of in previously unconsidered ways, repository managers are faced with management tasks of increasing complexity. Collections are being built which contain multiple data types, and organisations have discovered a need to archive and preserve complex. Finally, as collections grow in both size and complexity, the need to establish relationships between data objects in a repository becomes more and more apparent.

Five key research questions arose from consideration of these complexities:

1. How can clients interact with heterogeneous collections of complex objects in a simple and interoperable manner?
2. How can complex objects be designed to be both generic and genre-specific at the same time?
3. How can we associate services and tools with objects to provide different presentations or transformations of the object content?
4. How can we associate specialised, fine-grained access control policies with specific objects, or with groups of objects?
5. How can we facilitate the long-term management and preservation of objects?

Fedora's digital object model sets it apart from all other digital asset management solutions. Because the model is abstract, it makes no difference what kind of data are represented by the digital object (e.g. text, images, maps, audio, video, geospatial data). It is also flexible in that implementers can design their content models to best represent their data and the presentation requirements of their specific use case. In a Fedora object, data and metadata are tightly linked, making the object generic. Data referenced by a Fedora object may be stored locally or on any web-accessible server. And finally, Fedora's behaviour interfaces are extensible because services are directly associated with data within the

Fedora object, so as the services change, the objects change along with them.

Archiving and preservation needs are addressed in the Fedora architecture in four ways: encoding of Fedora objects in XML, content versioning, object to object relationships, and event history. Fedora objects' XML and the schema upon which they are based are preserved at ingest, during storage, and at export. Additionally, each Fedora object contains a persistent identifier that conforms to uniform resource name (URN) syntax. Fedora's XML format also allows for the storage of object to object relationships via the metadata included in the object.

Versioning of data objects in a Fedora repository is optional, but if utilised, implementers may store multiple versions of datastreams in Fedora data objects. When a data object is versioned, the object's audit trail is updated to reflect the changes made to the object, when the change was made and by whom and a new version of the modified data is added to the object's XML. This new datastream cascades from the original and is numbered to show the relationship between original and version. Every object also contains an audit trail, which preserves a record of every change made to the object.

Content stored in a Fedora repository may be easily repurposed by dynamically transforming it by the use of custom disseminators. Because of this inherent strength and flexibility, new views and data transformations are simple to add over time as the implementer's and user's requirements change.

Fedora is exposed via web services and can interact with other web services. The interfaces and XML transmission are defined using the Web Services Description Language WSDL. Fedora also supports any valid OAIPMH-2.0 request on the Dublin Core metadata datastream, and includes support for sets and allows requests on any metadata format datastream.

Fedora is not architected in such a way that any particular workflow or end-user application is assumed, which allows it to function as a generic repository substrate upon which many kinds of applications can be created and to take advantage, over time, of advances in web services.

All Fedora objects have a minimal Dublin Core metadata datastream added to them at creation. Dublin Core fields required by the implementing site's metadata standards can be added to this datastream as necessary. Fedora objects may also have additional metadata datastreams added to them as required by the institution's standards or by the nature of the data represented by the object.

Organisations need to manage their expanding volume of complex digital content. In the rapidly expanding Web, they want seamless integration of their own content with that served from remote servers. Finally, they want to exploit increasingly diverse and powerful web services, using them as tools to generate and transform new content.

Fedora is an open source digital repository service that gives organisations the tools for meeting these existing and emerging content management requirements. At its core is a powerful digital object model that supports multiple representations or views of each digital object. These representations may originate from data stored locally, from data referenced at other networked locations, or from data produced dynamically by local or remote web services. Relationships among digital objects can be stored and queried, providing the foundation for expressing rich information networks. These objects exist within a repository architecture that supports a variety of management functions such as fine granularity access control, version control, and ingest and export of information in standard XML formats.

This unique combination of features has allowed the deployment of Fedora in a variety of domains. Some examples of applications that are being built upon Fedora include library collection management, multimedia authoring systems, archival repositories, institutional repositories, and digital libraries for education.

The future of Fedora includes the following developments:

- *Object creation and workflow support*, where our proposed work will focus on content submission interfaces and industrial-strength batch processing.

- *Federated repositories and distributed collections*, where we will explore two approaches: peer-to-peer and development of an explicit federation service that would aggregate several Fedora repositories and act as a proxy or mediator to a set of distributed Fedora repositories.

- *Performance and longevity*, where we plan to directly address the issue of robustness for large-scale operations, as well as preservation.

- *Support for search and index services*, which are essential to enable indexing of metadata and content beyond the fields in the default Fedora index. Searching across a federation of repositories is also an important requirement in the next phase of work.

- *Sustainability*, which will require devising a sustainability model for the Fedora open-source software. We foresee a two-pronged approach: establishment of a maintenance organisation and of a development consortium.

- *Fedora source code standards and practices*, where we plan to improve the overall packaging of the code, and make it even easier for other programmers to modify and extend it.

Thornton Staples and Ronda Grizzle, University of Virginia Libraries; Sandy Payette and Carl Lagoze, Cornell University Digital Library Research Group.

Appendix F

OPUS: Online Publications of the University of Stuttgart

Programming languages	PHP 4
Native languages	German
Required software	Linux/Unix, MySQL, webserver
Online resources	Main installation at Stuttgart: *http://elib.uni-stuttgart.de/opus/doku/english/* Mailing list: *http://listserv.uni-stuttgart.de/mailman/listinfo/opus-l* Software: *http://opus.uni-stuttgart.de/opus/sw/*
Code licence	Stuttgart University R&D licence; free for trial or development use One-time fee of €250 for production use
Available as	Source
Components included	Web interface, storage layer, OAI-Interface

Online Publications of the University of Stuttgart (OPUS, or Online Publications System) was developed in 1998 by the University Library and the Computing Center of the University of Stuttgart. The project was made possible by funds from the German Research Net (DFN) and the Federal Department of Higher Education and Research (Bundesministerium für Bildung und Forschung). The goal of the original project was to provide a full-text information system by which faculty, students, and staff at the university could manage their electronic publications, including published and unpublished articles and theses and dissertations. The guiding principles for development were:

- freely available basic components (LAMP paradigm);
- core repository workflow automation;
- user driven metadata creation with maximum online support;
- container system for any given document format;
- document editing, peer review or long-term preservation handled outside the system.

The initial development project ended in October 1998. Ongoing development of OPUS is now funded by the University of Stuttgart. As the OPUS user base grew over time a more substantial part of development has also been done by other participating institutions. These include the University Library Center in the state of North Rhine-Westphalia (Hochschulbibliothekszentrum Nordrhein-Westfalen) as well as the Universities of Heidelberg, Regensburg, Saarbrücken and Hamburg-Harburg. Version 2.0, completely based on PHP4 and MySQL, was released in July 2002. Version 2.1 was released in January 2005, which was later superseded by version 3.0 in November 2005.

The OPUS software is currently used by more than 44 other German universities to manage the electronic publications of their university populations, and the system supports a search of metadata at participating German institutions (not all of which are using OPUS as their repository platform). Most OPUS implementations are managed and operated by an institution's university library, although some represent cooperative efforts of the library and the university's press and/or academic computing centre. OPUS is also being used by at least one disciplinary repository.

The OPUS interfaces and documentation are primarily in German, and all current implementations of the software are in Germany. Therefore, the system would appear to have its most direct appeal to repository implementations in German-speaking countries.

Functionality includes end-user (author) driven metadata creation (including controlled subject headings or classifications) and uploading of documents, internal metadata and document management as well as statistics and a variety of browsing (Dewey Decimal Classification or other classification schemes, document type, institutions) and searching (field, full-text, meta search) features for end users (reader). Internal metadata format is Dublin Core qualified based on a convention developed together with the Union Catalog for South-west Germany (BSZ) to which all metadata by institutional repositories in the region is exported. OPUS provides a special data provider service for this purpose but also the basic one based on OAI-PMH 2.0 and DC simple. Additional metadata formats supported by OPUS available for OAI based service providers are XMETADISS (DC qualified for the German National Library), XEPICUR (URN resolver service by the Germany National Library) and ProPrint (cooperative print-on-demand service). OPUS itself is not considered as a long-term preservation repository nor does it comply with the OAIS reference model, but the main organisations developing OPUS cooperate closely with the German Network of Expertise in Long-Term Storage of Digital Resources (NESTOR).

Functionality and workflow will be explained in more detail in the following section using persistent identifiers as an example. After metadata creation (and optional document upload) by the author using a web form, the data are only visible for OPUS administrators. The administrator can then calculate a persistent URN using the national bibliographic number (NBN) namespace from the German National Library (DDB) which the document will have once it is published. This URN can be sent back to the author for inclusion into their printed or electronic copies of the document. In the meantime metadata and documents can be reviewed and changed by administrators if necessary. Finally the document is published, which means that its metadata is accessible externally on the OPUS website as well as available via the OAI interface. From this interface it is harvested by the BSZ for the Library Union Catalog for South-west Germany. It is also harvested by the German National Library for the URN resolving service where the previously calculated URN is now registered. There is already a plug-in for Mozilla, Netscape or Firefox which allows for direct entering of URNs into the browser address bar.

OPUS systems at Heidelberg, Mannheim, Mainz, Tübingen, Saarbrücken, Stuttgart and Hohenheim Universities have been certified by the German Initiative for Networked Information (DINI) as reliable and standards compliant services (see *http://www.dini.de/dini/zertifikat/ dini_certificate.pdf*). Version 3.0 includes complete separation of code and content regarding the external user interface. This means that it becomes much easier to support different languages. In addition it will be possible to organise documents in any hierarchical structure thus supporting serial publications in a more efficient way. Last but not least there will an interface from the publishing workflow software GAPWorks to upload documents to OPUS which have been edited and reviewed there. GAPWorks has been developed within the German Academic Publishers (GAP) project to support the workflow within small- or medium-sized institutional or academic publishers including editing reviewing and layout. This interface from GAPWorks is currently being developed and follows the same approach as the interface from the Multimedia Document Versatile Architecture (MAVA) authoring system from which documents can directly be uploaded to OPUS. With this approach OPUS focuses on its core functionality as a repository for documents integrating with other specialised tools for authoring, editing or reviewing instead of trying to incorporate more and more functionality into one system. To sum it up, OPUS concentrates more on interfaces than on ever-expanding functionality.

Frank Scholze and Annette Maile, Stuttgart University Library.

Glossary

Abbreviations

AIP: Archival information package

API: Application programming interface

CSS: Cascading style sheet

DC: Dublin Core

DIP: Dissemination information package

GDFR: Global digital format registry

etd: Electronic theses and/or dissertation (see *E-Thesis*)

ETD-MS: The electronic thesis or dissertation metadata set

FAQ: Frequently asked questions

FOI: Freedom of information

FTP: File transfer protocol

GNU: 'GNU's not UNIX' (recursive acronym). The GNU project began in 1983 with the goal of creating a UNIX-compatible operating system composed of open source software. The GNU project is now carried out under the auspices of the Free Software Foundation (FSF).

GUI: Graphical user interface (see *User interface*)

HTML: Hypertext markup language

HTTP: Hypertext transfer protocol

IR: Institutional repository

IMS: Instructional Management Systems: a non-profit organisation (IMS Global Learning Consortium, Inc.) which promotes open standards in learning technologies.

JISC: Joint Information Systems Committee

LO: Learning object

LOM: Learning object metadata standard

METS: Metadata encoding and transmission standard

MPEG-21 DIDL: MPEG is the Moving Picture Experts Group, which develops standards for digital video and audio. DIDL is the digital item declaration language

OAI-PMH: Open archives initiative: protocol for metadata harvesting
OAIS: Open archival information system (reference model)
OCLC: Online Computer Library Center
OPAC: Online public access catalogue
OSS: Open source software
QDC: Qualified Dublin Core
RSS: Rich Site Summary
SCORM: Sharable Content Object Reference Model
SIP: Submission information package
SOAP: Simple object access protocol
SRU: Search/retrieve URL service
SRW: Search/retrieve web service
SRW/U: Search/retrieve web/URL service
TLO: Teaching and learning object (see *Learning object*)
TCO: Total cost of ownership
UI: User interface
URL: Universal resource locator
VLE: Virtual learning environment
XML: Extensible markup language

Definitions

Access metadata: Metadata whose primary purpose is to aid the discovery of an item.

Administrative metadata: Metadata which concerns the curation and administration of the item. This may include provenance, preservation and rights metadata as well as lifecycle information and access restrictions. It may also encapsulate technical metadata.

Aggregation: In repository terms, aggregation is the process of collecting metadata from a number of sources and collating into a single searchable set with a common interface.

Application programming interface (API): This is the set of instructions or requests that can be made of a particular piece of software or software module.

Archival information packet (AIP): A self-contained bundle of information which can be placed into an archive for long-term storage. Primarily refers to a digital bundle, which would contain both files and metadata of various types, as defined by the OAIS reference model.

Authentication: The process of determining that a user is who they say they are.

Authorisation: The process of determining that an authenticated user has the permissions within a system to perform the requested action.

Born-digital: An item is born-digital if it has been generated entirely electronically if it does not, or cannot, have a print analogue.

Bethesda Statement: The Bethesda Statement on Open Access Publishing is a statement of principle drafted during a one-day meeting held on 11 April, 2003 at the headquarters of the Howard Hughes Medical Institute in Chevy Chase, Maryland. The purpose of the document was to stimulate discussion within the biomedical research community on how to proceed, as rapidly as possible, to the widely held goal of providing open access to the primary scientific literature (*http://www. earlham.edu/~peters/fos/bethesda.htm*).

Berlin Declaration: The Berlin Declaration on Open Access to Knowledge in the Sciences and Humanities was drafted to promote the Internet as a functional instrument for a global scientific knowledge base and human reflection and to specify measures which research policy makers, research institutions, funding agencies, libraries, archives and museums need to consider. (*http://www.zim.mpg.de/openaccess-berlin /berlindeclaration.html*).

Big Deal: Subscription service to a portfolio of e-journals from a publisher or aggregator which offers a volume discount to encourage library purchasers to subscribe to the entire range rather than a subset.

Budapest Open Access Initiative: An international effort to make research articles in all academic fields freely available on the Internet. (*http://www.soros.org/openaccess/*).

Certificate: In authentication terms, the certificate is a digital signature to bind some public key to a particular user, thus verifying their authenticity.

Checksum: The result of applying a specific type of algorithm to a digital object which provides a practically unique identifier for that object, thus making it possible to quickly determine if the object has changed since the sum was last generated.

Community: A group of cooperating individuals. In OSS terms this is the group of people who will drive the development of the software.

Comparative evaluation: The process of comparing two or more systems undergoing *functional evaluation* in an attempt to determine the most suitable.

Controlled vocabulary: A set of *name authority* terms which make up the available input options for a particular metadata field. This aids greatly the standardisation and searchability of metadata records.

Copyleft: A play on *copyright*, it is used to indicate that a piece of software is free to copy, modify and re-distribute provided that any resulting software is shared under the same licence. A typical example of this sort of licence is the GNU General Public Licence (GPL).

Corporate assets: Any material produced within an institution which requires to be managed and preserved for future use (e.g. research papers, student records, statutory documents, learning materials).

Cross-walk: Translation of a metadata set from one schema to another. This usually involves creating a mapping from one metadata element in one schema to one in the other, although such one-to-one mappings are not always possible, and additional techniques may need to be employed.

Cascading style sheet (CSS): This is a way of indicating how an HTML or XHTML document should be displayed while abstracting as much of this away from the content as possible.

Data Protection Act: UK legislation which was introduced by Act of Parliament in 1998, giving citizens the right to access information held about them by organisations. The Act governs the way in which organisations can use the personal information that they hold: including the way they acquire, store, share or dispose of it.

Data provider (OAI): A repository which exposes its holdings via the OAI-PMH.

Deposit licence/agreement: The licensing terms that a submitter agrees to when they place an item in the institutional repository.

Descriptive metadata: Metadata whose primary purpose is to describe to the user what the item they are considering actually is. This would usually include the author, title, publisher and physical (or digital equivalent) dimensions.

Diffusion of innovations theory: The social sciences theory for how and why new ideas spread through cultures.

Digital asset: Any electronic resource which is of value to an organisation.

Digital preservation: The process and field of preserving digital assets in perpetuity in one form or another. It contains many complex challenges and remains a field of active research.

Dissemination information package (DIP): The files and metadata delivered to an end-user of a repository system, ideally one which is OAIS compliant. This is created from the stored *archival information package*.

Dublin Core (DC): A 'lowest common denominator' metadata set with 15 elements used to describe almost any object in a basic manner. Also, often referred to as 'simple Dublin Core' to draw a distinction from 'qualified Dublin Core', it is intended to facilitate the discovery of electronic uses through simplicity and extensibility.

E-print: An electronic version of an academic's research output. The term generally encompasses pre-and post-prints of journal articles, conference and working papers.

E-thesis (ETD): An electronic thesis or dissertation. Although it can be used to mean any thesis represented electronically, it is especially intended for born-digital theses.

Egress: The process of delivering material from a repository.

Electronic thesis or dissertation metadata set (ETD-MS): A metadata set defined as an extension to qualified Dublin Core to meet requirements for describing e-theses. It has 16 base elements, as it adds an extra 'thesis.degree' base element.

File transfer protocol (FTP): A common transport protocol allowing for remote management of file systems and for the transfer of files between a machines such as between the user and the FTP server for a repository.

Freedom of Information (FOI): Refers primarily to the Act of Parliament in the UK regarding the access status of information held by public bodies; this is also relevant elsewhere in the world where similar policies are also in effect. It guards the public right to view information which is not covered by one of the few exemptions.

Frequently asked questions (FAQ): Documentation which takes the form of a set of questions and their answers which are commonly asked about a particular service or system. These are best generated by logging questions from users and attaching the best solutions found by administrators.

Functional evaluation: The process of examining the behaviour of a system during evaluation.

Global digital format registry (GDFR): A registry of digital formats for the proper interpretation of otherwise opaque digital content streams and of how typed content is represented.

Gödelian: Refers to situations which are analogous to Kurt Gödel's incompleteness theorem (1931) which states that no formal system can be both complete and consistent. Often Gödelian flaws arise when a self-referential situations are encountered. In this book we indicate that the problem of persistent identifiers suffers from such a flaw, as to persistently identify an object requires a resolver which must be persistently identifiable. If followed to its logical conclusion, a truly persistent identifier needs an infinitely regressive chain of resolvers, each allowing the next to be persistently identified.

Graphical user interface (GUI): see *user interface*.

Grey literature: A term used to define scholarly material which is not formally published and is either difficult to find or generally ephemeral. Examples include e-theses or technical reports.

Harvest: The retrieval of metadata from websites and the subsequent storage of that metadata in an indexed file. See *Service provider*.

Holdings: The group of items 'held' in a library.

How-to: Documentation (often informal) which takes the form of a set of procedures to achieve a specific task. Mostly these are intended for non-experts.

HTTP GET: A query protocol which uses the URL requested from a server to pass a string for interpretation by the web server. This query string is indicated by starting with a question mark, followed by key=value pairs, separated by ampersands. For example: *http://www.myrepository.ac.uk/interface?action=help&user=me*.

HTTP POST: A query and transport protocol used for passing queries and other data to a server for interpretation. It is similar to HTTP GET but does not use the URL for passing information, and is capable of handling much more data. It is common to see web forms using HTTP POST to return user entered data to the server.

Hypertext markup language (HTML): This is a typical user interface language used on the web. It is used to mark-up plain text for display in a user's browser.

Hypertext transfer protocol (HTTP): This is the transport protocol used to deliver web content to browsers; that is, all websites are displayed by sending HTML over HTTP to the user.

In-house: Used to describe processes or software that an organisation has devised itself for its own purposes, rather than obtaining from a second party.

Ingest: The process of depositing material in the repository.

Interface: In software terms the set of requests that one software module may make to another software module. See also *user interface* and *application programming interface*. Effectively it is the boundary between parts of the system.

Learning object (LO): A self-contained piece of teaching information. Also referred to as *teaching and learning object (TLO)*. This is often combinable with other learning objects to create yet more. There is no universally accepted definition of exactly what constitutes a learning object. Current usage normally relates to files such as assessment objects (e.g. quizzes or multiple choice tests), course notes created by academic staff, and interactive or dynamic computer simulations.

MARC: The Machine-Readable Cataloguing standard, used by librarians to create digital metadata to describe printed books and journals.

Mediated deposit/submission: The process of placing an item into the institutional repository (in this context) on behalf of the actual creator. This is usually done by a repository manager to aid adoption of a service and to reduce burden on the academics.

Metadata: Information used to describe an object; in this context usually in a pre-specified language; literally: data about data. For librarians, metadata creation is a generic term for the activity they traditionally describe as 'cataloguing'.

Metadata element: A single piece of metadata in the metadata schema, usually part of a much larger whole. For example, 'contributor' is a metadata element in the Dublin Core metadata schema. It can also be used to refer to a single part of a populated *metadata record*, such as a single item's title.

Metadata record: The metadata for a single item. This is effectively an instantiation of the metadata schema with specific content regarding the item.

Metadata schema: The definition of the language and vocabulary allowed to describe an object.

Metadata encoding and transmission standard (METS): A complex object description language, formulated in XML, which allows for the bundling of many types of metadata regarding a digital asset, including access, descriptive, administrative, preservation and structural metadata.

Modularity: The concept that each small section of a piece of software should be an independent, self-contained (encapsulated) unit meaning that no external software needs to know how it works. This 'module' can then process requests via a standard *application programming interface* and return standard responses. This architecture aids the software engineering process by reducing overall complexity and making integration of new modules easier.

Name authority: A term, sometimes from a *controlled vocabulary*, which is not user or even cataloguer definable, but which comes from a standardised naming convention.

Open archives initiative: protocol for metadata harvesting (OAI-PMH): This protocol defines the request and response procedures for harvesting metadata from repositories using XML over HTTP.

OAI harvester: see *service provider (OAI)*.

On-the-fly: A software term used to mean that some process, calculation or customisation is performed as the software is being executed (run-time) rather than being hard-coded into it.

Online public access catalogue: A computerised library system for maintaining the catalogue of materials held by the institution that are available for public inspection. This includes both print and electronic holdings.

Open access: In the context of academic literature, open access describes the effort to grant access to a large variety of up-to-date information sources for free. The open access movement focuses on allowing all members of society to freely access relevant cultural and scientific achievements, in particular by encouraging the free online availability of such information.

Open archival information system (reference model): An ISO standard (ISO 14721) for long-term storage of digital data, initially developed by the Consultative Committee for Space Data Systems (CCSDS) for space data, and now finding adoption across the board for many preservation strategies.

Open source software (OSS): Software to which the source code is available under an open source licence such as the GPL or the BSD licences.

Operating system (OS): Software which mediates between applications and the hardware of a computer, providing a platform upon which those applications can then operate. Common examples of major operating systems include GNU/Linux, Solaris or Microsoft Windows.

Package profile: A short descriptive item concerning a piece of software which sums up its important and comparable elements. The appendices contains package profiles provided by the software developers for several common IR packages.

Peer-review: The process through which articles for journals pass where academic peers review each others' work to ensure correctness and suitability for publication in a refereed journal.

Permissive: A software licence which allows the source code to be copied or used without requesting the author's permission and without cost. A typical example of this sort of licence is the Berkley Source Distribution (BSD) licence. It differs from *copyleft* as there is not necessarily a condition to produce derived works under the same licence.

Policy: Effectively the same as a single *authorisation*.

Portal: A website that collocates content usually on a single topic or for a particular audience. A characteristic of portals is that they deliver content by means of a 'channel' architecture, delivering content produced elsewhere and syndicated for their use.

Post-print: The copy of a journal article actually included in the journal, or at least after peer-review. Sometimes publishers will permit this copy and not the pre-print to be deposited in an institutional repository.

Pre-print: A copy of a journal article which has not been peer-reviewed. Sometimes publishers will permit this copy and not the post-print to be the one deposited in an institutional repository.

Preliminary evaluation: A high-level review of options when performing evaluation, used to exclude inappropriate choices before moving on to evaluate in more detail.

Programming language: A standard set of instructions for a computer represented in a (relatively) human readable way. Common programming languages are C++, Java, or Perl. Some languages need to be compiled into the computer's native language (machine code), such as C++, while others are interpreted by another application (Perl). Languages in the latter case are often referred to as 'scripting languages'.

Protocol: A set of rules or standards for transferring information between systems. Examples of relevant protocols here are HTTP or OAI-PMH.

Provenance: The history of activity and ownership of an item.

Public domain: Term used of media generally to mean unrestricted content, including documents freely available on the web, broadcast television and radio programmes, newspaper content, etc.

Qualified Dublin Core: An extension to simple *Dublin Core*, this metadata schema defines 'refinements' to the base 15 elements of DC to allow for greater accuracy of description. The advantage is that it can be reduced to simple DC with a minimum of information loss, which is useful for transport over protocols such as OAI-PMH.

Query: In computer terms, this is a set of parameters which can be passed to a system specifying boundaries of a search on its data.

Representation information: Information which can aid in the understanding of how to render a particular file format. This is particularly important in the field of digital preservation, by aiding access in a meaningful way.

Rich Site Summary (RSS): An XML format for representing information about web resources. News stories are a common example.

Scholarly communication: The process of academics exchanging ideas for mutual benefit. This is typified by the peer-review journal system, but now includes many other types of digital communications aimed at academics and their institutions.

Scholarly literature: The materials that academics will often want to disseminate via the process of *scholarly communication*.

Search/retrieve URL service: A web service protocol similar, although more lightweight, to z39.50. This instance of SRW/U uses HTTP GET as its transport protocol, unlike SRW, which uses SOAP.

Search/retrieve web service: A web service protocol similar, although more lightweight, to z39.50. This instance of SRW/U uses SOAP as its transport protocol, unlike SRU, which uses HTTP GET.

Search/retrieve web/URL service: A web service protocol similar, although more lightweight, to z39.50. It can be broken down into component parts: SRW and SRU which are mainly differentiated by their access mechanisms (SOAP and HTTP GET respectively).

Self-archiving: The concept of an author depositing their own research, usually journal articles, into an online electronic archive, usually with reference to an open access institutional or subject-based repository.

Service provider (OAI): An OAI compliant system which queries data providers, aggregates their metadata into one larger record set and makes this available to search; also sometimes known as a 'harvester'.

Simple Dublin Core: see *Dublin Core*

Single sign-on: The idea that (and process by which) a user only authenticates once into a set of institutional services, and that authentication should be passed on to each subsystem that they interact with, thus eliminating the need to 'sign-on' to more than one system.

Simple object access protocol (SOAP): A lightweight, XML based transport protocol which has commonly been in use for web services.

Skin: An alternative interface to a website, usually incorporating graphical and design elements. With a skin applied, the appearance of the user interface changes, but the functionality of the site does not.

Source code: The human readable set of instructions which make up a piece of software.

Standard form: Cataloguing term indicating that a particular metadata field should be entered according to a pattern. A common example of this is the form that names are entered.

Structural metadata: Metadata describing the internal structure of a digital asset, such as the order or relationship between files.

Study initiation: In the process of evaluation, this is the stage where initial requirements are defined and a set of requirements is drawn up upon which to evaluate.

Subject heading: A *controlled vocabulary* term often taken from one of the standard subject heading libraries, such as the Library of Congress Subject Headings.

Subject repository: A digital repository whose content selection process is defined by the subject area of the material. A good example of this is the Los Alamos ArXiv.

Submission information package: The file and metadata package which makes up the submission, ideally into an OAIS complaint repository. This is converted by the system into an *archival information package*.

Super-user: The administrator of a system; these users have special privileges to have unrestricted access to all functionality.

Taxonomy: The theory and practice of describing, naming and classifying objects.

Teaching and learning object (TLO): see *learning object*.

Technical report: An in-depth report often too detailed for journal publication. May be for internal or external use.

Technical metadata: Metadata which concern the technologies associated with a digital item. This may include *representation information* for file formats, for example.

Total cost of ownership (TCO): The overall cost of owning and using a piece of software. This includes considerations such as cost of acquisition, staff training, installation time, hardware requirements and so forth.

UK E-thesis core set: A simple Dublin Core compliant metadata element recommendation using some non-standard refinements to the 15 base elements used to describe the UK's e-theses. It is not a metadata schema in its own right.

Uniform resource locator (URL): A name assigned to a web-based resource allowing for easy location; these usually take the form of a protocol, followed by the domain, followed by the location in the domain of the resource. For example, *http://www.era.lib.ed.ac.uk/index.jsp*.

Use case: A scenario describing how a user (not necessarily a human) might interact with a system.

Use licence: The licence under which an item is given to end-users. This defines what they are allowed to do without asking the author for permission.

User group: In technical terms this is a logical group of individually identifiable system users to whom operations can be applied as a single unit. Users can be members of multiple groups, and can be added and removed which effectively changes their state within a given environment.

User interface (UI): The point of communication between a human and a computer. Often this is a *graphical user interface (GUI)*, but not necessarily so. Typical examples of UIs (and GUIs) are web-based interfaces.

Verb: In OAI-PMH this is the action being requested of the data provider, such as *ListSets* or *GetRecord*.

Virtual learning environment (VLE): Application software, usually web-based, designed to allow academic staff to deposit teaching content, such as course notes, course readings, assignment topics and assessments, for access by authenticated members of the course to which these relate. The best known commercial systems are WebCT and Blackboard.

Web service: A service provided by a system which allows other systems to remotely request information in a structured manner, usually using XML over HTTP; in general web service interfaces are not for humans. To provide access to holdings via the OAI-PMH is one form of web service.

Workflow: A set of tasks held together in a logical network of pathways to achieve some objective. Often the controlled flow of information is supported by a software system.

Working paper: A paper in the process of being authored; not necessarily just a journal article.

eXtensible markup language (XML): An extensible language for the description and structure of many types of data and digital objects. Implementers may define their own schemas to match their particular needs, making it a powerful tool and excellent for standardisation.

z39.50: An information retrieval service definition and protocol specification for library applications.

Bibliography

Alston, R. (2002) 'Digital libraries: an overview: with special reference to English Studies'. Available at: *www.r-alston.co.uk/digitallibraries .htm.*

Andrew, T. (2003) 'Trends in self-posting of research material online by academic staff'. *Ariadne.* Available from: *http://www.ariadne.ac.uk/ issue37/andrew/* (Accessed: 14 September 2005).

Andrew, T. (2004) 'Intellectual property and electronic theses'. *JISC Legal.* Available from: *http://www.jisclegal.ac.uk/publications/ ethesesandrew.htm* (Accessed: 31 August 2005).

Antelman, K. (2004) 'Do open-access articles have a greater research impact?' *College & Research Libraries* 65(5): 372–82. Available at: *http://eprints.rclis.org/archive/00002309/* (Accessed: 27 September 2005).

Atkinson, R. (1996) 'Library functions, scholarly communication, and the foundation of the digital library: laying claim to the control zone', *The Library Quarterly* 66 (3): 239–65.

BBC (2002) 'Australian library may catalogue Internet porn' *BBC News World Edition.* Available at: *http://news.bbc.co.uk/2/hi/asia-pacific/ 2221489.stm* (Accessed: 27 September 2005).

Brownstein, I and Lerner, N (1982) *Guidelines for Evaluating and Selecting Software Packages.* New York: Elsevier.

Brunwin, V. (1994) 'A survivor's guide to workflow', *Management Development Review*, 7 (4): 27–9.

Buckland, M. (1997) 'What is a document?', *Journal of the American Society of Information Science*, 48 (9): 804–9. Available at: *www .sims.berkeley.edu/~buckland/whatdoc.html.*

Caplan, N., and Nelson, S. (1973) 'On being useful: The nature and consequences of psychological research on social problems'. *American Psychologist*, 28: 199–211.

CCSDS (2002) 'CCSDS 650.0-B-1: Reference model for an open archival information system (OAIS)'. *Blue Book.* Issue 1, January. Available from: *http://ssdoo.gsfc.nasa.gov/nost/wwwclassic/documents/pdf/CCSDS-650.0-B-1.pdf* (Accessed: 8 September 2005).

Clarke, R. (2005) 'A proposal for an open content licence for research paper (pr)eprints'. *First Monday*, 10 (8). Available at: *http://firstmonday.org/issues/issue10_8/clarke/index.html* (Accessed: 31 August 2005); *http://www.anu.edu.au/people/Roger.Clarke/EC/PrePrLic.html* (Accessed: 31 August 2005).

Cloonan, M and Dove, J. (2005) 'Ranganathan online: do digital libraries violate the third law?' *Library Journal* (April). Available at: *www.libraryjournal.com/article/CA512179.html*.

Copeland, S., Penman, A., and Milne, R. (2005) 'Electronic theses: the turning point'. *Program: Electronic Library and Information Systems*, 39 (3): 185–197.

Crow, R. (2004) 'A guide to institutional repository software'. Open Society Institute. Available from: *http://www.soros.org/openaccess/software/OSI_Guide_to_Institutional_Repository_Software_v3.htm* (Accessed: 31 August 2005).

erpanet (2004) 'erpanet workshop on workflow'. Available from: *http://www.erpanet.org/events/2004/budapest/* (Accessed: 8 September 2005).

Fischer, L. (ed.) (2002) *The Workflow Handbook 2002*. Lighthouse Point, FL: Future Strategies Ltd in association with The Workflow Management Coalition (WfMC).

Foster, N. F. and Gibbons, S. (2005) 'Understanding faculty to improve content recruitment for institutional repositories'. *D-Lib Magazine* 11 (1). Available at: *http://www.dlib.org/dlib/january05/foster/01foster.html* (Accessed: 27 September 2005).

Friend, F. J. (2003) 'Copyright policies and agreements: implementing the Zwolle principles'. White paper and discussion document. Available at: *http://www.surf.nl/copyright/keyissues/scholarlycommunication/implem_Zwolle_principles.pdf* (Accessed: 31 August 2005).

Gadd, E., Oppenheim C. and Probets S. (2003a) 'RoMEO Studies 4: The author-publisher bargain: an analysis of journal publisher copyright transfer agreements'. *Learned Publishing* 16 (4): 293–330.

Gadd, E., Oppenheim C. and Probets S. (2003b) 'RoMEO Studies 1: The impact of copyright ownership on academic author self-archiving'. *Journal of Documentation*, 59 (3), 243–77. Available at: *http://www.lboro.ac.uk/departments/ls/disresearch/romeo/RoMEO%20Studies%201.pdf* (Accessed: 31 August 2005).

Gadd, E., Oppenheim C. and Probets S. (2003c) 'RoMEO Studies 3: How academics expect to use open-access research papers'. Available at:

http://www.lboro.ac.uk/departments/ls/disresearch/romeo/RoMEO% 20Studies%203.pdf (Accessed: 31 August 2005).

Genoni, P. (2004) 'Content in institutional repositories', *Library Management*, 25 (6–7): 300–6.

Guédon, J.-C. (2002) *In Oldenburg's Long Shadow: Librarians, Research Scientists, Publishers, and the Control of Scientific Publishing*. Washington, DC: The Association of Research Libraries.

Harnad, S. (1990) 'Scholarly skywriting and the prepublication continuum of scientific inquiry'. *Psychological Science* 1: 342–3 (reprinted in *Current Contents* 45: 9–13). Available at: *http://eprints.ecs.soton .ac.uk/1894/* (Accessed: 27 September 2005).

Harnad, S. and Brody, T. (2004) 'Comparing the impact of open access (OA) vs non-OA articles in the same journals', *D-Lib Magazine*, 10 (6). Available at: *http://www.dlib.org/dlib/june04/harnad/06harnad .html* (Accessed: 27 September 2005).

Harnad, S., Brody, T., Vallieres, F., Carr, L., Hitchcock, S., Gingras, Y, Oppenheim, C., Stamerjohanns, H., and Hilf, E. (2004) 'The access/impact problem and the green and gold roads to open access'. *Serials Review*, 30 (4). Available at: *http://dx.doi.org/10.1016/j.serrev. 2004.09.013* (Accessed: 31 August 2005); *http://eprints.ecs.soton .ac.uk/10209/* (Accessed: 31 August 2005).

Hayes, M. J. (2003) 'Internet service provider liability: overview of internet service providers liability by the JISC legal information service'. Available at: *http://www.jisclegal.ac.uk/ispliability/ispliability .htm* (Accessed: 31 August 2005).

Hoorn, E. and van der Graaf, M. (2005) 'Towards good practices of copyright in open access journals: a study among authors of articles in open access journals. The report of a study funded by JISC and SURF'. Available at: *http://www.jisc.ac.uk/* (Accessed: 31 August 2005).

Johnson, R. K. (2002) 'Institutional repositories: partnering with faculty to enhance scholarly communication'. *D-Lib Magazine*, 8 (11). Available from: *http://www.dlib.org/dlib/november02/johnson/ 11johnson.html* (Accessed: 31 August 2005).

Jones, R. (2004a) 'DSpace vs ETD-db: Choosing software to manage electronic theses and dissertations'. *Ariadne*. Available from: *http://www.ariadne.ac.uk/issue38/jones/* (Accessed: 14 September 2005).

Jones, R. (2004b) 'Technical issues for repository software. Edinburgh University Library'. Available from: *http://www.thesesalive.ac .uk/archive/ePrintsUKWorkshop2.ppt* (Accessed: 8 September 2005).

Jones, R. (2004c) 'The Tapir: adding e-theses functionality to DSpace'. *Ariadne*. Available from: *http://www.ariadne.ac.uk/issue41/jones/* (Accessed: 14 September 2005).

Jones, R. (2004d) 'Initial proposal for DSpace workflow procedure for e-theses. Edinburgh University Library'. Available from: *http://www .thesesalive.ac.uk/archive/EThesesWorkflowProposal.html* (Accessed: 14 September 2005).

Jones, R. (2004e) 'Edinburgh Research Archive (ERA) administration guide. Edinburgh University Library'. Available from: *http://www .thesesalive.ac.uk/archive/ERA1.0AdminGuide.htm* (Accessed: 14 September 2005).

Jones, R. (2004f) 'Theses submission procedure at Edinburgh University. Edinburgh University Library'. Available from: *http://www.thesesalive .ac.uk/archive/ThesesSubmissionProcedure.html* (Accessed: 8 September 2005).

Jones, M. and Beagrie, N. (2001) *Preservation Management of Digital Materials: A Handbook*. The British Library. A web version is available from the JISC website: *http://www.jisc.ac.uk/* (Accessed: 31 August 2005).

Jones, R and Andrew, T (2005) 'Open access, open source and e-theses: the development of the Edinburgh Research Archive', *Program*, 39 (3), 198–212.

Lau, H. C. W., Lee, W. B. and Lau, P. K. H. (2003) 'Flexible workflow integration: an object technology approach', *Industrial Management and Data Systems*, 103 (3): 167–76.

Lavoie, B. (2004) 'Technology watch report: the open archival information system reference model: introductory guide'. *Digital Preservation Coalition*. Available from: *http://www.dpconline.org/ docs/lavoie_OAIS.pdf* (Accessed: 8 September 2005).

Lawrence, S. (2001) 'Online or invisible'. Published in print as 'Free online availability substantially increases a paper's impact' *Nature*, 411 (6837): 521 (May). Available at: *www.neci.nec.com/~lawrence/ papers/online-nature01.* (Accessed: 31 August 2005).

Lesk, M. (1997) *Practical Digital Libraries*. San Francisco: Morgan Kaufman.

Library of Congress (1993) 'Collections overviews: general statement'. Available at: *http://www.loc.gov/acq/devpol/colloverviews/generalstmt .html* (Accessed 5 October 2005).

Lynch, C. (2003) 'Institutional repositories: essential infrastructure for scholarship in the digital age'. Association of Research Libraries.

Available from: *http://www.arl.org/newsltr/226/ir.html* (Accessed: 31 August 2005).

MacColl, J. (2002a) 'Electronic theses and dissertations: a strategy for the UK'. *Ariadne*. Available from: *http://www.ariadne.ac.uk/issue32/theses-dissertations/* (Accessed: 14 September 2005).

MacColl, J. (2002b) 'Theses Alive! Project Proposal. Edinburgh University Library'. Available from: *http://www.thesesalive.ac.uk/archive/proposal030408.html* (Accessed: 14 September 2005).

McGuire, W. J. (1989) 'Theoretical foundations of campaigns', in Ronald E. Rice and Charles K. Atkins (eds), *Public Communication Campaigns*, 2nd edn, Newbury Park, CA: Sage, pp. 43–65.

NISO Press (2004) *Understanding Metadata*. Available at: *http://www.niso.org* (Accessed: 31 August 2005).

Nixon, W. (2003). 'DAEDALUS: initial experiences with EPrints and DSpace at the University of Glasgow'. *Ariadne*. Available from: *http://www.ariadne.ac.uk/issue37/nixon/* (Accessed: 31 August 2005).

Online Computer Library Center (2004) *2003 Environmental Scan: Pattern Recognition*, OCLC: Dublin OH.

Open Archives Forum (2003) 'OAI for Beginners – the open archives forum online tutorial'. Open Archives Forum. Available from: *http://www.oaforum.org/tutorial/* (Accessed: 8 September 2005).

Oppenheim, C. (1999) *The Legal and Regulatory Environment for Electronic Information* 3rd edn. Tetbury: Infonortics.

Powell, S., and Green, M. (2005) 'Confidentiality of PhD theses in the UK: a report and discussion paper'. United Kingdom Council for Graduate Education. Available at: *http://www.ukcge.ac.uk/filesup/PhDTheses.pdf* (Accessed 27 September 2005).

Ranganathan, S. R. (1931) *The Five Laws of Library Science*, Madras: The Madras Library Association.

Research Councils UK (2005) 'RCUK position statement on access to research outputs'. Available at: *www.rcuk.ac.uk/access/statement.pdf* (Accessed: 27 September 2005).

Rogers, E. M. (1962) *Diffusion of Innovations*. 1st edn. New York: The Free Press.

Rogers, E. M. (1995) *Diffusion of innovations*. 4th edn. New York, London: Free Press.

Rogers, E. M., and Agarwala-Rogers, R. (1976) *Communication in Organizations*, New York: Free Press, p. 26.

Roosendaal, H., and Geurts, P. (1997) 'Forces and functions in scientific communication: an analysis of their interplay' Cooperative Research Information Systems in Physics, Oldenburg, Germany; Aug–Sept.

Available at: *www.physik.uni-oldenburg.de/conferences/crisp97/ roosendaal.html* (Accessed: 27 September 2005).

Swan, A. and Brown, S. (2004a) 'JISC/OSI journal authors' survey report'. Available at: *http://www.jisc.ac.uk/uploaded_documents/ JISCOAreport1.pdf* (Accessed: 31 August 2005).

Swan, A. and Brown, S. (2004b) Authors and open access publishing', *Learned Publishing* 17 (3): 219–24. Available at: *http://www .ingentaselect.com/rpsv/cw/alpsp/09531513/v17n3/s7/* (Accessed: 31 August 2005).

Swan, A. and Brown, S. (2005) 'Open access self-archiving: An author study'. Technical Report, Joint Information Systems Committee (JISC), UK FE and HE funding councils. Available at: *http://cogprints .org/4385/* (Accessed: 31 August 2005).

Thompson, J. (1982) *The End of Libraries*, London: Bingley.

Van de Sompel, H. (2000) Closing Keynote Address, Coalition for Networked Information Fall Conference 2000 (San Antonio, Texas; 8th December).

Van de Sompel, H., Payette, S., Erickson, J., Lagoze, C., and Warner, S.. (2004) 'Rethinking scholarly communication: building the system that scholars deserve' *D-Lib Magazine* 10 (9). Available at: *www.dlib.org/ dlib/september04/vandesompel/09vandesompel.html* (Accessed: 27 September 2005).

Wellcome Trust (2005) 'Wellcome Trust position statement in support of open and unrestricted access to published research'. Available at: *www.wellcome.ac.uk/doc_WTD002766.html* (Accessed: 27 September 2005).

Wheatley, P. (2003) A way forward for developments in the digital preservation functions of DSpace: options, issues and recommendations. DSpace.org. Available from: *http://www.dspace .org/news/articles/DpAndDSpace.pdf* (Accessed: 31 August 2005).

Wheatley, P. (2004) 'Technology watch report: institutional repositories in the context of digital preservation'. Digital Preservation Coalition. Available from: *http://www.dpconline.org/docs/DPCTWf4word.pdf* (Accessed: 13 September 2005).

Zaltman, G., Duncan, R. and Holbek, J. (1973), *Innovations and Organizations*, New York: Wiley and Sons.

Zwolle Group (2001) *Copyright Management for Scholarship*. Available at: *http://www.surf.nl/copyright/* (Accessed: 31 August 2005).

Index

Printed in the United Kingdom
by Lightning Source UK Ltd.
108272UKS00002B/43-48

9 781843 341383